20.00

REGIONAL GOVERNMENT IN ENGLAND

REGIONAL GOVERNMENT IN ENGLAND

Edited by
BRIAN W. HOGWOOD
MICHAEL KEATING

CLARENDON PRESS · OXFORD
1982

Oxford University Press, Walton Street, Oxford OX2 6DP

London Glasgow New York Toronto
Delhi Bombay Calcutta Madras Karachi
Kuala Lumpur Singapore Hong Kong Tokyo
Nairobi Dar es Salaam Cape Town
Melbourne Auckland

and associate companies in
Beirut Berlin Ibadan Mexico City

Published in the United States
by Oxford University Press, New York

British Library Cataloguing in Publication Data

Regional government in England.
  1. Regionalism—England
  2. Great Britain—Politics and government—1964–
  I. Hogwood, Brian II. Keating, Michael
  352'.0073'0942   JS3025
  ISBN 0-19-827434-3

Set in IBM Baskerville by Graphic Services, Oxford
Printed in Great Britain
at the University Press, Oxford
by Eric Buckley
Printer to the University

And what should they know of England who only England know?

Rudyard Kipling, *The English Flag*

Preface

THIS book is the result of the observation by each of us separately while based in Scotland that the recent interest in the territorial aspects of United Kingdom government had tended to neglect the arrangements for administering the English regions. Since Brian Smith's work in the early 1960s there has been no systematic analysis of the operation in practice of regional government in England. Thornhill's book, *The Case for Regional Reform*, was, as its title suggested, concerned mainly with the case for institutional change rather than describing what actually exists. Throughout the 1960s and 1970s, the debate about English regions was largely about the case for regional planning or the establishment of devolved regional assemblies or governments. However, an appraisal of how government actually operates at regional level is surely an essential preliminary to analysing the implications of proposed changes. Our task in moving quickly from the original idea of editing such a book to completion was assisted by the fact that the papers commissioned for this book are all based on research work which was already being undertaken by a number of people from different academic disciplines. By drawing on this range of expertise we have been able to provide a much wider picture than we could possibly have done from a single research project. The picture is not a complete one, we recognize. Perhaps the most obvious omission is the lack of a chapter on the regional operations of the nationalized industries.

The book has benefited immeasurably from the fact that most of the contributors were able to gather at a small conference to discuss draft chapters at the Madeley campus of North Staffordshire Polytechnic (on the borders of the North

West and West Midlands regions, with a Cheshire postcode but in a district of Staffordshire). All chapters were rewritten in the light of comments made at the conference and our task as novice editors was made much easier. In particular we would like to thank the discussants of the draft chapters and those who made comments in discussion at the conference; although their names do not appear in the contents list of this book, we would nevertheless like to acknowledge them as contributors: Mike Goldsmith, Brian Jacobs, Don McIver, Bob Smith, and Mike Tappin. The conference was made possible by funds made available to us by the Centre for the Study of Public Policy, University of Strathclyde, from a Ford Foundation grant to promote the study of intergovernmental relations.

Although both of us are currently based in the University of Strathclyde (in different departments) we have both by coincidence studied in the past in the same part of England— Brian Hogwood at the University of Keele, Michael Keating at North Staffordshire Polytechnic. Accordingly, we would like to dedicate this book to the friends that each of us made while in North Staffordshire.

University of Strathclyde   BRIAN W. HOGWOOD
May 1981   MICHAEL KEATING

Contents

Maps

Notes on Contributors

Brian W. Hogwood is Lecturer in Public Policy at the University of Strathclyde.

Michael J. Keating is Lecturer in Administration at the University of Strathclyde.

Howard J. Elcock is Head of the School of Government at Newcastle-upon-Tyne Polytechnic.

Clive Gray is Lecturer in Public Administration at the Polytechnic of Wales

Stuart C. Haywood is Honorary Research Fellow at the Health Services Management Centre, University of Birmingham.

Peter D. Lindley is Senior Research Officer in Public Administration at the Civil Service College.

John F. McDonald is Economics Teacher at Howell's School, Cardiff.

Malcolm Rhodes was formerly Research Assistant in Public Administration at North Staffordshire Polytechnic.

John Short is an economic consultant and was formerly a member of the team producing the Northern Regional Strategy.

Stephen Young is Lecturer in Government at the University of Manchester

CHAPTER 1

Introduction

BRIAN W. HOGWOOD

THE chapters in this book are primarily concerned with apprais-
ing how British government operates at regional level within
England rather than with suggesting how such operations could
be reformed. In stressing our concern with description of what
currently exists rather than prescribing what changes should
be made, it would be wrong to assume that the description is
of formal characteristics only—the statutory tasks, the number
of people employed, how people are appointed, what the formal budgetary procedures are, etc. As the chapters on the
health and water authorities in particular show, to list only the
formal characteristics of the authorities and their relationship
with other bodies would be misleading as a description of what
actually happens. Accurate description therefore inevitably
involves analysis and interpretation. This introduction attempts
to draw together and develop some of the analytical themes
which emerge from the chapters about specific aspects of
regional government.

SEEKING PATTERNS IN THE COMPLEXITY

Being based in Scotland in the aftermath of the devolution
debate provides a perspective which leads one to ask questions
about English regions which might not occur to someone in
England. England as a whole is rarely a satisfactory unit for
comparison with Scotland, so it is natural to look for a set of
regional units within England for comparison. Scotland is quite
different from all English regions in terms of its political and
administrative arrangements, yet, as John Short's chapter in
this volume shows, it also shares certain characteristics such as

economic problems and public expenditure with areas of England, particularly those close to the Scottish-English border.[1] So Scotland is different as a geographical and political unit from the English regions in many ways, but what is it different from?

The most striking feature of the English regions in terms of their role in British government is a complete absence of a coherent definition of their boundaries, their size or even of the concept of a region. Neither geographers nor economists can offer an unambiguous guide to defining what constitutes a region. That is not to say that there are no available definitions or discussions of the concept of a region.[2] Geographers and economists have developed very sophisticated models to analyse the properties of regions.[3] However, these models are often concerned with abstract analysis or define regions in terms of limited sets of criteria. In contrast to the view held by many academics in the early twentieth century that there were 'objective' or 'natural' regions, the general view now is a 'subjective' one—that regions are descriptive tools, defined according to selected criteria, and used for a particular purpose.[4] Unfortunately, delineation of regions according to one set of criteria may not coincide with those drawn on the basis of another set of shared characteristics, and these in turn may differ from definitions stressing functional interaction between city and hinterland or definitions according to administrative criteria. In terms of our concern to relate government activity to territory, we find that in the literature there is a lack of intergration of spatial, economic, and social concepts in discussing relationships between territory and social structures and social structures and activities, including the activities of government.

If we look to administrative practice as a guide, we find, as Chapter 2 shows, that the problem is not so much the lack of any definition of boundaries, but of a proliferation of inconsistent boundaries. Chapter 3 shows by examining a range of regional organizations in the West Midlands that there is no consistency in terms of the functional division between central government in London and the regional organization. In contrast to Scotland, Wales, and Northern Ireland (since 1972) there are no government departments or ministers for individual English regions.

The pattern of regional government in Northern Ireland is different from that in all parts of Great Britain as a result of the historical legacy of the Stormont system, abolished in 1972, under which a separate Northern Ireland Government and Parliament legislated on and administered most aspects of domestic policy, though having to negotiate with HM Treasury about the financing of provisions at or above 'parity' with service provision in Great Britain.[5] This pattern of relatively self-contained administration, though with financing issues having to be referred to London, has continued under the Northern Ireland Office.[6] Security policy has, of course, a special UK dimension. Northern Ireland now has a (non-Northern-Irish) Secretary of State in the UK Cabinet, but he is inevitably perceived to a greater extent than the Scottish and Welsh Secretaries as the representative of the United Kingdom government in the territory rather than a special voice for the territory at the centre of government in London.

As Chapter 2 shows, the boundaries of Scotland and, to a lesser but increasing extent, Wales are much more likely to be used for administrative purposes by government departments and other bodies ('quangos') than the English regions. In addition, Scotland in particular is more likely than English regions to have separate 'quangos' established for a territory rather than regional offices of British or English-wide bodies.[7] There is, as Chapter 10 in this volume indicates, a greater chance of issues being labelled as 'regional' (i.e. Scottish or Welsh) than is the case in the English regions. Such issues also have a specifically territorial channel in the Scottish and Welsh Offices through which demands can be articulated, even where the issue is not the direct responsibility of the territorial departments. The existence of the Scottish and Welsh Offices enables the initiation and maintenance of distinctive policy features and a potential for greater discretion in the administration of some policies than exists in the English regions. However, one of the key contrasts between Scotland and Wales and the English regions is not the extent to which powers are decentralized to the Scottish and Welsh Offices but the way which Scottish and Welsh Office Ministers and civil servants are plugged in to the Cabinet system and the parallel interdepartmental committees of civil servants. This gives the territorial departments an opportunity to ensure that their views are taken into account in a way which is not available to any individual English region. This access to the centre is certainly considered very important by the Scottish and Welsh Offices themselves: Nicholas Edwards, Secretary of State for Wales, told the House of Commons Committee on Welsh Affairs in 1980: 'Do Wales have an advantage in this process?—I say quite clearly that we do; because in a way that, for example, the English regions cannot, we are present and taking part in those general policy decisions; we contribute to them'.[8]

However, it is important not to exaggerate the differences between government arrangements in the English regions and those in other parts of the United Kingdom. As Richard Parry has pointed out: 'The Scottish and Welsh Offices account for only a small minority of civil service employment in their nations—18 per cent in Scotland, 6 per cent in Wales—because the big civil service numbers are in functions administered on a United Kingdom or Great Britain basis, such as social security payments'.[9] Similarly, many of the organizational units analysed in Chapter 2 in this volume operate in Scotland (31 out of 60) and Wales (46 out of 60) as well as the English regions. Thus Scotland and Wales also have complex (though more coherent) patterns of regional government, but with the highly important difference that the Scottish and Welsh Offices form part of that pattern.

Faced both with a lack of clear conceptual underpining and the complexity of the observable pattern, the temptation is to give up in despair at the possibility of adopting a regional focus in studying the activities of British government in England. However, as one of the participants of our conference pointed out, there may not be a clearly identifiable 'regional level of government' in England, but there is certainly a lot of government acitivity going on in the regions.

Ideally, we should be able to relate the existence of regional institutions and their activities to a broader theory of the state, the allocation of functions and intergovernmental relations. One possibility as a general explanation can fairly quickly be dismissed, and that is that there is something intrinsically 'regional' about many of the activities of government, i.e. that the target population or area exists at regional level. This can be shown when we look at the government's 'regional' policy and the history of its evolution (see Chapter 5); we find that the target areas are not always defined in terms of broad regions, let alone areas corresponding to the boundaries of the regional units responsible for administering the policy. Similarly we find from the discussion of the origins of the Regional Water Authorities in Chapter 7 that apparently technical arguments for a regional level (e.g. hydrological boundaries) may turn out to require an understanding of the operation of professional and organizational factors. A possible exception is the idea of regions as a suitable unit for land-use and economic planning. However, as Chapter 8 shows, this entered only weakly into the substantive acitivity of most regional institutions.

As Michael Keating brings out in the concluding chapter to this volume, one of the confusions which bedevils discussions of 'regional' demands is the failure to draw adequately the distinction between demands or 'needs' relating to a region and questions of regional institutions and of regional autonomy.[10] It is difficult to pin down anything intrinsically 'regional' about political demands on the state even where these have an explicitly territorial focus. This in turn, however, may be partly a reflection of the structure of the state itself, which provides no clear regional point of entry in England for articulating demands. Even where there is a clear regional definition of demands, it does not necessarily follow in all cases that regional government or regional autonomy is necessary to pursue them. Arguments for regional government based on the need to pursue regional demands need an explicit theory of how the instrument of regional government would enable this to be done more effectively. Conversely, it is not necessary for there to be pre-existing regional characteristics or a regional identity to advance arguments justifying the establishment of 'regional' government; such justifications might include inadequacies of central and local government or a theory of the allocation and balance of powers within the state.

If we can find little help in our quest to find an explanation of the existence of regional institutions in England from the concepts of region or regional demands and activities, a basic starting point is the necessity for government to subdivide its activities both functionally and geographically. It would be impossible for all government functions to be carried out by one department in London. However, this does not in itself explain the need for a regional level either between central and local government, between field offices and central government or for *ad hoc* regional bodies.

Nor can we look to any constitutional allocation of powers, based on a concept of 'division of powers' for the origins of regional government activities in England. This is in striking contrast to the situation in other countries with a wide range of constitutional and political structures; what all these countries have and Britain lacks is a constitutional or public law framework defining the basis of territorial management.[11] In Britain there is neither a constitutional basis of division of powers or roles between centre and defined territories, as in the United States or the Federal Republic of Germany, nor a systematic basis of territorial management by the centre as under the French prefect system. In each of these countries one can find an identifiable intermediate 'level (or levels) of government' between centre and local government, though the use of a blanket terms such as 'intermediate level of government' obscures the wide variety of roles performed as the intermediate level in different countries. In England, as Keating and Rhodes show in their detailed study of the West Midlands in this volume, it is not possible to demarcate such an intermediate 'level' because of the wide variety of geographical boundaries, roles, organizational forms, and channels of responsibility involved. Other writers, comparing Britain to other countries, have also commented on the absence of a coherent intermediate level of state administration.[12]

Contrasts with the apparent ease of defining the statutory tasks of local authorities or of the constitutional functions of states in federal systems can be exaggerated, since, as studies of centre-local relations and federal systems have shown, statutory or constitutional allocations of tasks may provide a poor guide to dynamically evolving relationships.[13] However, whatever the inadequacies of the ideas of the American Founding Fathers as a description and explanation of contemporary American federalism, their theory of federalism and the allocation of powers did provide a basis for the establishment of the system. As Chapter 11 shows, the debate about regional reform in England has not been based on any common starting point for arguments for regional government. Similarly the evolution in practice of regional institutions has not resulted from any theory of intermediate administration.

Detailed study of the history of individual organizations can offer us explanations at individual level. But given the range and variety of such explanations there is a temptation to throw up one's hands at the task of arriving at any kind of generalization. However, this despair is unnecessary since we can see recurring themes which enable us to see patterns in the diversity as well as some limited integrating insights. Further, it is possible to conceive of analytical frameworks which will assist us in understanding the interaction of organizations at regional level with each other and with other organizations.

ADMINISTRATIVE ARRANGEMENTS AT REGIONAL LEVEL IN BRITAIN

Certainly, it would be misleading to attempt to analyse regional government in England in terms of a simple model of 'administrative devolution' by which for reasons of administrative convenience, span of control etc., it made sense to interpose a regional tier between central government and local authorities (although this is a partial explanation, as we will show). Although the term 'administrative devolution' is widely used, it is ambiguous since, quite apart from the fact that regional level activities are sometimes highly political, it is unclear whether the term relates to territorial dispersal of personnel or degree of discretion or form of accountability or other linkage to government in London. Amongst the 'administrative' arrangements to be found at regional level in Britain are':

(*a*) Deconcentration within departments or other bodies of administration of a particular area, but in strict conformity with standardized rules devised at the centre. The administration of Regional Developments Grants described in the Hogwood chapter is of this type. Such regional units are effectively geographical extensions of the headquarters organization.

(*b*) Deconcentration with discretion. Tasks are carried out at regional offices within departments or other bodies, but the officials have important discretion in deciding on the application of policy to individual cases. They are, of course, answerable for the exercise of this discretion to the departmental headquarters. Much of the work of the regional directors of the Departments of Environment/Transport described in Young's chapter is of this type.

(*c*) Decentralization with a cabinet minister. This does not apply to the English regions, but does to Scotland, Wales, and Northern Ireland. Here a separate department for a defined area exists, with *Ministerial* responsibility for the conduct of policy in the defined territory. This arrangement is characterized by political access to the Cabinet, separate budgetary arrangements and scope for policy variation, though often within a requirement to conform to general British government policy.

(*d*) Quasi-autonomous organizations at regional level. Here separate organizations are constituted for each defined territory. (Regional Electricity Boards are of this type, while British gas regions are of type (*b*).) A whole range of budgetary arrangements and (more or less well) defined relationships with central government departments is possible within this category, as the examples of the health and water chapters show.

The lack of a theory of intermediate administration in England—or indeed of the general status of such bodies—has left unresolved a number of issues of the accountability and responsibility of type (*d*) organizations. More generally, the extent to which organizations at regional level are accountable or sensitive to what Keating and Rhodes describe as 'constituencies' of clients, voters, and central and local government is not accurately described in the formal allocation of powers to those organizations. Certain mixtures of formal allocation of powers, internal composition and structure, and operating ideology can produce organizations at regional level which are almost 'independent fiefdoms', to use a phrase which cropped up in our discussions of water and health authorities. The obvious 'remedy' for this apparent insensitivity to outside influence might appear to be to make such bodies directly accountable to elected regional assemblies. However, a pause for careful thought is in order here. One of the interesting findings of the chapters on water and health is the gap between members of the 'authority' and the full-time officers. In other words the issue is one of *intra*-organizational relations as well as *inter*-organizational relations and might not be resolved in the way expected by adjusting the inter-organizational aspects.

THE VARIETY OF TASKS

Just as it is possible to observe a variety of degrees of types of autonomy at regional level, so it is possible to observe that regional organizations or regional levels within organizations perform a variety of tasks; any given organization may perform more than one of these tasks:

(*a*) Direct provision of a good or service. For example, Department of Industry regional offices are the access points for selective financial assistance.

(*b*) Supervision of field offices within the organization at regional level.

(*c*) Strategic allocation of resources to separate organizations covering smaller areas or separate functions. The Regional Health Authorities are largely concerned (in terms of budget) with strategic allocation to Area Health Authorities rather than direct provision.

(*d*) 'Oversight' functions over organizations covering smaller areas. This includes the role of acting as an intermediary between departmental headquarters in London and local authorities, and is a major role of the regional offices of the Departments of Environment/Transport.

Both (*c*) and (*d*) constitute a 'bridging' function between Whitehall and organizations at subregional level. This bridging function is both a geographical one and a functional one. The geographical one is the obvious bridge between a large number of authorities covering small areas and a single headquarters covering the whole country. The functional bridge is the involvement of regional institutions in the chain of decisions involved in delivering public policy. Thus Regional Health Authorities carry out the more detailed allocation of funds which they have in turn been allocated by central government (see Chapter 6). Offices of the Department of the Environment perform crucial roles in the land use planning process (see Chapter 4). The relationships involved are far from being purely hierarchical—the relationship is often a two or three way communication and adjudication one. The relationships also often involve questions of 'distancing' from central government or professional or local autonomy. Both Chapter 11 and Chapter 3 raise the question of whether it would still be necessary to retain a bridge between newly established regional governments and pre-existing organizations at local level. Would Regional Health Authorities continue to exist, or would AHAs be made directly responsible to the regional assembly? Issues of distancing from government, professional autonomy, and vested interests would all suggest the survival of at least some aspects of the work of the RHAs. An interesting parallel here is that the ill-fated Scotland Act 1978 envisaged the retention of the Scottish Office as a 'bridge' between the Assembly and Westminster, though this was at least in part a consequence of the design of this specific devolution proposal.

EXPLANATIONS FOR THE DEVELOPMENT OF REGIONAL BODIES

Given the existence of this variety of degrees of autonomy and variety of tasks, we should not expect to find a single simple cause. Each instance of regional organization owes its origins and continuing existence to its own blend of the following explanations.

(*a*) Although unacceptable as a single explanation, straightforward administrative convenience lies behind the existence of many regional arrangements. Considerations here include span of control—there are too many local authorities or social security offices for them to be readily supervised by an undifferentiated headquarters organization, and around eight regional offices appear in turn to be a suitable number for inter-regional communication and headquarters scrutiny. Mundane explanations such as the need for a suitable labour force should not be overlooked—it would be difficult if not impossible to find all the necessary labour in London. Ease of access in both directions in the exercise of supervisory or oversight functions clearly points to the need for regional offices in many organizations. Similarly, convenience of clientele was a consideration in allocating functions to regional offices of the Department of Industry.

(*b*) There are technological arguments which may point to a regional rather than a local level of organization. Economics of scale arguments are relevant to the provision of utilities and certain aspects of health care. 'Technological' arguments may also influence the size of area covered and the drawing of boundaries (e.g. the apparent need to have a teaching hospital in each hospital region; hydrological boundaries). However, such arguments may not in themselves be overwhelming but reflect professional and organizational priorities. These priorities are determined through essentially political processes. Indeed, a decision by government to define regional institutions on the basis of a particular set of professional or technical values is a *metapolitical* activity, since it defines the parameters for future decision-marking.

(*c*) The central government's search for control over time without swamping itself during a period of expansion of total government activities. This explanation will be developed further in the context of the dynamics of the evolution of intergovernmental relations in Britain.

(*d*) The existence of quasi-autonomous organizations can be regarded as the geographical aspect of the 'distancing' from government explanations of the existence of 'quangos'.[14] Central government departments and ministers would find it inconvenient to be held accountable for the detailed actions of 'commercial' concerns like the nationalized industries or 'sensitive' matters like clinical decisions.

(*e*) Finally, individuals or groups may have a vested interest in the establishment or maintenance of a regional level. This comes across quite clearly in the health and water chapters where 'professional' arguments for autonomy provided the reciprocal argument for distancing from government to (*d*). A regional rather than local basis also severs the link with local authorities and this enhances the potential autonomy in that direction. Regional organizations are also bigger and therefore provide scope for 'empire-building'. The existence of vested interests in the autonomy of regional bodies is often overlooked in discussions of the implications of devolution or other forms of reorganization.

RELATING THE REGIONAL LEVEL TO THE BROAD CHARACTERISTICS OF BRITISH GOVERNMENT

The above explanations should not, of course, be abstracted from their historical setting, and we will later attempt to analyse the development of regional institutions in relation to the growth of government. Similarly, we must relate characteristics at regional level to other broad characteristics of British government. Various chapters in this book (particularly Keating and Rhodes, Hogwood and Lindley) show that there is a high degree of functional fragmentation at regional level, sometimes even within the same department. However, there is no grand co-ordination at central level either. Functional fragmentation at central level is the main reason both for functional fragmentation at regional level and for the diversity of geographical arrangements. This point can be made in terms of Fig.1.1, which compares ideal type 'prefect' and 'regional planning' models with the reality of fragmentation and complexity. The 'descriptive' model is, of course, a gross oversimplification—it ignores the varying degrees of autonomy, variety of tasks and diversity of geographical arrangements. Above all, it appears to retain the concept of levels, whereas we find that most government policies involve *interaction* between a number of organizations rather than a single organization pursuing its activities in isolation.

Are we now in a position to return to the issue of attempting to place regional government in England in the context of broader theories of government? Consider the following passage taken from Maass:

. . . dynamic—a mechanism by which functions are assigned to the several levels of government, exclusively or jointly, according to the demands of the time.
. . . by limiting our concern for area division of powers to the allocation of functions among the several levels of government— by building one scheme on top of another often without returning to basic reasons for the division in the first place, we have lost sight of liberty, equality, and welfare and of how these values can be realised in part by dividing government power.[15]

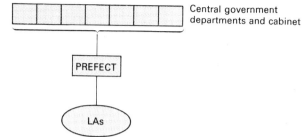

Central government
departments and cabinet

PREFECT

LAs

(b) *Ideal type 'regional planning' model*

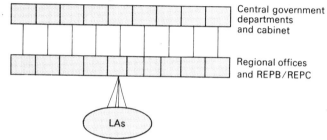

Central government
departments
and cabinet

Regional offices
and REPB/REPC

LAs

(c) *Simplified description of actual English regional arrangements*

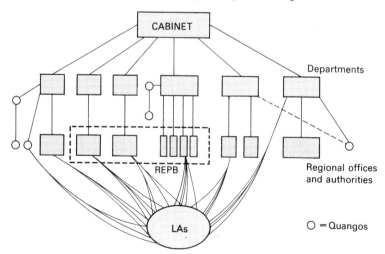

CABINET

Departments

REPB

LAs

Regional offices
and authorities

○ = Quangos

Fig. 1.1 Models of regional government

Maass is not, in fact, describing regional government in England, but the 'new federalism' in the United States, which contrasts with the old federalism which attempted an exclusive separation of functions. Thus, there is an analogy between regional government and federalism, but it is not with the constitutional separation of powers, but with the 'marble-cake' federalism of modern America.[16] Thus regional government in England is 'marble-cake' regionalism.

Grodzins argued that rather than see American government as a three-layer cake, 'A far more accurate image is the rainbow or marble cake, characterised by an inseparable mingling of differently colored ingredients, the colors appearing in vertical and diagonal strands and unexpected whirls.'[17] Grodzins arrived at a similar conclusion about American government as we did above on regional government in England: 'It is difficult to find any governmental activity which does not involve all three of the so-called "levels" of the federal system.'[18] Of course, we must not push the analogy with marble-cake federalism too far: in the United States there is the crucial role of the constitutional definition of the existence and powers of the states (however ambiguous, however subject to changing interpretations) as an ingredient in the marble cake; in the United Kingdom the central government has a much bigger role in listing the ingredients. Similarly, the lack of constitutional definition of English regions has led to a wide variety of boundaries, thus making the English cake even more mablecakey than the American federal brand. Before we finally lay aside the culinary metaphor, it is worth reflecting on its implications for the allocation of functions to a regional government: it is extremely difficult to cut a marble cake in such a way as to ensure that all of one colour (function) falls within a single horizontal slice (level of government).

The diversity of forms of organization at regional level, of the relationships between regional level and central and local level, and between different organizations at regional level all point to the need to analyse regional government not in terms of a 'regional level', but in terms of a regional focus within the broader study of intergovernmental relations. Such a framework must also be one that allows for how regional bodies operate in practice rather than simply formal definitions of their tasks and relationships. A useful and influential framework for analysing centre-local relations in Britain, with potential for being developed into a framework for analysing intergovernmental relations generally, has been devised by R. A. W. Rhodes.[19] This framework stresses the *complexity* of the environment in which an organization operates, an environment which includes other organizations which supply needed resources. Variations in the degree of discretion of an organization are a product of the goals and relative power potential of interacting organizations; this relative power potential is seen as a product of the resources of each organization, of the 'rules of the game' (more or less informal rules which set approximate limits to acceptable behaviour), and of the process of exchange between organizations. A particularly valuable feature of the framework is that the relevant resources are taken to include not only constitutional, legal, and financial resources, but also political and informational resources (including expertise) possessed by members of organizations. Chapter 3 demonstrates the usefulness of the framework as a means of illuminating the degree of discretion available to a number of organizations in the West Midlands.

The framework can usefully be developed further by including considerations of the strategic sequential position of organizations—the extent to which the activities of an organization have to be carried out prior to or parallel with the activities of other organizations.[20] The implications of this are not always as clear-cut as they might seem. For example, Grey points out that while the Regional Water Authorities have a statutory obligation to consult the local authorities in their area during their respective planning processes and a further duty to 'have regard to' structure and local plans, in practice the regional focus of the Water Authorities gives them what is called here a strategic sequential position so that the Water Authorities actually play a major role in the production of those plans.

THE EVOLUTION OF REGIONAL GOVERMENT OVER TIME

Three caveats should be made about the potential for developing the Rhodes framework as a model of intergovernmental relations focusing on the regions. These relate to the fact that the framework is atheoretic and, partly as a consequence, can offer no explanation of the dynamics of the evolution of relations over time (as opposed to the dynamics of a sequence of rounds of interaction in the 'game').[21]

The first of these relates to responsibility for the rules of the game, and for changing those rules. In the case of the regional focus on the 'game', even more than on the centre-local government focus, the central government (leaving aside for the moment the fact that the centre is itself multiple actors) is not merely the most significant actor but has special legitimacy and power in defining rules and in changing those rules to suit the changing needs of the centre. This includes changing the form of other key actors—their composition, their functions, and the boundaries of the territory in which they operate. This power to change rules and actors is not absolute—other organizations do have relevant resources, and numerous chapters in this book emphasize that formal allocations of authority are often poor guides to the realities of decision-making in practice. Yet it remains true that, in important contrast to federal systems with entrenched constitutions, the central government in Britain has a greater unilateral capacity to change rules and actors, especially those covering territory intermediate between local government and the whole of the country.

This is brought out by the discussion elsewhere by Richardson and Jordan of the reorganization of the water industry in 1973 which led to the establishment of the Regional Water Authorities (RWAs) which are examined in Chapter 7.[22] Richardson and Jordan used this example to illustrate their concept of a 'negotiated order'; even though central government had clear ideas about the nature of changes it wished to undertake, it tried to involve local authorities (who would lose water functions) in consultations. The resentment of the local authorities at the refusal of central government to modify its proposals was such that for a while the local authorities refused to co-operate in arrangements for the transition to the new structure. However, this policy of non-co-operation was rescinded after nine months and the government made certain concessions such as allowing district councils to act as sewerage agencies of the RWAs. The implication drawn from this episode by Richardson and Jordan is that the local authorities were reluctant to refuse co-operation and ended their boycott because 'It appeared to be recognised that such action was outside the "rules".'[23] Without rejecting this interpretation, it can also be pointed out that water reorganization showed the ability of central government to push through without substantial amendment an important reallocation of functions and major organizational change in the face of substantial opposition from other organizations because there were no constitutional restraints on its ability to do so.

The remaining two ways in which a model of inter-governmental relations needs to be developed relate to the dynamics of change over time. The first of these is concerned with the technical, professional, and other values which not merely help to determine individual decisions of regional organizations but shape the frameworks considered appropriate for taking such decisions. We have already noted that such technical or quasi-technical factors are one influence on the development of regional institutions and that the determination of such values is ultimately a political issue. However, these sets of values and the role which they are accorded in shaping public policy institutions and decisions are themselves subject to change over time. Such technological or professional 'imperatives' should not be regarded as independent variables in the interplay of intergovernmental relations but are themselves the outcome of a process of political bargaining which may lead to changes over time in the extent to which particular values are given prominence.[24] The key role of the central state in defining the parameters of the 'game' is reflected in the way in which some professions have been able to persuade central government to devise territorial organizational forms which effectively amount to a 'grant of autonomy' to determine the delivery of services in the policy area of their professional interest. This is true of the Regional Health Authorities and, to a lesser extent, of the Regional Water Authorities.

Finally, we need to relate changes in intergovernmental relations involving regional institutions to changes in the activities of government and how the state tries to manage territories over which it claims responsibility. Earlier in this chapter, it was suggested that one of the reasons for the development of regional institutions has been the central government's quest for control without swamping itself. This dilemma has to be seen in the context of the continuing growth of total government activity in the thirty years after 1945. It is not intended to discuss here the various explanations which have been offered for this growth, but it is suggested that this growth is relevant to the growth of regional institutions and their relationships with other organizations.[25] It is suggested here that two different aspects of the quest for control without being swamped by the need to take decisions, working in apparently opposite directions, point to the evolution of regional institutions in England.

In the first place, central government has since the Second World War taken a number of functions away from local authorities—health, water, and other undertakings. For a mixture of some of the reasons outlined earlier, the central government did not want to absorb these functions into London headquarters, but handed them over to regional authorities. Relevant reasons include administrative convenience in administering services which had to be delivered throughout the country, technical or quasi-technical considerations, and a desire to avoid being held responsible for the details of commercial or professional decisions. Also of relevance here is the 'central autonomy' model outlined by Bulpitt, which argues that far from wanting to control every decision, the centre will be quite happy for matters of 'low politics' (such as which health area within a region should get how much of a marginal increase) to be decided by organizations in the 'periphery', since this will enable the centre to concentrate its limited decision-making resources on matters of 'high politics' such as foreign affairs and economic management.[26]

Secondly, despite the removal of these functions from local authorities, the scale and scope of local authority activities has expanded enormously. The centre by no means wanted to carry out these functions itself, but it did want to oversee their execution. Reasons of administrative convenience as outlined earlier in the chapter often pointed to regional offices as the most suitable way of exercising this oversight function.

The present organizational form and regional boundaries of organizations reflect their individual organizational histories.

On the other hand, there have been variations over time in the central government attitude to regions. There was an upsurge in regional organization in the 1940s, and a downturn in the 1950s. The 1960s saw renewed interest in regional aspects of government, and the 1970s saw the establishment of the regional water and health authorities. The early 1980s appear to be a period of relative lack of interest in the regional dimension of English government. The present pattern of regional institutions contains residues from each of these periods.

The creation of regional institutions thus itself shapes the future structure and processes of changing those structures. One of the most interesting ways in which this can occur is through the creation of a regional identity or 'regional office culture' among officials in regional institutions, even though we have noted that the delineation of English regions is often confused. The development of such a regional office culture is possible even in the regional offices of central government departments if transfers of staff take place within or between regional offices rather than by frequent and systematic exchange of Whitehall headquarters and regionally based staff. Thus, regional officials may cease to see themselves solely as representatives of the centre in the region and 'go native'— acting as spokesmen for their perceptions of the needs of their region at the centre. Stephen Young's chapter discusses the significance of this in the Department of the Environment.

A 'TWO NATION' ENGLAND?

The complexity and diversity of English regional government is such that one is tempted to say that it is complex and diverse and leave it at that. However, there is one pattern which does emerge, even if it is difficult to establish a definite explanation of the pattern. A number of chapters note the substantial variations which exist between different English regions in terms of systematic use of boundaries, allocation of functions, and expenditure patterns. It is worth nothing that the most northerly regions and, to a lesser extent, the South West, show up as systematically distinctive. Thus these regions tend to have a more systematic use of regional boundaries, (see Chapter 2), to have certain functions (selective financial assistance,

NEB subsidiaries) allocated to regional organizations only in those parts of England (see Chapter 5), and have higher levels of total public expenditure (see Chapter 9). Conversely, London and the South East have traditionally been better off in terms of health provision, and special arrangements are made for London for some functions. The linking thread to at least part of this pattern of variation is clearly the social and economic characteristics of these 'peripheral' regions. What it is not possible to determine on the basis of the evidence presented in chapters in this book is how far this pattern of variance also reflects cultural differences or the peripherality of the regions as such.

CONCLUSION

The previous section reminds us that regional government in England is not simply about the internal operations and inter-organizational relations of regional bodies, but about coping with the problems of those areas and delivering services to citizens. The growth and changing pattern of those services has helped to shape the regional dimension of government in England. The argument advanced in this chapter for relating intra- and inter-organizational studies of regional bodies to the broader context of British government is not concerned simply with the internal rituals of British government but with the contribution this can make to understanding how policies are delivered to the citizens of the English regions.

CHAPTER 2

Variations in regional boundaries

BRIAN W. HOGWOOD AND P. D. LINDLEY

INTRODUCTION

OUR purpose in this chapter is to analyse the variations in regional boundaries in England used by government departments and other agencies.[1] In doing so we attempt to go beyond the merely negative point of drawing attention to the fact that standard regions are not uniformly used for administrative purposes. Our aim is to *measure* the use of regional boundaries by government departments and agencies.[2] This enterprise involves considerable conceptual and practical problems. We attempt to measure:

(*a*) variations between departments and agencies in the extent to which they conform to standard regional boundaries:
(*b*) variations between standard regions in the extent to which they are used by departments and agencies.

The history of standard regions illustrates the difficulties facing attempts to produce a definitive set of regional boundaries. During the Second World War, Regional Commissioners were appointed for Scotland, Wales, and ten English regions. Because the central government was never destroyed by invasion or other causes, the Regional Commissioners were never required to assume the direction of government in their areas. However, a substantial amount of decentralization of domestic departments to the English regions did occur, with departments appointing Divisional Officers to each region. After the war, the Treasury attempted to get all departments to conform in their regional organization to standard regions (see Map 2.1), though it was always prepared to give latitude 'to amalgamate

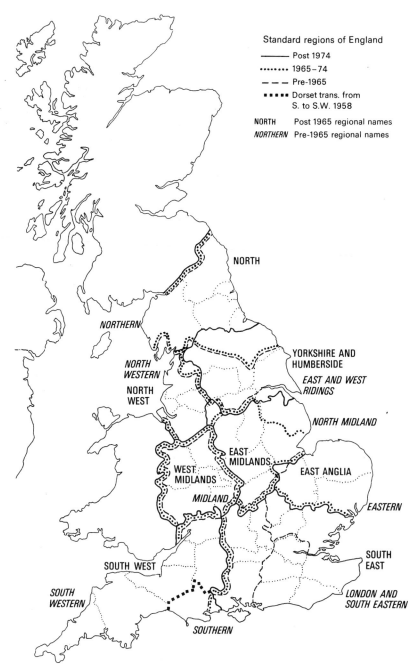

Standard regions of England

——— Post 1974
•••••• 1965–74
– – – Pre-1965
▪▪▪▪▪ Dorset trans. from
        S. to S.W. 1958

NORTH   Post 1965 regional names
NORTHERN   Pre-1965 regional names

NORTH

NORTHERN

YORKSHIRE AND
HUMBERSIDE

*EAST AND WEST
RIDINGS*

*NORTH
WESTERN*

NORTH
WEST

NORTH MIDLAND

EAST
MIDLANDS

WEST
MIDLANDS

EAST ANGLIA

MIDLAND

EASTERN

SOUTH WEST

SOUTH
EAST

*SOUTH
WESTERN*

*LONDON AND
SOUTH EASTERN*

SOUTHERN

Map 2.1. Changes in standard regions since 1945

regions and to make adjustments in boundaries where this effects economies in staff and suits the convenience of the Department concerned'.[3] The standard regions defined after the war differed from the wartime regions established under the Regional Commissioners in that Cumberland and Westmorland came under the Northern region rather than the North-Western, and the war time London and South-Eastern regions were combined to form the London and South-Eastern standard region. After about 1956, the Regional Organization Committee (a committee of civil servants under Treasury chairmanship set up after the war to review the development of regional organization, including the delineation of regional boundaries) fell into disuse and individual departments no longer had to obtain Treasury sanction for deviations from standard regional boundaries.[4] This led to a proliferation of individual departmental sets of boundaries. The 1950s saw a general decline in the use of regional offices by departments.

With the election of the Labour Government in 1964, there came a new emphasis on regions with the establishment of Regional Economic Planning Councils and Regional Economic Planning Boards for each economic planning region, the boundaries of which also became the new standard regions (see Map 2.1). To foster co-ordination between departments at regional level, departments were encouraged to establish regional offices in the same location. This is not the place to discuss the failure of this new system to produce much by way of regional economic planning or co-ordinated decision-making at regional level but since only those departments most concerned with regional planning were actually encouraged to bring their administrative boundaries into line with the new standard regions, the renewed regional focus therefore did little to prevent a continued proliferation of systems of regional boundaries.[5] The most recent changes in standard regional boundaries occurred in 1974, and were associated with local government reorganization in England in that year. While many of these post-1974 regions are used by many government departments, we show below that the pattern remains one of substantial deviation from the standard region boundaries, with no department conforming to all the boundaries, not even the Department of the Environment, which has inherited the regional co-ordinating role of the Department of Economic Affairs.

The abolition of the Regional Economic Planning Councils by the new Conservative Government in July 1979 removed one of the most visible bodies using the standard regions. It will be interesting to see whether the abolition of the REPCs leads to a reduced use of standard regions by departments and other organizations in future internal reorganizations. Indeed, the significance of standard regions as anything except areas for statistical purposes must now be in question.

An examination of Map 2.1 reveals that only one English region has retained the same regional boundaries for the past twenty-five years: the West Midlands. All other regions have undergone some change, in some cases on two different occasions. However, the significance of these changes in standard regions should not be exaggerated (apart from the fact that they are often ignored in delimiting departmental boundaries!). If the regions are considered in terms of whether the bulk of the population has been affected, we find that the changes in the North, Yorkshire and Humberside, East Midlands and South West are less significant than a simple glance at the map might indicate. The really major change occurred in 1965 with the replacement of the three old Eastern, Southern, and London and South Eastern regions by two regions, East Anglia and South East.

This review of changes in standard region boundaries has helped to clarify the extent to which the current standard regions can be regarded as long-term standards, and is of significance for the study of current departmental boundaries, since some of the regions used by some departments are still based on *old* standard regional boundaries (i.e., pre-1974 or pre-1965 boundaries): for example, the Department of Industry's North West region still includes Barrow and High Peak.

These changes in the boundaries of the standard regions and the fact that many departments do not use them for many of their own regions pose problems of measuring variations in the use of regional boundaries. In this chapter, despite some disadvantages, we have used the current standard regional boundaries as the base from which variations are measured. However, we also comment on certain regional configurations other than the standard regions which occur regularly. In measuring deviations from standard region boundaries, we are not simply concerned with a crude classification of whether or not a particular region is used. We wish to identify separately cases where there are only minor deviations from the standard regions (by minor we normally mean small parts of counties, e.g., the treatment of the High Peak area of Derbyshire). We will also be interested in cases where even though the standard region boundary is not used it is not actually cross-cut by the departmental regional boundary. However, our biggest problem in designing the analysis lay not with the territorial basis for measurement but with the organizational unit of analysis. This is particularly important, given our interest in aggregate measures of the use of regional boundaries rather than simply a detailed narrative of each set of boundaries used by each organization. We faced the kinds of problems of establishing a suitable unit for measurement and of classifying types of organizations which will be familiar to those who have read reports of the work of the Machinery of Government project at the University of York.[6]

As far as government departments are concerned, we had to discard the idea of treating each as a single unit for the purposes of analysis, both because several departments themselves contain a large number of sets of regional boundaries, and because of the existence of 'interdepartments', i.e., organizations which transcend normal departmental structures, such as the Departments of the Environment/Transport regional offices system under which the same individual acts as Regional Director of the Departments of the Environment and Transport (and also as Chairman of the Regional Economic Planning Board). Accordingly we have devised the artificial concept of a 'unit', which we define as an organizational system with its own set of regional boundaries and a presence in those regions as indicated by a chief regional official. In some cases this produces relatively clear cut units—such as those dealing with social security and social work in the Department of Health and Social Security. In other cases the picture is more complicated since a regional controller may oversee other regional officials who work on the basis of different sets of regional boundaries! This is the case in Environment/Transport, where the Regional Director has under him Regional Controllers for Housing and Planning and for Roads and Transportation. Here our decision was to treat Roads and Transportation etc. as separate units and to 'invent' a unit consisting of the Regional Directors and the Regional Establishment Units of Environment/Transport. Clearly, then, some of our units are more artificial than others. We provide a full list of our departmental units, grouped by departments, in the appendix to the chapter. It must also be recognized that our units vary considerably in their significance in terms of their importance within a department, the size and rank of the staff involved, the degree of discretion accorded to officials in the regions, and the nature of the tasks carried out by the regional office.

Our other problem relating to the organizational unit of analysis concerns the distinction between departmental regional structures and other organizations. As Hood *et al.* have pointed out, even the government doesn't seem to be sure which organizations are government departments and which are not.[7] Our main concern in this chapter is with government departments, but it soon became clear that an over-rigid separation of government departments from other bodies would cause problems. For example, the Department of Employment is now virtually a 'holding company' for a number of organizations delivering employment services: the Manpower Services Commission (MSC), the Advisory, Conciliation and Arbitration Service (ACAS) and the Health and Safety Executive (HSE). Another example is the health service: one of the main functions of the DHSS, the regional system on the health side, is not part of the DHSS but a set of separately constituted Regional Health Authorities. We have been unable to devise a satisfactory criterion for separating out organizations which are close to government, in this sense of close to their department's core functions, from other organizations set up by government which have their own regional organizations. Accordingly, we have fallen back on a fairly arbitrary classification system which has the merit of being very easy to use: we have classified as departmental units those units listed in the 'Ministers and Departments' chapter of the *Civil Service Year Book*; as listed bodies those bodies listed as 'Other Organisations' in the *Civil Service Year Book*; and as 'other bodies' selected public bodies not so listed. The purpose of devising the classification system is, of course, to determine whether the pattern of regional boundaries used by government departments differs from that used by other public organizations with regional structures. Because of time constraints and data gaps, our coverage of 'other bodies' in this chapter is incomplete, and is confined to bodies whose operations have a reasonably direct impact on the general public. This classification gave us a total of thirty-seven departmental units, eleven units for bodies listed in the *Civil Service Year Book* and twelve units for other public bodies. All these units are listed in the appendix to this chapter.

ANALYSIS BY TYPE OF ORGANIZATION

This section analyses variations within and between types of organization in the extent to which they use standard region boundaries. The main conclusions which emerge are:

(*a*) the overall low use of standard regions for administrative purposes in all three categories, and a particularly low usage by selected other public bodies;
(*b*) the wide variations in the use of standard regions between the various organizations in each category, including in many cases variations between different units of the same organization.

The first conclusion is revealed by the results in columns (4) and (6) of Table 2.1. The scores in column (4) represent the number of times standard regions or standard regions with minor modifications are used. Thus for government departments the score is 93 out of a possible maximum total of 296 if all 8 standard regions were used by each of the 37 units, for listed bodies the score is 32 out of a possible maximum total of 88, and for selected other public bodies the score is 14 out of a possible maximum total of 96. (The number of standard regions used by each unit is listed in the appendix.)

The scores in column (6) provide a general indication of the degree of deviation from standard region boundaries. They represent the number of times standard regions or standard regions with minor modifications are used, plus the number

Table 2.1. Use of English standard regions by government departments, other organizations listed in the Civil Service Year Book, and other selected public bodies.

Type of unit (1)	Geographical coverage (1)	No of English standard regions used (2)	No. of standard regions used with minor modifications (3)	(2)+(3) (4)	No of standard regions not cross-cut (excl. (3)+(4)) (5)	(4)+(5) (6)	Maximum possible score* (7)	Comment (8)
Government departments	United Kingdom 10 Great Britain 4 England and Wales 12 England 11 Total 37	78	15	93	93	186	296	There are five cases where unit subdivisions aggregate to a standard region, and five unit subdivisions which comprise two standard regions.
Other organizations listed in the Civil Service Year Book	United Kingdom 1 Great Britain 8 England and Wales 1 England 1 Total 11	25	7	32	21	53	88	There are four unit subdivisions which comprise two standard regions, and two unit subdivisions which aggregate to a standard region.
Other selected public bodies	United Kingdom 2 Great Britain 6 England and Wales 2 England 2 Total 12	7	7	14	23	37	96	There are two unit subdivisions which aggregate to a standard region.
Totals	United Kingdom 13 Great Britain 18 England and Wales 15 England 14 60	110	29	139	137	276	480	

* i.e. if all standard regions had been used by all units in the category.

of times the boundaries of other standard regions are not cross-cut by the boundaries used by units. Thus for government departments the score in column (6) is 186 out of a possible maximum of 296 (i.e., if no standard regions were cross-cut by any of the 36 units), for listed bodies the score is 53 out of a possible maximum of 88, and for other selected public bodies the score is 37 out of a possible maximum of 96. These scores reveal a higher level of deviation from standard region boundaries among the units of other selected public bodies than among those of the listed bodies or government departments.

One interesting sidelight cast by Table 2.1 is that column (1) shows that England is governed by organizations with a variety of territorial jurisdictions ranging from those covering England only to those covering the whole of the United Kingdom. England as such is covered by only about a quarter of the units. The territorial coverage of units operating in England is determined not by whether special arrangements are made for England but whether separate arrangements are made for one or more of Northern Ireland, Scotland, or Wales (normally in that order) Thus 'England' is a residual category. (The geographical coverage of individual units is listed in the appendix.)

These findings may be further illuminated by examining the variations in the use of standard region boundaries among the units in each category, including variations between different units in the same organization. These variations are shown for each type of unit in Table 2.2 (Column (1) shows that government department units are much more likely than other units to use five or more standard regions, though this accounts for only 10 out of 37 departmental units. Column (3) shows that none of the selected other public bodies uses more than 3 standard regions.

Examination of the difference among the government department units reveals a tendency for units represented on the Regional Economic Planning Boards (REPBs) to use more standard regions than other units. Thus, whereas all units which use 6 or more standard regions are represented on the REPBs, 14 of the 15 units which do not use any standard regions, including 3 from the Home Office and 3 from the

Table 2.2. Variations in use of English standard regions or standard regions with minor modifications

No. of English standard regions used + minor modifications	Government departments (1)	Listed bodies (2)	Other selected bodies (3)	Total
8	1	—	—	1
7	—	—	—	—
6	6	2	—	8
5	3	—	—	3
4	4	4	—	8
3	2	—	4	6
2	5	2	—	7
1	2	—	2	4
0	14	3	6	23
Total	37	11	12	60

revenue departments, are not represented. The average number of standard regions used by units represented on the REPBs is 4.2, whereas the average number of standard regions used by the remaining units 1.5. (The units which are represented on the REPBs are indicated in the appendix.)

It may at first sight appear that low use of standard regions is simply due to the fact that the number of regions used by some units is substantially higher or lower than the number of standard regions (8). Table 2.3 shows that in fact over half of the units have between 7 and 9 regions. Of these, only one —the Regional Economic Planning Boards themselves—uses all 8 regions, while no others use more than 6. Half of the units with 8 regions use *none* of the 8 standard regions (even allowing for minor modifications). Table 2.3 shows that the propensity of units to use some standard regions is greater if the number of regions they use is between 7 and 10. The average number of standard regions used by all units is 2.2, while the average number of standard regions used by units with between 7 and 10 regions is 3.3. However, it is clear that the existence of units within a number of regions substantially higher or lower than the number of standard regions is insufficient in itself to explain the generally low use of standard regions by units, since even units with numbers of regions the same as or close to the number of standard regions have a generally low propensity to use more than a few of the standard regions.

Table 2.3. Relationship between number of unit regions and use of standard regions (or minor modifications)

Number of regions used by unit	Number of standard regions (including minor modifications)									
	0	1	2	3	4	5	6	7	8	Total
2	1									1
3	3									3
4	4									4
5	1									1
6	2									2
7		1	5		5					11
8	5			1		1	2		1	10
9		2		1	1	2	6			12
10	1		1	2	1					5
11	2	1								3
12	1			1						2
13										0
14				1						1
15		1			1					2
16 and over	3									3
Total	22	4	7	6	8	3	8	0	1	60

To sum up, this section has shown an overall low use of standard regions, with the selected other public bodies scoring lower than the other types of unit, and a wide variation in the use of standard regions both between different units in the same category and, in some cases, between different units of the same organization.

ANALYSIS BY REGION

The previous section showed that government organizations vary in the extent to which the boundaries of regions they use for administrative purposes conform to those of the standard regions. This variation was not simply a contrast between those who used all standard regions and those who used none but variation in the number of standard regions used. This section examines the implications of this fact from a regional perspective—are there significant variations between standard regions in the extent to which they are used for administrative purposes? Table 2.4 summarizes the results of an analysis by standard region of the regional boundaries used by units.

Table 2.4. Relationship between each standard region and regions used by departments and other public bodies

Region and type of unit*	No. of units using standard region boundaries	As (1) with modifica-tions	(1)+(2)	No. not subdividing region (ex-cluding (1), (2))	No. using boundaries aggregating to standard region	Others	Not applic:
	(1)	(2)	(3)	(4)	(5)	(6)	(7)
NORTH							
Departmental	11	4	15	7	0	15	0
Listed bodies	7	0	7	0	0	4	0
Other bodies	1	1	2	2	1	7	0
Totals	19	5	24	9	1	26	0
YORKS & HUMBER							
Departmental	15	1	16	12	0	9	0
Listed bodies	8	0	8	0	1	2	0
Other bodies	1	1	2	2	0	8	0
Totals	24	2	26	14	1	19	0
E. MIDLANDS							
Departmental	12	1	13	5	0	18	0
Listed bodies	2	1	3	1	0	7	0
Other bodies	2	0	2	0	0	10	0
Totals	16	2	18	6	0	35	0
EAST ANGLIA							
Departmental	1	0	1	30	0	5	1
Listed bodies	0	0	0	9	0	2	0
Other bodies	1	0	1	7	0	4	0
Totals	2	0	2	46	0	11	1
SOUTH EAST							
Departmental	1	0	1	1	1	33	1
Listed bodies	0	0	0	0	0	11	0
Other bodies	0	0	0	0	0	12	0
Totals	1	0	1	1	1	56	1
SOUTH WEST							
Departmental	14	4	18	8	0	11	0
Listed bodies	3	3	6	0	0	5	0
Other bodies	1	0	1	1	0	10	0
Totals	18	7	25	9	0	26	0
W. MIDLANDS							
Departmental	15	0	15	14	1	7	0
Listed bodies	2	0	2	5	0	4	0
Other bodies	2	1	3	2	0	7	0
Totals	19	1	20	21	1	18	0

Region and type of unit*	(1)	(2)	(3)	(4)	(5)	(6)	(7)
NORTH WEST							
Departmental	9	3	12	12	2	11	0
Listed bodies	3	3	6	1	0	4	0
Other bodies	0	4	4	2	1	5	0
Totals	12	10	22	15	3	20	0
SCOTLAND‡							
Departmental	34	0	34	1	2	0	0
Listed bodies	7	0	7	0	4	0	0
Other bodies	6	3	9	0	2	1	0
Totals	47	3	50	1	8	1	0
WALES‡							
Departmental	24	0	24	6	1	6	0
Listed bodies	9	0	9	0	2	0	0
Other bodies	4	1	5	0	0	7	0
Totals	37	1	38	6	3	13	0

* Departmental units are those in departments listed as such in the *Civil Service Year Book*; listed bodies are units in other bodies listed in the *Civil Service Year Book*; other bodies are selected public sector bodies not listed in the *Civil Service Year Book*; for full list see Appendix to this chapter.

† Regional Development Grant Offices; East Anglia and the South East have no assisted areas.

‡ Tabulated according to corresponding type of body in England; Scotland and Wales have additional bodies of their own, and departments and other bodies may have their regions within Scotland and Wales.

Three general points emerge clearly from the figures in Table 2.4:

(*a*) In no English region is the standard region (plus minor modifications to the standard region) used even as much as half the time—the highest figure is 26 out of 60.

(*b*) There is very substantial variation between the regions in the extent to which the standard regions are used, with the highest score being 26 out of 60 and the lowest 1 out of 60.

(*c*) Where the standard regional boundaries (or minor variations) are not used, there are very substantial variations between regions in the relationship between the standard regions and the boundaries actually used by the unit. Thus cases where such boundaries do not subdivide the standard region (col. 4) vary between 1 and 46, and cases where subdivision does occur but the regions do not aggregate up to the standard region (col. 6) vary between 11 and 56. In all English regions, there are either no or very few cases where the regions used aggregate up to the standard region, the highest being the North West with 3.

These variations enable us to group four of the standard regions as having similar characteristics, with each of the other four constituting a type of their own.

North, Yorkshire and Humberside, South West, North West

All these regions share the following general characteristics:

Moderate use of standard regions (or minor variations) (col. 3)	22-6 out of 60
Low number of 'not subdivided' cases (col. 4)	9-15 out of 60
Moderate number of 'other' cases (col. 6)	19-26 out of 60

These regions are those where there is the greatest use of standard regions (or minor variations). The fact that the three northernmost regions all have similar characteristics should not be regarded as a coincidence. Since the Scottish border almost always forms a boundary (see below), the scope for deviation from the North standard region in that direction is limited. Where the North region as a whole is used as a region by a unit there is a very high chance that Yorkshire and Humberside and the North West will also be used. Conversely, where, say, Cumbria is not included with the rest of the North region, and the rest is lumped in with all or part of Yorkshire and Humberside, this automatically implies that the North West and Yorkshire and Humberside will not be used. In fact, the joining of Cumbria with the North West rather than the North standard region occurs regularly, 11 times among other body units. In the case of the South West, its relatively high score for use of the standard region can be explained by its peninsular nature. Its relatively low score for 'not subdivided' (col. 4) and its relatively high score for 'other' (col. 6) may in part be explained by its great length, and in part by its proximity to the South East (see below).

Both the North West and the South West have a relatively high amount of use of the standard region with minor modifications. In the North West this reflects the inclusion of the

Barrow enclave (from Cumbria) and/or High Peak (from Derbyshire), and in the South West to the treatment of the Ringwood
employment exchange area by the Department of Employment Group and the treatment of Bournemouth by some
other bodies.

Turning to the use of these four standard regions by different types of bodies, we can see that these four regions are
much less likely to be used by 'other bodies' than by 'listed
bodies' or departmental units. This is particularly the case in
Yorkshire and Humberside and the South West where the bulk
of other bodies use boundaries which cross-cut the standard
regions. In part, this reflects the 'functional' criteria for drawing boundaries of bodies such as British Rail or the Water
Authorities, but it also in part reflects the institutional history
of some of the bodies.

West Midlands

In the West Midlands the results show:

Moderate use of standard region (col. 3)	20 out of 60
Moderate number of 'not subdivided cases' (col. 4)	21 out of 60
Low-moderate number of 'other' cases (col. 6)	18 out of 60

The West Midland (or minor variations) is used slightly less
often as a region by all units only). The particularly distinctive
feature of the West Midlands is the relatively high number of
units which use regions which wholly contain the standard
region but are larger than the region. To a small extent, this
reflects the use of a combined Midlands region by some bodies,
e.g. in the Department of Employment Group, but as we will
see when examining the East Midlands, this only explains a
small number of cases. What happens most frequently is that
parts of the North West, East Midlands, or South West are combined with the whole of the West Midlands to form a region.
Thus, while the West Midlands scores lower than North, Yorkshire and Humberside, North West, and South West on the number of times the standard region itself is used, it scores higher
than them in terms of not being cross-cut by the boundaries

used by units. In just over two-thirds of the cases, the counties forming the West Midlands are all in the same region.

East Midlands

In the East Midlands the results show:

Low-moderate use of standard region (col. 3)	18 out of 60
Very low number of 'not subdivided' cases (col. 4)	6 out of 60
High number of 'other' cases (col. 6)	35 out of 60

It can readily be seen that the East Midlands is not simply the 'twin' of the West Midlands. The East Midlands has a slightly smaller number of units using the standard region boundaries and, more significantly, has a very much higher number of cases which cross-cut the standard region boundaries and join part of the East Midlands to the whole of or parts of East Anglia, Yorkshire and Humberside, West Midlands, and the South East. The explanation for this contrast is not immediately obvious. Population does not provide an obvious answer, since although the East Midlands has a smaller population than that of the West Midlands and three of the other four regions so far considered, the difference is not sizeable (see Table 2.5). In

Table 2.5. Populations of standard regions (1978)

	Millions	
North	3.1	
Yorkshire & Humberside	4.9	
East Midlands	3.8	
East Anglia	1.8	
South East	16.8	
South West	4.3	
West Midlands	5.2	
North West	6.5	
England		46.3
Scotland	5.2	
Wales	2.8	
Great Britain		54.3

Source: *Regional Statistics* 15, 1980, Table 2.1

any case, we would expect smaller size to lead to a greater number of 'not subdivided' rather than 'other' cases. Part of the explanation may lie in the changes in boundaries of the region twice in the past fifteen years, and even a change in name in 1965 from North Midland to East Midlands (see Map 2.1). This is bound to have reduced the extent to which the component counties would be regarded as a group which should be administered together. However, this can at best be considered a partial explanation, since Yorkshire and Humberside, which has a much higher use of standard regions, underwent boundary changes of a similar scale.

East Anglia

In East Anglia the results show:

Very low use of the standard region (col. 3)	2 out of 60
Very high number of 'not subdivided cases' (col. 4)	46 out of 60
Low number of 'other' cases (col. 6)	11 out of 60

Apart from the Regional Economic Planning Board, which is supposed to co-ordinate the work of departments in the region, the only other unit conforming to the 'standard' region is the Regional Health Authority. Even the Regional Director of the Departments of Environment/Transport, who is the Chairman of the Regional Economic Planning Board, is responsible for a wider area in his Regional Director role. By far the majority of cases consist of the whole of the East Anglia region being included with part or whole of another standard region, with the most common occurrence being the combination of East Anglia with varying numbers of the northern counties of the South East. The explanation for this pattern is the small size of the population of East Anglia, particularly when related to the very large size of the neighbouring South East (see Table 2.5). (The existence of Northern Ireland, which has an even smaller population but which almost always has its own separate region of UK-wide bodies, reminds us that population has to be seen in the context of geographical contiguity and political and administrative history.) The obvious conclusion to draw is that East Anglia is normally considered too small to form a region for administrative purposes.

A glance at Map 2.1 will confirm that there are good

geographical reasons why the three counties forming East Anglia are normally kept together, though there are eleven cases when the region is split up and added to parts of other regions. Thus we have the apparent paradox that though the identity of the East Anglia region is very low in terms of its use as a standard region, East Anglia scores the highest of any English region in terms of its component counties being grouped together rather than split up.

South East

In the South East the results show:

Very low use of standard region (col. 3)	1 out of 60
Very low number of 'not subdivided' cases (col. 4)	1 out of 60
Very high number of 'other' cases (col. 6)	56 out of 60

Apart from the Regional Economic Planning Board, the South East is split up into a varying number of areas, with istrative purposes. The main explanation is fairly simple, and can be seen from Table 2.5—the South East is regarded as too large in terms of population to be used as a single administrative unit. However, it is interesting to note in terms of the use of the regional boundaries, that the approach adopted is not simply to subdivide the standard region (col. 5 of Table 2.4); there is only one case where this is done. Rather, the South East is split up into a verying number of areas, with one or more of these being joined up with part or whole of another standard region or regions to form the administrative region used.

Because the overwhelmingly dominant pattern is one of total disregard for the standard region, measurement of the extent of deviation is not a very helpful way of describing the pattern of regional administration which does exist in the South East, so it is worth commenting briefly on some of the configurations which do occur. A very common pattern is for Bedfordshire, Hertfordshire, and Essex or all counties north of London and the Thames to be grouped with the whole of East Anglia to form an Eastern region. A less frequently occurring configuration is the use of a Southern region in the west of the South East, sometimes taking in part of the South West standard region. (Dorset is taken in to a Southern region by fourteen units.) London is sometimes treated as one or more separate regions, with the boundaries not always coinciding with those of the GLC. (A related feature is that London is sometimes dealt with as a headquarters function rather than as a region.) In addition to various combinations of these configurations, there are also a number of idiosyncratic arrangements.

Comparison with Scotland and Wales

Although this study is concerned with the English regions, comparison with Scotland and Wales is of interest to establish whether the existence of the Scottish and Welsh Offices is accompanied by a greater use of standard regions for administrative purposes.

Taking Scotland first, and confining ourselves to units corresponding to those we analysed for the English regions (see note to Table 2.4) we find that Scotland has the following characteristics:

Very high use of the standard region (col. 3)	50 out of 60
Very low number of 'not subdivided' cases (col. 4)	1 out of 60
Very low number of 'other' cases (col. 6)	1 out of 60

It is also worth noting that Scotland has a higher number of cases where Scotland is subdivided into regions which aggregate up to Scotland (8 out of 60) than any of the English regions, though the number is still low. Scotland and the South East of England can be seen as opposite extremes; whereas the South East standard region is virtually never used for administrative purposes, Scotland is virtually always used. The main reason for the use of Scotland as a unit is its political and administrative history, with this being reinforced by its suitable population size. Of the 60 units, Scotland has a separate department or organization for 31 of them. In other words the Scottish border represents not simply a regional boundary, but a departmental or system boundary. For GB or UK units 11 out of 14 departmental units use Scotland as a region (1 includes Scotland in a larger region, and 2 subdivided Scotland), 4 out of 8 'listed' body units use Scotland (the other 4 subdividing it), and 3 out of 9 'other' units use Scotland (plus 3 using it with minor modifications, 2 subdividing it, and 1—the IBA—joining part of Scotland with part of the North region in England).

Turning to Wales, we find that it has the following characteristics:

High use of the standard region (col. 3)	38 out of 60
Very low number of 'not subdivided' cases (col. 4)	6 out of 60
Low number of 'other cases' (col. 6)	13 out of 60

Wales can be seen as lying intermediate between Scotland and the group of four English regions—North, Yorkshire and Humberside, South West, and North West—which were identified as sharing common characteristics. This intermediate position can again be attributed to the political and administrative history of Wales, with a steady increase in the functions administered by the Welsh Office since its establishment in 1964 but with many functions still being administered on an England and Wales basis. Of the 60 units, the Welsh Office or a separate Welsh body are responsible for 19. There is a noticeable tendency for 'other' bodies to be less likely to use Wales as a region than departments or 'listed' bodies; 7 out of 12 'other bodies' (7 out of 10 of those operating on a Great Britain or England and Wales basis) split Wales up and join one or more of the parts with part of England. We should expect a continuing trend towards treating Wales as an administrative unit; for example, Wales is due to become a separate Traffic Area instead of being split and joined up with parts of England.

Variation between English regions

The use of English standard regions for administrative purposes can be seen to differ from that in Scotland and Wales. At least as significant as this, however, is the wide variation between English regions. Viewed solely in terms of use of the standard region (or minor variations) we can rank the regions in the following order: Scotland (50), Wales (38), Yorkshire and Humberside (26), South East (25), North (24), North West (22), West Midlands (20), East Midlands (18), East Anglia (2), and South East (1). However, as Fig. 2.1 shows, this simple

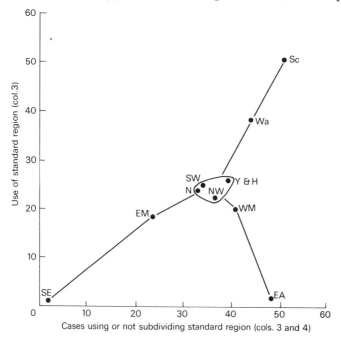

Fig. 2.1. Compatibility with standard regions

ranking conceals an important difference among English regions. We can group the regions of Great Britain in terms of the 'central' group of four English regions—North, Yorkshire and Humberside, South West, North West—with three groups of two regions 'radiating' out from this group. Wales and Scotland lie on an axis which represents both increasing use of the standard region itself and increasing use of all boundaries which do not subdivide the standard region. Conversely, the East Midlands and the South East lie on an axis which represents decreasing use of the standard region and increasing cross-cutting of the standard region. The West Midlands and East Anglia lie on an axis which represents decreasing use of the standard region at the same time as increasing use of all boundaries which do not subdivide the standard region. Thus, East Anglia is hardly ever used for administrative purposes, yet it is cross-cut less often than Wales, which is used as a region by two-thirds of units.

It can be seen that the four English regions with the highest scores for use of standard regions are also those which are the most 'peripheral' in England, while the two regions in the South Eastern 'core' are those with the lowest scores. We discussed above some of the possible geographical factors explaining this pattern. The high score for the most peripheral regions may also be related to their relative distancing from 'spillover' effects from the South East, though the South West is affected by this to some extent—Dorset is excluded from the South West standard region and included in a separate Southern region by fourteen units. The four peripheral regions are also the regions which are perceived to have 'regional problems' and have contained almost all the designated Assisted Areas. This is reflected in the special functions of the Department of Industry regional offices for these regions (these functions are discussed in detail in the chapter by Hogwood on the regional dimension of regional policy administration).

Our analysis of the (lack of) use of standard regions for administrative purposes in the South East and East Anglia confirms that the major difficulty in attempting to delimit regional boundaries in England for administrative, economic planning or legislative devolution purposes is to delimit the areas to be covered by the region or regions in the South East. This reflects both the sheer size of London and the area which looks towards it and the special problems of devising arrangements for the metropolitan centre.

IMPLICATIONS AND CONCLUSIONS

Our analysis has shown both an overall low use of standard regions in England as a systematic basis for the administrative regions used by government departments and other public bodies and a high degree of variation between organizations and between regions in the use of standard regions. The first issue which has to be tackled in the light of this analysis is how this state of affairs has arisen and developed despite the Treasury's post-war attempt at standardization and the mid-1960s emphasis on regional co-ordination and planning. Short of detailed research into the drawing up of the boundaries of each organization, no definitive answer can be given to the question of how regional boundaries are chosen, but certain suggestive factors can be explored. Among these are the 'function' being carried out, the span of control of the chief regional officers, the optimum level of population to be served, the organizational history, and the extent to which the organization is open to pressures to conform to standard boundaries and the boundaries used by other organizations. These factors may be mutually reinforcing or at times pulling in opposite directions.

Taking first the 'functional' argument, it is clear that there are a number of organizations, mainly the listed bodies and other bodies, where activities are structured territorially in such a way as to make it sensible for the boundaries to cut across standard regions or even counties. Thus the Water Authorities follow watersheds. In the case of British Rail it would make little sense in railway management terms to treat Wales as a region, since the three separate pieces of track do not connect with each other. However, not all such boundaries are wholly justifiable in purely functional terms: it is not clear why gas should be able to treat Wales as a region while electricity cross-cuts it. Deviations from standard regions by Regional Health Authorities (RHAs) are justified on the grounds that each RHA should contain a teaching hospital, but the need for access to a teaching hospital could, in principle, be handled by agency arrangements. To understand such boundaries in full we also have to understand the organizational history of the bodies concerned, including the areas covered by predecessor organizations and the 'convential wisdom' within the organization about the appropriate criteria for determining boundaries.

Related to the 'functional' criterion is the question of the optimum population, if any, to be served by a regional office, since the population to be served may not be directly related to the whole human population. In the case of the Forestry

Commission the relevant population is trees, which explains why Scotland has four regions, Wales has two, and England only five. For the Ministry of Agriculture, Fisheries, and Food (MAFF), the relevant population is farmers, and relating to 'functional' considerations, we can understand why a MAFF regional boundary goes right through the middle of Greater London—it would not make any difference whether it went to the north or the south.

It has to be stressed that in looking at the regional bound-aries used by a unit we are not dealing with a fixed set of boundaries but a set which changes over time for internal organizational reasons, with the changes at any given time not necessarily being related to the standard regions of the time. Such changes may occur when a unit decides to build up or run down its regional outposts, or when the workload faced by particular regional offices has changed. Organizational mergers, whether internal mergers or divisions or mergers with other organizations, are quite likely to lead to changes in re-gional boundaries. Thus for example, the Manpower Services Commission (MSC) recently went through a whole cycle of changes associated with its merger with the formerly separate Employment Services and Training Services Agencies, the allo-cation of responsibility for manpower services to the Scottish and Welsh Offices, and the establishment of seven new regional offices in England, which also involved changes in the regional boundaries of the Employment and Training Services, and the delineation of new MSC regional boundaries. Such adjust-ments may lead to greater standardization within an organiz-ation or departmental group, but may not lead to a greater standardization in all cases with the standard regions, or with the regions used by other departments. It has to be stressed that organizational mergers do not automatically lead to in-ternal standardization. Although the total number of differ-ent sets of regions within the Departments of Environment/ Transport is slightly smaller than at the time of the original formation of the Department of the Environment in 1970, considerable diversity still remains, and, for example, the Traffic Areas, Road Construction Unit Areas, and Roads and Transportation Controllers Regions still have different sets of boundaries.

Although decisions about which boundaries to use are essentially taken by each individual department or other organization, it is clear that many of them do take into account the standard regions existing at the time when the boundaries are drawn, and some are adjusted to take account of changes in standard region boundaries. However, changes by some units (perhaps relating only to some regions) to conform to standard regions while others stick to the pattern of old standard regions or regions of their own design may *decrease* the common use of boundaries. Thus we have the paradox that partial moves towards 'standardization' may lead to greater proliferation of sets of boundaries.

Clearly, there are both costs and benefits attached to any move towards greater standardization. The boundaries chosen by each department or agency may be optimal or acceptable from the perspective of each, but viewed in terms of the operation of government as a whole the proliferation of boundaries may be suboptimal and pose problems for the co-ordination of related activities at regional level.

Our findings raise an issue connected with administrative co-ordination and the role of REPBs and (prior to their demise) the REPCs which has not, to our knowledge, previously been raised. This is that the variation between standard regions in the use of these regions for administrative purposes must result in differences *between* standard regions in the nature of administrative co-ordination between units at regional level and in the role of the REPBs. We are not implying any simple determinism: for example, the task of administrative co-ordination and planning is clearly much more complex (and arguably more necessary) in the South East than in any other region, but this could lead to anything between the extremes of co-ordination and planning at the level of the South East planning region being merely shadow play to extra effort being exerted to overcome this complexity. Unfortunately, the literature on regional economic planning and on the operation of regional offices offers us little guidance about how the implications of variations between regions work out in practice. Either only one or a very small number of regions are studied in detail, or the issue is discussed largely in general terms.[8]

Clearly the task of regional co-ordination must be made

West Midlands

County Council

Planning Department

more difficult in all cases by the lack of standardization of boundaries. For example Hennessy reported that when Regional Emergency Committees were established during the road haulage dispute in the winter of 1978/9 the ones which worked best were those where departmental boundaries were co-terminous.[9] However, that is not to say that standardization of boundaries would itself lead to greater co-ordination between departments; the problems posed by differing degrees of discretion accorded to regional offices and the essentially vertical lines of control to London would still remain.[10]

Where civil servants or other administrators are responsible for different areas the development of a regional identity and of a 'regional community' corresponding to the 'village community' of Whitehall is bound to be hindered, even where regional offices are in the same location. From the perspective of a local authority, it may find itself in different regions according to which department or agency it is dealing with. Similarly, identification by MPs and citizens with regions used for administrative purposes can only develop when common regions are used. It should be stressed that we are not implying some kind of 'boundary determinism' by which standardization of regional boundaries would lead to a greater political identification with regions and the greater exercise of power at regional level. Rather, we are suggesting that the absence of standardization both reflects a lower political and administrative identification with English regions compared to Scotland and Wales, and may hinder the development of such identification.

Set against such possible potential benefits from greater standardization of regional boundaries are the undoubted costs arising both from the process of standardization and the continuation of standardization. In many cases it would be relatively easy to change regional boundaries where these are the product of historical accident (though some disruption would inevitably result from changes), but where existing regional functions are substantial or there is a 'functional' or 'population served' basis to the existing agency boundaries (as is arguably the case with, for example, water and railways) some costs of a continuing nature would be incurred by the standardization of boundaries.

If the issue of devolution to English regional assemblies or even of regional assemblies to 'oversee' the operation of the regional organization of *ad hoc* bodies were ever to develop, then the questions of standardization of boundaries discussed above would inevitably emerge. This would be true both for the functions to be taken over by regional assemblies and for those remaining with the London departments which had to be co-ordinated with the devolved functions. The issue is not, of course, simply one of standardization, but what to standard-ized to. In the North of England, the standard regions, perhaps with some modifications, are not obviously unsuitable as the basis for devolved regional assemblies. In the South East, how-ever, there are no obvious regional boundaries based on admin-istrative practice, nor is it even clear how many regions would be drawn. The designation of regional boundaries for devolved assemblies would not, of course, simply be a matter of admin-istrative considerations.

The analysis of regional boundaries cannot be seen in iso-lation from other aspects of government at regional level. The *ad hoc* process of boundary determination and the variety of systems resulting from this reflects the generally *ad hoc* ap-proach to regionalism in England. This *ad hoc* approach applies both to the pattern at any one time and to the processes of bringing about change over time. The analysis in this chapter is largely based on a 'snapshot' at a particular point in time (1979), but we have also shown that boundaries are continually being revised. We would expect the pattern we have described to change in future, for example, as a result of possible cut-backs in regional offices, but we would expect that diversity of boundary systems would continue to be the most obvious characteristic of the overall pattern.

APPENDIX

Names of units and use of regions, 1979

	Geo-graphical coverage	Number of unit regions in England	Number of standard regions used (inc. minor modifications).
Departmental units			
Department of Employment (unemployment benefit)	GB	7	4
Department of Industry regional offices*	E	8	6
Department of Industry Regional Development Grant Offices	GB	3	0
Departments of Industry/Trade Export Services*	E	8	6
Export Credit Guarantee Department	UK	8	0
Regional Economic Planning Boards*	UK	8	8
Departments of Environment/Transport Regional Directors*	E	8	6
Department of Environment Housing regions*	E	9	6
Department of Environment Planning regions*	E	9	6
Department of Environment Rent Assessment Panel Areas	E	15	4
Department of Environment Ancient Monuments Works Areas	GB	7	2
Department of Environment Audit Districts	E & W	11	1
Property Services Agency*	UK	8	0
Department of Transport Roads and Transport Controllers*	E	9	6
Department of Transport Road Construction Units	E	7	1
Department of Transport Traffic Areas	E & W	9	3
Home Office: Prison Service Regions	E & W	4	0
Home Office: Fire Inspectorate Regions	E & W	4	0
Home Office: HM Inspectorate of Constabulary	E & W	6	0
Home Defence Regions	E & W	9	4
Lord Chancellor's Office: Court Circuits	E & W	6	0
Ministry of Agriculture, Fisheries, and Food regions*	E	7	2
Ministry of Agriculture, Fisheries, and Food: Agricultural Development and Advisory Service	E & W	7	2
HM Land Registry	E & W	11	0
Department of Education and Science: HM Inspectors Divisions*	E & W	7	2

	Geo-graphical coverage	Number of unit regions in England	Number of standard regions used (inc. minor modifications).
DHSS: Social Work	E	9	5
DHSS: Social Security	GB	10	4
Ministry of Defence: TAVRA regions	UK	10	3
Ministry of Defence: Army Districts	UK	7	2
Ministry of Defence: Naval Flag Officers	UK	4	0
Civil Service Department regional offices	UK	8	5
HMSO	UK	3	0
Inland Revenue: Tax Organization	UK	12	0
Inland Revenue: Valuation Office Regions	E & W	23	0
Customs & Excise: Collections	UK	23	0
Central Office of Information*	E	9	5
Charity Commission	E & W	2	0

Units of bodies listed in Civil Service Year Book

Manpower Services Commission:			
Regional Manpower Services Directors*	GB	7	4
Employment Services Division	GB	15	2
Training Services Division	GB	7	4
Special Programmes Division	GB	7	4
Advisory Conciliation and Arbitration Service	GB	7	4
Health and Safety Executive	GB	18	0
Price Commission	UK	10	2
Countryside Commission	E & W	9	6
Nature Conservancy Council	GB	8	0
Sports Council	E	9	6
Forestry Commission	GB	5	0

Units of selected other public bodies

Tourist Board regions	E	12	3
Post Office: Postal regions	UK	8	0
Post Office: Telecommunications regions	UK	8	0
Regional Water Authorities	E & W	9	1
Housing Corporation regions	GB	8	3
British Rail regions	GB	4	0
National Bus Company regions	E & W	3	0
Electricity Boards	E & W	11	0
Gas Regions	GB	10	3
BBC regions	UK	9	1
IBA regions	UK	10	0
Regional Health Authorities	E	14	3

* Unit represented on the Regional Economic Planning Boards.
Note: Information about regions used by the Commission for Racial Equality and about the Department of Trade's Official Receivers Districts, Marine Offices and Marine Survey Offices was not available at the time of carrying out the analysis.

CHAPTER 3

The Status of regional government: an analysis of the West Midlands

MICHAEL KEATING AND MALCOLM RHODES

THIS chapter is a review of the nature and status of regional administration in England. While the data is derived from the study of one region, the West Midlands, the analysis is intended to be applicable to other English regions.

Regional administration poses a number of theoretical and practical problems for the British political scientist. We have a clear set of canons of the constitution at the level of central government, such as the sovereignty of Parliament, ministerial responsibility, and civil service anonymity. However abused these ideas have become in practice, they at least provide a starting point for analysis. At the local level, we have a strong municipal tradition and a rationale for local government in terms of local choice over divisible services and local responsibility within specific limits. However, there is no tradition of intermediate government and no set of conventions to provide ground rules for establishing intermediate institutions. As Nevil Johnson comments, 'we have a feeble grasp of the potential relationship between territory and power'.[1] The consequence has been a haphazard growth of bodies of very different types 'with nothing by way of an operational and co-ordinating middle level of the state administration'.[2]

These bodies include regional outposts of central government, *ad hoc* authorities such as the regional water and health authorities, the regional planning machinery, and a variety of regulatory and promotional bodies and quasi-governmental agencies. As a group, they have been characterized in a variety of ways—as a 'level of government',[3] as 'intermediate government',[4] as 'administrative convenience',[5] as *'ad hocracy'*[6]. Stemming from these characterizations has been a variety of proposals for reform. However, the characterizations have often suffered from a lack of rigour in definition and there has been little attempt to show how existing regional bodies fit into the overall pattern of administration in England.

The chapter is in four parts. Firstly, we consider the structure of regional administration, briefly describing the bodies in our sample and applying a framework for the analysis of structure. Then we consider the issues of power and discretion in regional administration. Then we consider regional institutions from two perspectives, as extensions of the centre and as 'intermediate government'. Finally, we consider the implications of our findings for prescriptions for reform.

THE STRUCTURE OF REGIONAL ADMINISTRATION

Our framework for the analysis of structure is adapted from Maass' framework for studying the division of governmental powers.[7] Maass sees powers as divisible by process, by function, and by constituency. As Maass does not give precise definitions of these terms and as we wish to adapt his usage, we give here our own definitions. Division by *process* refers to the familiar division of executive, legislative, and judicial powers as well as to the various stages in the policy process, such as policy formulation or implementation. By *function*, we mean distinct policy areas, such as education or agriculture or, within these, primary education or agricultural price support. *Constituency* is possibly the most difficult of the categories to operationalize, as Maass seems to reserve it for the electors of a unit of government. However, as most of the bodies involved in regional administration in England do not have electorates, we expand the term to include those to whom the body is responsible or in whose interests it is operating. Thus, it would make sense in our terms to talk of a body having the central government or local authorities as its constituency.

Powers can be divided by process, function, or constituency amongst bodies at the centre (the 'capital division of powers'), between the centre and the locality (the 'areal division of powers'), or between government and the private sector. They can be exercised exclusively by one unit or they can be shared.

A further concept needed for our analysis is that of

legitimacy by which bodies seek to justify their activities and their authority. There is a variety of ways in which authority is legitimized in British government but the principal ones are by reference to the sovereignty of the Crown in Parliament, by election or other means of ensuring that decisions reflect what Dahl[8] has called the criterion of personal choice; and by what Dahl has called the criterion of competence according to which decisions are taken by those most qualified to do so. Legitimacy is thus closely associated with our concept of constituency, as one of the means of legitimizing an agency's activities is by reference to a democratic, sovereign, or expert constituency.

We have chosen for our sample of regional institutions a group of bodies including examples of the main types which have featured in the debate about English regionalism. They comprise four government departments with regional outposts, two *ad hoc* authorities, two promotional agencies and one 'hived-off' agency.

Ministry of Agriculture, Fisheries, and Food (MAFF)

MAFF has organized itself into seven regional units in England; its internal structure has been largely determined by two features of its work. Firstly, decentralization has been considered essential to the efficient execution of its responsibilities since the Ministry is highly client-oriented and this arrangement facilitates the establishment of close relationships with the farmer and farming organizations. Secondly the Ministry is functionally split between the administrative side and the Agricultural Development and Advisory Service. The regional organization is headed by an Assistant Secretary who, as Chief Regional Officer, is responsible for the efficient and economic performance of the Ministry's functions in the region. Although the ADAS staff are directly responsible in technical matters to their respective divisions in London, the Regional Management Board, under the chairmanship of the Chief Regional Officer includes ADAS staff.

Exports Credits Guarantee Department (ECGB)

The ECGD is a separate department of government although it is accountable to the same ministers as the Department of

Trade. It operates mainly on a commercial basis although subject to Treasury and parliamentary control. At the London headquarters are the main administrative divisions and those responsible for underwriting long-term credit and the provision of special facilities for capital goods. The ten regional offices— three of which are located in London—are exclusively concerned with the marketing function, selling insurance and export advice. It is in the regional context that the ECGD is most visibly a commercial insurance company and its status as a government department is deliberately obscured. However, matters of policy are in the hands of headquarters.

Department of Industry (DI)

Although the old Department of Trade and Industry (DTI) has been split up in terms of ministerial responsibility there are common services at the regional level for the successor departments of Industry, Trade, and Energy (and until May 1979, Prices and Consumer Protection). The regional office of the Department of Industry, headed by a Regional Director at Assistant Secretary grade, is largely concerned with industrial assistance. The regional office is responsible for the initial sifting of companies applying for assistance and the preliminary appraisal of these applications and some decisions are made in the region.

Department of the Environment (DOE)

The DOE has a wide range of responsibilities, including planning, housing, construction, local government, water, environmental protection, and building research. While responsibility for transport has been given to a separate department in Whitehall, at the regional level transport and environment retain their common organization. Most of the responsibilities of the DOE are represented in the region, making its regional office the largest among government departments. It comprises three divisions: Plans and Planning, Housing and Environment, and Transport. These are headed by Assistant Secretaries who are responsible to the Regional Director who, as an Under Secretary, is the most senior civil servant in the region. The Regional Director is normally chairman of the Economic Planning Board and the Department provided secretarial facilities for the former Economic Planning Council. The DOE also acts as sponsor to the construction industry, operating through the Regional Joint Council, of which the Regional Director is chairman. The DOE is responsible at the national level for sport and recreation but this responsibility is not reflected at the regional level. The communications links between the regional office of the DOE and the Regional Council for Sport and Recreation and the West Midlands Countryside Commission are functionally specific and tend to be more infrequent and tenuous than the headquarters relationship might suggest, though the Regional Director of the DOE does chair the liaison committee for Sports and Recreation.

Regional Water Authorities: The Severn-Trent Water Authority (STWA)

The Water Act, 1973, created ten regional water authorities in England and Wales, to assume responsibility for water conservation and supply, sewerage and sewage disposal, pollution control, land drainage and flood prevention, and water recreation and fisheries. Responsibility for promoting a national policy rests with the Secretaries of State for the Environment and for Wales and the Minister of Agriculture, Fisheries and Food. The creation of the regional water authorities stemmed from a recognition of the functional interdependence of all stages of the hydrological cycle within a given river basin or catchment area. The STWA is headed by a corporate management team led by a chief executive but, as a statutory requirement, the members of the authority include a majority of local authority nominees.

Regional Health Authorities (RHA)

In 1974, fourteen Regional Health Authorities were created in England. In the three tier system of health service administration, the task of the Regional Health Authority mainly concerns strategic planning and the monitoring of Area Health Authorities. The Districts are concerned with the practical delivery of health care, while the Area Health Authorities are in a position to engage to a certain degree in both activities. Originally the members of the Regional Health Authority were appointed directly by the Secretary of State but currently the requirement is that one third of the membership should be local authority nominees.

Regional Arts Associations: West Midlands Arts (WMA)

An arts association has existed in the Midlands since 1957 and in 1970 separate associations for the East and West Midlands were created and in conjunction with local authorities have since that time assumed a major role in the planning and development of the arts in the region. West Midlands Arts is an independent charity—that is neither a regional branch of the Arts Council of Great Britain, nor a purely local authority agency. Membership of WMA is available to all the local authorities and any interested corporate organizations in the region. It comprises a Management Council of which half the members (41) are local authority representatives, one from each principal council in the region, an Executive Committee which is accountable to the Management Council for the general administration of WMA, and the Director and staff who together with the Executive Committee constitute the focal point of the organization in terms of the conduct of business. The primary function of WMA is the administration of grant-aid and it is to this that the greatest emphasis is given. WMA is distinguished in its status as an independent charity and this is reflected in the organizational structure, mode of operation, in the absence of a management relationship with a parent body outside the region, and of course in its funding arrangements.

The Countryside Commission

In 1968 the Countryside Commission replaced the National Parks Commission as an independent statutory body and assumed its functions and responsibilities when the Countryside Act became law. This Act in combination with the National Parks and Access to the Countryside Act 1949 and the local Government Act 1974 provide the statutory basis for the operation of the Commission. A major part of the Commission's work concerns the designation of national parks subject to confirmation by the Secretary of State for the Environment. The Commission advises on the planning and management of national parks. These are administered either by national park boards (e.g. in the Peak District) or as in the majority of cases, by county council committees. Since the formation of the Commission the staff has been tied to the Civil Service. The Commission is considered to have '. . . unique status amongst public bodies . . . it was never divorced from the Civil Service like its grant-aided cousins (The Forestry Commission, the English Tourist Board, the Design Council). It is a limb of the Department of the Environment.'9 The Commission acts primarily as an advisory body whose major tasks centre upon the functions of research and publicity, and the statutory responsibilities to advise government at both national and local level in the implementation of policy. It is now clear that the Commission finds increasing difficulty in fulfilling the vast range of commitments which is implied in a regional recreational strategy and this difficulty stems primarily from staffing shortages and acting, as it does, in an advisory capacity and through a system of grant-aid.

Manpower Services Commission (MSC)

While employment policy in general, industrial relations, and pay policy are the responsibility of the Department of Employment proper, the Manpower Services Commission, which was established in 1974, is charged with the task of administering the public employment and training services and has the responsibility for the development and operation of a comprehensive manpower policy. MSC maintains a continuing assessment of manpower resources and requirements both for the whole economy and for particular industries and occupations. The Commission, which is separate from government but accountable to the Secretary of State for Employment, has seven regional manpower services boards, each with a director. The Boards have the task of representing the Commission in the regions and are funded by an annual grant-in-aid from the Department of Employment.

One of the most striking features of regional administration in England, as Hogwood and Lindley show, is the diversity of boundaries among the various agencies. Essentially, this is a consequence of the English tradition of dividing administration vertically by function, rather than by territory. Viewed from the centre, there is no obvious or natural way of dividing

England into regions, nor is any body at the centre able to take such an overall view. Boundaries, then, have usually been chosen for the convenient administration of individual functions. The West Midlands—defined here as the counties of *Staffordshire, Salop, Hereford and Worcester, Warwickshire,* and *West Midlands metropolitan county,* is one of the more cohesive regions but even here we find that the MAFF region includes Cheshire for reasons of 'agricultural affinity' with the other counties. The Manpower Services Commission uses different boundaries for different functions, an inheritance from the Training Services Agency and the Employment Services Agency which it has absorbed. The Severn-Trent Water authority has boundaries which differ substantially from those of any other agency, reflecting the needs of technical efficiency in the water management function.

In recent years, some progress has been made by the DOE in rationalizing regional boundaries on the basis of the planning regions. Its own structure is based on this as is that of the DTI group. Other bodies have also been prevailed upon to use planning region's boundaries. These include West Midland Arts, the Sports Council, and the Countryside Commission. The latter represents a rare instance of territorial tidiness being preferred to functional logic as the boundary of the Commisson's West Midlands region passes through the Peak District National Park and the Wye valley.

Division of Powers

We now apply the framework developed earlier for analysing the areal division of powers in terms of process, function, constitutency, and legitimacy. The division of functions in regional administration, in particular, has been a source of considerable confusion. For example, Crowther-Hunt and Peacock say of the organization of regional offices of government:

The general principle on which departments have devolved functions to their regional and local offices is that policy matters and the formulation of policy are dealt with at departmental headquarters while the administration of policy and the attendant casework ... is handled and decided at the department's regional office.[10]

We would call this a division of *process*, reserving the term *function* for policy areas. There is, in the case of most government departments, no functional differentiation between the centre and the region. The organization of departments is dictated largely by administrative convenience and historical circumstances rather than by whether there is a distinct policy area best dealt with at the regional level. Departments have the task of carrying out the centre's policy in the regions so that their constituency is central government. Their authority and legitimacy are derived from the sovereignty of the centre. So it is most useful to regard the regional offices as the end of functional chains, each with its place in a functionally-based hierarchy. This is clearly illustrated in the case of MAFF, where there are two hierarchies, one for administration and another for technical services, each stretching from the field to headquarters. The regional level is distinguished by its geographical location and the stages in the policy process in which it is involved. The picture is similar in the MSC, where the different divisions are divided, in terms of function, from each other, but not from their respective headquarters organizations.

In the case of the ECGD, the division between region and headquarters is a little more than that between policy-making and execution. The regional offices are concerned with the marketing function of selling insurance and export advice, while headquarters is responsible for the rest of the work. However, although there may be a functional split here, it is between closely complementary functions. There is no territorial division in terms of constituency, which comprises central government and its client firms. (The issue of legitimacy and authority did arise with the Labour Government's attempt to use the ECGD in furtherance of its incomes policy but this did not raise *territorial* issues.)

The DTI group of regional offices represent the ends of functional hierarchies in several policy areas, the main one of which concerns industrial development and selective industrial assistance. There is some areal division by process, with a range of detailed decisions effectively given to the regional offices but formally taken by London but they are taken within a national policy framework and for a national constituency. So, at least until recently, the main task of the Department of Industry has concerned the location of industry nationally and the balance *between* regions. In the West Midlands, this meant refusing Industrial Development Certificates and persuading industrialists to invest elsewhere.

In the DOE, too, functions tend to be divided among divisions both at headquarters and in the region but not areally between headquarters and region. An attempt was made to create an integrated regional structure by stipulating that the three divisions, for Plans and Planning, Housing and Environment, and Roads and Transport, should be responsible to the Regional Director. In practice, however, it appears that, at least in the case of Roads and Transport, it was the functional links between the division in the region and the corresponding division in Whitehall which were more important. Thus it was possible to separate the departments of Environment and Transport in Whitehall without disturbing the formal allocation of functions in the region. The constituency of the DOE, too, is largely national, with the regional offices being responsible for implementing national policy, mainly through local authorities.

In the case of the DOE, however, there are qualifications to this picture. A distinct function has emerged at the regional level, that of regional planning, closely associated with the processes of co-ordination and communication among local and regional bodies. To some extent, the regional offices of the DOE have developed a distinctive constituency in that not only do they represent central government in the region but, as Young[11] shows, they represent local authorities at the centre. This point is developed further below.

The Water Authorities are distinct in terms of function and process and, indeed, were ostensibly created in order to unify the water management function (though there have been suggestions that their creation owed more to the needs of a professional constituency). In terms of constituency, their position is certainly confused. It seems that the Water Authorities were designed primarily with managerial efficiency in mind but modified to take account of the need for participation. The STWA reports to the Department of the Environment and thus has strong links with central government. At the same time, local interests are represented by the majority of local authority nominees on the authority, though it is an unsettled question whether the local authority members are there to represent their local interests to the authority or to act in a corporate capacity for the whole Severn-Trent area. Communication links with local interests and citizens are extensive but not formalized, an arrangement which has given rise to problems when the Authority sought to reflect public opinion.

An example of this, involving both the water authority and the health authorities, was the proposal to fluoridate water supplies in the West Midlands. The Health Authority decided on a policy of fluoridation for health reasons and asked the Water Authority to co-operate. The STWA however, conscious of the criticisms of it as an unelected and unaccountable body, refused to co-operate unless it was clearly demonstrated that public opinion favoured the scheme. The problem here was that there is no way of ascertaining public opinion in the STWA region. Local authorities were divided and in many cases the three levels of local government in a given area failed to agree. There was a confused process of consultation through county, district, and parish councils and local referendums, yielding no clear result.

The STWA, like the water authorities, has thus failed to develop a clear constituency other than its own professional membership. This raises problems of authority and legitimacy. In general, the water authorities have sought to justify their activities in terms of the competence criterion, claiming that the questions which they had to resolve are ones of professional and technical judgement, but the representation of local authorities among their membership and the attempts to measure public opinion show an awareness of the need to satisfy the personal choice criterion.

The same is true of the Regional Health Authorities. Here there are functional and process divisions between the centre and the region but corporate accountability of each tier to the one above it. Again, the composition of the membership indicates a diverse constituency including, as it does, professional and ministerial appointees as well as local authority members. Authority and legitimacy are also confused, being drawn from central government through the system of formal accountability and from the claim to competence of the medical professions, with an acknowledgement of the elective criterion in the representation of local authorities.

In the MSC, the Regional Manpower Services Director has line responsibility for the Special Programmes and exercises general oversight for the delivery of manpower services acting as chairman of the Regional Manpower Services Board. While the senior Employment and Training Services Managers in the regions sit on the Board there is not a line management relationship between these divisions in the region and the Regional Manpower Services Director. Consequently this position carries no executive powers over TSD and ESD in the region. Functional lines of responsibility exist for these divisions to the counterparts at the London-based headquarters. Indeed each Division operates through a different number of regional, area, and district offices, which makes for an extremely complex organizational structure. Essentially, however, the division between centre and region is one of process rather than function and the constituency is national, despite the existence of district manpower committees. The MSC thus represents a capital division of powers taken into the region, rather than an areal division of powers.

The Countryside Commission and West Midland Arts are both quasi-governmental agencies, with the former towards the governmental and the latter towards the non-governmental end of the spectrum. This adds the dimension of division of powers between government and non-government to the areal dimensions we have been considering. Both bodies are distinct in terms of function and process, with the Countryside Commission having functions bestowed on it by statute and West Midlands Arts assuming functions which it is not considered proper for government to discharge itself. In terms of their constituencies, however, they differ. The Countryside Commission see their responsibilities as being to a national constituency. Their reaction to the proposals for Welsh devolution makes this clear. They pointed out that their responsibilities were national in scope and unsuitable for devolution to a body with a territorially limited constituency.[12]

West Midland Arts, on the other hand, is concerned with the promotion of the arts within the region and would see its constituency as comprising local and regional artistic interests and local authorities within the region.

Both bodies derive legitimacy and authority from their

claims to special competence and their role in mediating between diverse constituencies though, in the case of the Countryside Commission, considerable authority is derived from its close links with central government.

Thus the regional institutions in our sample vary greatly in terms of territory, function, process, constituency, and legitimacy. This confirms the findings of an earlier paper by the present authors,[13] that there is not a regional level of government in England. Later, we will consider the region as central government and as intermediate government but first we examine the issue of discretion and power in regional administration.

DISCRETION AND POWER IN REGIONAL ADMINISTRATION

A useful framework for analysing the potential power and discretion of regional bodies is that devised by R. A. W. Rhodes[14] for the study of central-local relations. Rhodes points out that organizations exist in complex environments, which include other organizations. This imposes mutual constraints and gives rise to a process of exchange in which organizations mobilize their potential power resources. These resources include constitutional-legal powers; hierarchical authority, distinguished from the first by the fact that it may have no legal base; financial resources; political resources, by which is meant the legitimacy derived from election and the right to build public support; and informational resources, including the expertise possessed by professionals. The use of these resources is determined by goals. As imputing goals to organizations risks the errors of reification—only individuals really have goals—and formalism—'real' goals may not correspond to 'official' goals—the goals considered relevant are those of the 'dominant coalition' within an organization. Here, we are concerned with analysing the potential power and discretion of regional organizations, linking our earlier discussion of structure with the concepts derived from the Rhodes framework.

Let us take the government departments first. There is, as we have seen, little formal division of functions between the centre and the region but a system of bureaucratic hierarchies reflecting their role as agents for the pursuit of centrally determined goals. Financial allocations are usually made for specific purposes defined nationally by function and not by area. There are exceptions. In the MAFF, in particular areas —travel, promotions, laboratory expenditure, and experimental work—the Regional Management Board has a certain discretion to reallocate finance between activities which are funded by block grant. The financial discretion available to the regional offices of the DI varies among regions though this reflects the overall national goal of inter-regional discrimination. Selective assistance to industry is given under Sections 7 and 8 of the Industry Act. Under Section 7, offices in certain regions classified as predominantly 'assisted' areas were given the authority, within a policy framework laid down by departmental headquarters and the Treasury, to grant assistance of up to £2m. per project. In the West Midlands, there is only one small assisted area (Oswestry) and most financial assistance is given under Section 8. This deals with 'rescue cases' involving the National Enterprise Board, with Accelerated Project Schemes and selective sectoral assistance. All formal decisions on Section 8 assistance are taken at the London headquarters although the initial sifting of companies applying for financial assistance and appraisals of up to £1½m. are made in the region. Case papers are prepared on all applications by the Regional Industrial Director. These are submitted to the Regional Industrial Development Board (a non-statutory body) and, although responsibility for the final decision rests with London, the recommendations of the regional office are usually accepted. Applications beyond the authority of the regional office go to the Industrial Development Advisory Board. In general, regional offices of government departments lack political resources in the form of a separate constituency available for mobilization.

A partial exception to this, though the point should not be pushed too far, are the regional offices of the DOE. While formally in a hierarchical relationship with headquarters, the regional offices have evolved a distinctive planning function growing out of their tasks in mediating among local authorities and promoting co-ordination and communication among governmental agencies at the regional level. They have also developed a distinct constituency with the local authorities, which gives them added political resources. Further, the possession of local knowledge in the regional offices gives them a measure of informational resources. Within the national policy framework, regional offices are able to develop somewhat divergent goals[15] and use the resulting discretion in mediating among local authorities in planning matters and in financial allocations. Thus they do possess financial resources as a source of power over the locality, though not over the centre. The Regional Office makes financial allocations through the Housing Investment Programme System. The Transport Division has a certain discretion over finance for trunk-road improvement schemes. It has complete responsibility for financing all improvements up to £1¼m. and those to £½m. are selected, developed, and programmed in the region. The Regional Controller also recommends the Transport Supplementary Grant. Local authorities submit their Transport Policies and Programmes to the regional office and on the basis of this receive loan sanction for their local road schemes. In theory, the approval of TPPs rests with the departmentl headquarters but in practice the recommendations of the regional controller have great influence.

The Water Authorities possess a great deal in the way of power resources. As we have seen, they have statutory functions for which they are responsible, though the independence stemming from this is limited by their hierarchical relationship with central government, to which they report. Their independent source of finance gives them a great deal of discretion which is increased by the presentation of the water service as a 'technical' one in which the views of experts should be paramount. It is in political resources that the Water Authorities are weakest. As we have seen, their constituency is uncertain and their perceived lack of political support has inhibited their decision-making, particularly where this would take them beyond their official goals, into issues of planning and health.

The Regional Health Authorities have the task of translating national policy directives into a regional strategy. Thus, while they have a degree of legal independence, they are part of a hierarchy stretching from the local level to central government, a hierarchy officially united as to goals. They possess a considerable degree of discretion in the allocation of financial resources though not, like the Water Authorities, in determining the level of financing. Their political resources are similar to those of the Water Authorities, with a weak base in elected local government. Their informational resources, however, derived from the key position of the medical professions in the delivery of services, are considerable. Indeed, the distinction between informational and political resources may begin to break down if, as we have done, one sees the constituency of the authorities as including key holders of scarce expertise.

West Midlands Arts possesses legal independence and is not in a hierarchical relationship with any other body. Although it receives 75 per cent of its funds from central government, it derives considerable discretion from its legal position, its control of artistic expertise and the willingness of politically strong central and local governments to respect this as a condition of achieving their goal of promoting the arts.

The Countryside Commission is tied closely to the DOE and possesses few independent resources other than the expertise derived from its advisory function. In particular, it has failed to build up political resources in the region.

The MSC regional organization possesses no distinctive functions or legal independence and none of the other potential power resources, has no distinctive goals, and so possesses little effective discretion.

Thus the potential for discretion in regional administration varies greatly among the bodies surveyed. The goals of the bodies are also varied and so, accordingly, is the use of this discretion. To examine properly the exercise of this discretion, we would need case studies of regional decision-making which are beyond the scope of this paper. What we can do next, however, is to distinguish two main types of regional body, according to their formal structure and functions. These are central government bodies and 'intermediate' institutions.

THE REGION AS CENTRAL GOVERNMENT AND AS INTERMEDIATE GOVERNMENT

We have seen the regional institutions of government vary greatly in terms of their delineation by territory, function, process, and constituency and in the type and degree of discretion available to them. In particular, it has proved difficult to isolate distinctive regional functions and distinctive regional constituencies. Some of the bodies in our survey are best seen as extensions of central government into the regions or, to use Maass' terminology, the regional end of a capital division of powers. This is clearly the case with most government departments, the regional offices of which cannot be differentiated in terms of function, constituency or legitimacy from their respective headquarters and possess little in the way of power resources. Their existence has allowed central government to expand without changing the nature of the state or raising serious constitutional issues, as they so clearly represent the centre and have been able to avoid being 'captured' by local or regional interests. We would maintain that this is true, for instance, of the DTI, the MSC, and the ECGD, whose links with client groups tend to be at national level.

On the other hand, some of the bodies we have surveyed are distinguishable from both central and local government in terms of function and constituency and possess varying degrees of autonomy. These institutions we see as 'intermediate', illustrating the role of the region as a meeting place of bodies representing diverse interests. These interests include, on the territorial dimension, central and local government and, on the 'functional' dimension, governmental and non-governmental interests. The STWA can be seen as an intermediate institution, with its mixture of centrally and locally appointed members and its claims to be responsive to all interests. So can the Regional Health Authority, which draws members and legitimacy from central and local government as well as professional interests. West Midlands Arts is clearly intermediate between the public and private sectors. The reasons for the establishment of these intermediate institutions are varied and, in many cases, contentious. It is said in the defence of the regional health and water authorities that there are inherently 'regional' functions demanding special institutions to perform them efficiently. It is said in criticism of them that their real *raison d'être* is to place power in the hands of the special interests which control them. Our scheme of analysis can help to illuminate this controversy by distinguishing between differentiation by function and differentiation by constituency. So where, if anywhere, there is a distinctively regional function, it is possible to have it administered by a body answerable to any of a variety of constituencies. So the STWA could be made responsible to central government, local government, or an elected regional government. On the other hand, intermediate institutions, answerable to diverse constituencies, could be established even where there was not a distinct 'regional' function, as with West Midlands Arts.

One function which is inherently regional, which necessarily brings together a number of diverse constituencies and which has been of importance in recent years is that of regional planning and the promotion of communication and co-ordination among agencies operating at the regional level and below, including local authorities. Thus Gillingwater and Hart see regional planning as involving policy, control, and communication, and write:

> It is the interlocking of all three of these components which gives meaning to the idea of regional planning . . . for the public administration of planning being divided into large functional parts, rather than being wholly collective or atomised, no single political administration has the basic ability to effectuate its proposals without the prospect of having them changed by some other administration with an interest in the policy field. This is an almost continuous prospect for regional planning because . . . it is to be found located somewhere in the opportunity space between the two principal tiers of government—central and local.[16]

This point could be adapted for our purpose by noting that space can be both geographical and functional, and that central government itself is functionally fragmented at the regional level.

Policy, control, and communication were some of the tasks for which the new regional economic planning machinery was established in 1964, the policy content being provided by the National Plan. The other major task of the machinery was to provide a regional input into policy-making and feedback on the impact of national planning in the regions. The machinery had two main elements—the Economic Planning Boards and the Economic Planning Councils. The Boards comprise the senior civil servants in the region, including those responsible for housing and land use planning, transport, employment, industry, and investment in public utility services. Originally, the chairman was from the Department of Economic Affairs. The Economic Planning Councils, until their abolition in 1979, were advisory bodies, with members drawn from local government, industry and commerce, and the universities. Their original terms of reference were 'to assist in the formulation of regional plans having regard to the best use of the region's resources, to advise on the steps necessary for implementing the regional plans on the basis of information and assessments provided by the economic planning boards, and, to advise on the regional implications of national economic policies'.[17]

The councils and boards were intended to be part of a single integrated system of planning, linking central and local government planning, breaking down, or at least bridging the functional division between 'economic' and 'physical' planning and providing a distinctive regional input to planning. However, there were ambiguities from the start in both the functions and the constituency of the Councils and Boards.

Some observers saw the functions of the new bodies in an optimistic light. Paterson welcomed the 'much greater emphasis (placed) on the need for co-ordinated plans of regional development covering the provision of physical services as well as the stimulation or control of industrial growth'.[18] Others pointed to the fact that the prefix 'economic' had had to be inserted in the title of the Councils and Boards and Powell maintained that 'the old dichotomy between economic and physical planning was sharply revived in 1964 with the creation of the Department of Economic Affairs and the Regional Economic Planning Councils'.[19]

Even more serious were the criticisms directed at the status and constituency of the new bodies. It was not clear whether they were intended to represent central government, local interests, or a new 'regional' constituency. Ministers seemed to view them as an extension of central government. Before coming into office, Labour's then spokesman, Michael Stewart, had made clear his view of the machinery required:

My other reason for rejecting building up from local authorities is that, in the region, we are executing national policy.[20]

Yet the Councils, when established, did include authority

members. Mackintosh saw a need to build up a regional constituency:

Cohesive regional planning activity in England was being inhibited by the absence of the kind of political authority that might be provided by an elected regional assembly and also by the pessures arising from the hierarchical structure of government departments.[21]

So it was not clear whether the planning machinery was to be a means of channelling demands *upwards* from local and regional constituencies, of transmitting orders *downwards* from the centre, or of forming the basis of a new, regional tier of government. These contradictions could only be reconciled by an assumption of consensus, which plainly was not present in the West Midlands, where the interests of the centre's regional policy demanded restrictions on industrial development and the transfer of industry to other regions; or by a coherent theory of intermediate government as a level where these conflicts could be mediated and negotiated.

These contradictions soon undermined the authority and legitimacy of the Councils. They could not claim to be the voice of local government in the regions, nor could they claim to represent a regional constituency. They had limited claims to special competence or expertise and they could not claim to be the representatives of central government in the face of the Boards and the conflicts of interest referred to above.[22]

The role ambiguity was also reflected in the uncertainty of the relationship between the Councils and the Boards. Originally, it had been intended that the Boards should draw up the regional plans advised by the Councils, but in 1966 the responsibility for preparing the plans was transferred to the Councils. Lindley[23] suggests that this may have been intended to enable the Government to avoid being committted to the plans. However, the separation of Boards and Councils was far from complete, as the Councils had no separate staff and so relied on the Boards for information and servicing. The shift of responsibility for plan-making led to further role ambiguity. The regional civil servants as the representatives of central government, now had to pronounce on plans drawn up by the Councils with the advice and assistance of those same civil servants.[24]

After 1966, the problem was eased by the demise of the

National Plan. Thereafter, the Councils, lacking a regional constituency and without support from local government, declined in importance until their final extinction by the incoming Conservative Government in 1979. However, a continuing need was felt for machinery to promote communication and co-ordination at the regional level, and the Boards continued to develop slowly and hesitantly under the leadership, from 1970, of the Department of the Environment. In the West Midlands, the Board's membership has been expanded to include the chief executive of the Regional Health Authority but there is still no representation from the social services or effective input from education. Generally, the Boards provide a network of communication among government departments in the regions and serve as the 'eyes and ears' of the departments. Modest claims have been made about the success of this network. Friend, Power, and Yewlett quote an official as saying that 'he believed that a spirit of genuine co-operation was evolving both among the officials of different government departments with the regional office and also between regional and central officials within his own departmental establishment'.[25] They conclude:

Despite the low profile of the regional structure in terms of public political debate . . . the processes of innovation and interactive learning which have been developing in Britain in recent years—and which we believe may have parallels in a number of other countries—are of much potential significance.[26]

The DOE itself has developed an 'intermediate' role, mediating among local authorities, particularly in planning matters, and promoting regional strategies. The latter involve co-ordination and consensus-seeking among a wide variety of bodies representing diverse constituencies. In the West Midlands this has required a further set of *ad hoc* machinery bringing together the DOE, the Economic Planning Council before its abolition, and the West Midlands Planning Authorities Conference, a local government body.

However, despite these developments, Johnson's comment about the lack of an operational and co-ordinating middle level of administration remains true. The failure of the Regional Economic Planning Councils to develop and their later abolition have meant that there is no politically powerful body representing a regional constituency. Local authorities, divided politically and geographically, are largely unable to operate together at the regional level. The DOE has increased in importance but is far from becoming a comprehensive Ministry of the Interior, monopolizing access to Whitehall and exercising a prefectoral tutelage over local government. It is likely, therefore, that there will be a continued development of *ad hoc* machinery for mediating intergovernmental conflict and promoting communication at the regional level.

CONCLUSION

Our survey of the pattern of regional administration in the West Midlands has shown that there is no consistent definitiom of the region and no consistent concept of regional government. Instead, there is a variety of bodies covering different areas, with different functions and answering to different constituencies. The distribution of power in regional administration reflects this. There are few regional power bases or vested regional interests. The 'regional' institutions of government which exist can in most cases be seen as either part of central government or as 'intermediate' government. Intermediate institutions often lack authority and legitimacy in their own right, drawing these from their varied constituencies, and their constitutional status is uncertain.

It has often been suggested that regional government could be reformed by placing the existing regional institutions under the control of elected assemblies. We do not see this as a viable option. Central government will wish to retain its national and inter-regional responsibilities whatever happens to its regional outposts. Similarly, intermediate institutions will continue to be required as meeting places for representatives of differing constituencies. So even elected regional authorities would need some machinery for mediation between themselves and local authorities and private interests in, for example, the arts, unless they were going to take over these completely and run them themselves.

This is not an argument against any form of elected regional government but it is an argument against basing it on the present institutions. Regional government would involve the recognition of new constituencies and interests and, for this, the creation of new institutions.

Regional offices of the Department of the Environment: their roles and influence in the 1970s

STEPHEN YOUNG

INTRODUCTION

THIS chapter[1] analyses the roles and influence of the regional offices of the main government departments in England. It concentrates mainly on the Department of the Environment (DOE), but draws on the Departments of Transport and Industry (DOI) as well, The main part of the chapter analyses the different roles that were played under a series of headings designed to illustrate the wide variety of tasks that were performed during the 1970s. The last section discusses some of the main issues that are raised in preceding sections.

Regional offices were dismantled in the late 1940s and early 1950s. The first moves to re-establish them came in agriculture. The Ministry of Agriculture found that a regional office had more impact on real problems as it was closer to them than a remote office in Whitehall.[2] This principle was followed in 1962 when the Ministry of Housing and Local Government (MHLG) established regional offices in Manchester and Newcastle to spearhead the drive behind the slum clearance programme. Regional offices of most other government departments were set up in the mid 1960s, following moves to develop a comprehensive set of regional plans. These were initiated by the Conservatives in 1963/4 and taken further by the Labour Government elected in October 1964. Regional planning was the main focus of the regional offices of MHLG and the Department of Economic Affairs in the late 1960s, and of the regional offices of the DOE in the early 1970s. However, although such plans were relatively straightforward to prepare, the process of implementing them proved more difficult and elusive. Attempts at regional planning did not cease during the 1970s. These are discussed in a separate chapter in this book.

What is important from the perspective of this chapter is that some civil servants appear to have questioned whether it was worthwhile for regional offices to concentrate so much on regional planning. Pure regional planning ceased to be such a central concern for regional offices of the DOE during the 1970s when compared to the 1960s. This appears particularly to have been the case outside the West Midlands and the South East: in these two regions there were greater pressures for growth. Focusing less on regional planning created the opportunity for civil servants to act on different, often more specific issues. There was thus scope to develop their influence using both established and new channels and techniques.

THE DIFFERENT ROLES OF REGIONAL OFFICES IN ENGLAND

Formal Executive Responsibilities

The first role of the regional offices is to carry out a wide range of jobs which have been delegated by Whitehall. Some of these, like responsibilities over listed buildings, are quite straightforward. A regional presence enables civil servants to operate more effectively, visiting archives departments or specific buildings or conservation areas to discuss details of listing, boundaries, grants, or demolition problems with local authority officials. Regional offices also have an important formal role to play over planning appeals.

Other tasks involve a great deal of administrative work to implement national policy. Transport is a clear example. Although such work may appear to be mainly administrative, the resource allocation problems have important political implications. Each year the County Councils have to prepare their Transport Policies and Programmes (TPPs). These are five-year rolling programmes with expenditure planned under a series of headings including, where appropriate, bus and rail subsidies, road improvement schemes, highway maintenance, and car parking. They are submitted to the Department of Transport which allocates finance to the counties via the

Transport Supplementary Grant (TSG). In outline the annual timetable is as follows. In March the regional office tells the counties what level of resources are likely to be available over the next five years. Informal discussions take place between each county and its districts, and between the county and the regional office, prior to submission in the autumn. The regional office offers advice to the centre about the most appropriate way to allocate the funds.

A similar procedure is followed each year with the Housing Investment Programmes (HIPs). This allocates funds for new buildings, improvement of local authority property, and local authority mortgages. These are capital allocations, and are made in one block covering all local authority housing activity. The regional office advises local authorities as they prepare their submissions, often getting involved in intensive discussions. Regional DOEs make recommendations to Whitehall about how best to allocate funds within the region. As with the TSG, the regional office 'recommendations' often amount to *de facto* decisions. Although ministerial approval is still necessary, these recommendations are very influential. In the late 1970s servicing the inner city partnership committees became a major preoccupation for the regional offices with partnerships in their areas.[3]

Regional offices also carry out some financial responsibilities which are delegated by London. Applications for Urban Aid Grants, Derelict Land Grants, and before 1981 Community Land Act (CLA) grants are all typical examples. The DOI can also approve finance for regional development schemes of up to £2m. without reference to the centre. Above that they have to be referred to the centre. Some of the industry schemes under Section 8 of the 1972 Industry Act are located in regional offices—clothing in Manchester for example.[4]

Whitehall's Co-ordinator in the Region

The DOE (or a predecessor department) has chaired the Regional Economic Planning Board (REPB) ever since its establishment in the mid 1960s when regional planning was the overwhelming concern. The REPB is made up of the senior civil servant from each department in the region. The REPBs parelleled on the official side the Regional Economic Planning

Councils until the latter were abolished in 1979 by the incoming Conservative Government.

The DOE's role as Whitehall's co-ordinator in the region manifests itself in a variety of ways. It acts as a clearing house giving the collective reaction of all government departments at the regional level to other government agencies that ask for comment on plans or programmes. The DOE at the regional level sees the Regional Health Authority programmes, the Development Commission proposals and schemes being put forward by other parts of government. It talks to the regional offices of other government departments about the way in which projected ideas fit in with others' investment strategies. The DOE is also responsible for civil defence in its widest sense, and carries out any emergency planning work that is thought necessary by Whitehall, as for example it was during the lorry drivers' strike in 1978. The DOE thus attempts to co-ordinate different policies. In so far as any point in central government exists which provides some sort of corporate link to local authorities, it is the regional DOE that most approximates to it.[5]

Active Promotion of Government Policies

The third main role of the regional offices is a promotional one. This role is vitally important to central government because one of the main characteristic features of British central/local relationships is the straightforward fact that local authorities are responsible for the implementation of many nationally determined policies. The extent to which a Labour or Conservative government can, for example, implement its housing policies depends largely on its ability to persuade and cajole housing authorities to adopt national policies. In these circumstances it falls to the regional DOE to 'promote' central government's policies.

The move in the 1970s in housing away from policies based on clearance and redevelopment towards policies based on rehabilitation of old property is a good example of this promotional role. The 1969 and 1974 Housing Acts led to the introduction respectively of GIAs and HAAs. Each Act was naturally followed by a circular explaining the powers and finance available to local authorities. However circulars and guidance notes leave some issues unclarified in the minds of councillors and officers at the local authority level. The regional offices of the DOE have the job of answering queries and explaining the detailed points.

This was particularly important in the context of the 1975 Community Land Act which was widely regarded as the most complicated piece of legislation ever to have been introduced.[6] The Treasury and the DOE were divided in Whitehall over the priorities of the scheme. The Treasury's view appeared to be that the CLA should aim to earn income immediately, through local authorities acquiring prime sites for sale to the private sector, so that the public expenditure costs of the scheme—especially after the 1976 IMF loan and the subsequent public expenditure cuts—could be limited. The DOE on the other hand, and particularly John Silkin the minister who saw the scheme through Parliament, argued that the CLA should be planning-led, not finance-led. The original aim of the scheme was to enable planners to acquire what were from the planning point of view, the most appropriate sites for public sector development, even if this meant that during the early years of the scheme there were public expenditure costs that had to be carried until CLA got off the ground and generated income. This dispute led to an enormously complex series of circulars and guidance notes in the late 1970s. It fell to the DOE regional offices to explain the twists and turns of the centre's approach to CLA to local authorities. It was particularly important for local authority finance and planning departments to understand the evolving criteria used by the DOE for allocating CLA finance so that they knew which sites would be most likely to meet with grant approval.

The DOI regional offices also have an important promotional role explaining to local firms for example, the variety of assistance available to potential exporters via the British Overseas Trade Board schemes; the details of regional assistance policies, and the government's energy conservation policies as they apply to industry. This promotional role enables some regional offices to take the initiative and develop a more active, somewhat interventionist, style. Explaining the details of housing or transport policies does not necessarily confine regional civil servants to answering the phone and replying to letters. There is considerable scope for approaching local authorities and actively encouraging them to adopt new ideas, by, for example, showing councillors and officers films illustrating how other local authorities have made use of the GIAs legislation and circulars. This can extend to site visits to discuss the boundaries of proposed GIAs, or the details of a road improvement scheme. An important part of this promotional role is the way that some regional offices also seek to spread new ideas that come up from local authorities, as opposed to down from Whitehall. An example here is the way in which the Manchester office has tried to persuade other metropolitan authorities in the North West to adopt the Wirral approach to local plans.[7] Wirral have used it as a means of co-ordinating expenditure from different sources, as opposed to merely seeing it as a land use plan.

'Mothership'

On occasions the promotional role grows into something where the regional office takes the initiative and becomes more intimately involved with some of the more specialized areas of policy-making within the local authority. On these issues the regional office plays what amounts to a 'mothership' role. On some specialized issues some small district councils lack knowledge, experience, and skilled manpower. The regional office may take the view that there is central government or EEC money available for the region, but that it is not being claimed by areas where it would have an impact.

Regional civil servants can move to fill this vacuum by encouraging local authorities to develop particular proposals, even to the extent of providing specialized assistance. One example has been the EEC Regional Development Fund. Basically this makes EEC grants available towards development schemes like road improvements or industrial estates in deprived regions. They are available to local authorities within Assisted Areas. The process of applying for one of these grants, and meeting all the criteria, is complex, and some of the smaller district councils lack the skills necessary to put together an application in such a way that it will pass easily through all the hoops.

Derelict Land Grants provide another example where there

is scope for regional civil servants not just to encourage local authorities to put in applications in a promotional way, but to go further and provide expert assistance in the preparation of the application. This is a highly specialized area that not many local authorities are manned up to cope with. In the era of retrenchment and public expenditure cuts in the late 1970s specialized posts relating to non-statutory functions were often the first to be frozen. Local authorities are glad of help from the regional office in preparing applications which are, after committee and council approval, forwarded to the same regional office for processing.

The mothership role is an extension of the promotional role, but appears sufficiently different to justify emphasizing by its inclusion as a separate category. There is a touch of benign paternalism as the regional office goes beyond actively promoting government schemes, and provides direct expert advice in the choosing and preparation of projects which are eligible for finance from sources outside the local authority. Such expertise also appears to be forthcoming, on occasion, in more mainstream policy areas like preparing GIA applications.

The Regional Office as Arbitrator

Sometimes the regional offices of the DOE find themselves having to act as arbitrator between two local authorities with conflicting ideas. Housing has provided a number of examples over the years. Manchester's protracted attempts to get planning permission to build extensive overspill estates in Cheshire in the 1960s provoked great opposition from Cheshire County and many pre-reorganization Urban and Rural District Councils on the grounds that this would unnecessarily erode the green belt.[8] The Manchester Regional Office played an arbitrating role first in trying to persuade the Cheshire authorities to agree, secondly in promoting the Central Lancashire New Town idea as a strategic solution to Manchester and Salford's need for new housing. Similar disputes took place between Birmingham and some surrounding, predominantly-rural authorities in the West Midlands in the 1960s.[9]

The reorganization of local government in 1974 left housing as a district responsibility. However the falling forecasts of future population level did not reduce the demand for new housing. The average size of household was decreasing and inter- and intra-regional migration continued. In addition county councils became interested in housing in the context of structure plans. Further they were responsible for strategic aspects of development control. The conflicts between authorities over the release of land thus remained. In the South East, for example, there has been conflict between counties and districts over the granting of planning permission for housing on white land. Sometimes the attempts at mediation fail, as in the dispute over Salford's plans to develop a thousand house site at Linnyshaw in the mid-1970s. Salford wanted to build on a partially derelict site in the Green Belt which was affected by old coal workings and spoil tips. The site was within Salford's boundaries and it provided an opportunity to help alleviate the shortage of land for new council house building. Greater Manchester County Council argued strongly that it was more important to retain the green belt around the conurbation and find other uses for the derelict land. As no agreement could reached the issue went to a public inquiry where the inspector and then the minister found against Salford.[10]

It is important to draw a distinction between what might be termed the diplomatic negotiating work where the regional office is trying to settle a dispute, and its much more aloof formal role when it is processing planning appeals and inquiries. Regional offices clearly do act as arbitrators over some contentious cases while they are being discussed. However, in the last resort this arbitrating role is constrained by the existence of the inquiry processes. If a particular case reaches the public inquiry stage, then the regional office has to step back from arguing a particular viewpoint, and revert to playing the more formal disinterested aloof role referred to on page 76 above.

It seems that regional civil servants do not relish being pulled in as arbitrators. When writing about the late 1950s and early 1960s Griffith makes the same point.[11] However, with responsibility for development control in the 1970s being divided between the counties and the districts,[12] it has been important for regional civil servants to keep an eye open for potentially controverisal planning applications. Their growing collective experience has led them to try and head off trouble by arranging meetings to resolve conflicts before they reach confrontation stage. Another area where the regional office sometimes has to try and sort out differences before they erupt into something much worse, arises over local plans where a county is concerned that it may contradict the structure plan, whether the latter is still being prepared or has been approved. It is not clear precisely what criteria regional civil servants use to decide when to allow themselves to be pulled into a fluid situation as potential arbitrators.

Directly Influencing Local Authority Policy-Making Within the Authority

The 1970s have seen civil servants in some regional offices apparently moving to involve themselves directly in the policy formulation process within local planning authorities. This is not a new approach. Its significance is that it has grown. Griffith notes that it existed in the late 1950s and the early 1960s with regard to the development plan process. 'The influence of the Department (of Housing and Local Government) is normally felt from the beginning of the process of preparation and continues through the subsequent negotiations until the plan is finally approved.'[13] He sees the significance of civil servants' involvement as being that 'they see and comment upon nearly all development plans . . . when many . . . are in a very early stage of preparation'.[14] However, he notes that the civil servants concerned worked in London, and contact was closest in places that were easily accessible from London. The strength of the links appears to have varied. In the 1970s, with the existence of regional offices in the regions, and with fewer local authorities after reorganization, it has been possible for civil servants to become involved to a greater extent than before in the policy-making process within local authorities. This seems to be a significant central government control technique which affects a variety of issues. The evidence suggests that it has been considerably developed during the 1970s, especially in the context of structure planning. Here civil servants have responded to another of Griffith's findings —local authority planners felt by the early 1960s that they needed more policy advice and more technical advice.[15]

Structure plans have to be prepared by county councils

under the 1968 and 1971 Town and Country Planning Acts. They are the main planning documents drawn up to guide development in a county over a ten or fifteen year time horizon. They outline the expenditure priorities on subjects like transport and public sector developments generally, and detail (without specifying sites) the areas where industry, commerce, and shopping and housing development will be allowed to develop, and where they will be prevented from growing. The basic procedure has been for county councils to prepare these documents over a period of several years, during which time they have gone through several annual statements, and consulted the public, the district councils, and statutory undertakers like the water authorities. The final draft plan is submitted to the minister who sets up a panel of experts to debate the issues in the plan at the Examination in Public (EIP). After reading the Panel report the minister sends the local authority his decision letter outlining the parts of the plan he approves and the parts he wants amending.

Structure Plans are clearly significant documents as they will guide public and private sector resource allocation for the subsequent decade. Thus it is clearly most important from central government's standpoint to ensure that a county's structure plan fits in with its own view of the priorities facing that county, and the implied demand for public sector resources. It has fallen to the regional offices of the DOE to ensure that the structure plans accord to Whitehall's view of what in outline terms they should or should not contain. The regional office offers advice to the county councils as they prepare their structure plans; it comments in tremendous detail on the draft plans at the various stages; it is influential in picking the individuals who form the Panel for the EIP (and they sometimes include a senior DOE regional civil servant); it chooses the issues that will be debated at the EIP; it picks the groups who will be invited to debate the issues with the county and the districts; it advises the minister on the Panel's report after the EIP; and it is heavily relied on when the Secretary of State announces his final verdict even to the extent in some cases of drafting the modifications to the structure plan.[16]

The process of preparing a structure plan thus takes a period of several years from the initial stages through to the minister's decision letter. The regional office is involved throughout that period. Initially the links between the county and the regional office are informal at civil-servant/senior-officer level. Later they become more formalized. In the initial stages while different potential strategies are being developed and examined there is a clear opportunity for the regional office to use the informal talks to shape policies as they are created.

In the West Midlands, Yorkshire and Humberside, and the South East an important source of influence has been the regional strategies. The 1971 Town and Country Planning Act requires that structure plans should 'have regard to' regional strategies. In the case of the West Midlands it was prepared by the West Midlands Planning Authorities Conference (WMPAC) which represents local planning authorities. In Yorkshire and Humberside the regional strategies were prepared by the Economic Planning Council which was advised by the regional DOE civil servants. In the South East the Review of the Strategic Plan was prepared by committees and officer panels from central and local government in the Standing Conference on London and the South East. In these cases the Whitehall view of the priorities and strategic issues is outlined in the strategies, and it is made clear to the local planning authorities from the outset that the structure plans must broadly conform to the regional strategies. The Birmingham DOE appears to have been the first to take this approach for the simple reason that the structure planning authorities began their work on their structure plans earlier than elsewhere in the country. Although it was not actually represented on WMPAC it was still able to influence the content of the Regional Strategy.

In the South East the regional strategy picked out Area 8 as a growth point. This referred to the area between Aldershot, Camberley, and Bracknell, which spills into three separate counties—Surrey, Berkshire, and Hampshire. The issue has been clouded by the fact that Peter Walker granted some of this land interim green belt status when he was Secretary of State for the Environment in the early 1970s. Local authorities used this point to argue against plans to allow development.

It seems that in the South East and West Midlands civil servants have used the regional strategies as a means of controlling the content of the structure plans, advocating ideas that dovetail into the strategies, especially over land release for industry and housing. Behind lay the implied threat that if there was too much divergence from the regional strategy, then the minister's decision letter would amend it. In the case of the West Midlands, Tony Crosland, Secretary of State for the Environment decided there should be more industry and public sector housing at Solihull. In 1979/80 his successor but one, Michael Heseltine, called for more land release in the parts of Area 8 in Surrey and Berkshire in his decision letter on their structure plans.[17]

Some would argue that this interpretation goes too far in suggesting that regional civil servants take the initiative and have an important influence on policy-making with regard to structure plans. These people would argue that the regional office only gives 'technical advice' about the preparation of structure plans. In some parts of the country the structure plans differ from the strategies in important respects—in Greater Manchester and Merseyside for example. However, it seems that this illustrates that the regional strategy was out of date, rather than the inaccuracy of the argument presented here. Even if the regional strategy was out of date it was still apparently possible for civil servants to influence the general approach of those counties to their structure plans.

The essential point is that the act of saying that some ideas are more likely to prove acceptable than others clearly implies an element of control if the advising civil servants have considerable influence over the content of the minister's decision letter at the end of the day. The West Yorkshire structure plan changed as it went through the various annual statements. It moved away from the strategy of supporting the declining westerly parts of the county to be more in line with the Regional DOE's view, outlined in the 1975 Regional Strategy, that growth, if it was to come, would be best encouraged in the east of the county. It appears in short that the county planners came to accept the Leeds DOE view partly because of pressure from DOE civil servants, and partly because they knew that at the end of the day the Leeds DOE would act as judge and jury and advise the minister how the plan should be revised at the decision letter stage.

This general interpretation is further illustrated by the Regional DOE in the West Midlands moving to revise the Regional Strategy a year before the counties started on their five year reviews of their structure plans. The main object appeared to be to use the strategy as a means of influencing the content of the structure plans.

It is important to emphasize that structure plans are not the only example there appears to be of the widening attempts by regional civil servants to influence policy-making within the local authority. Regional civil servants also advise local authority officers during the preparation of the HIPs and TPPs. It may be the case that in those areas too, regional civil servants have become more directly involved in the policy-making process within local authorities.

This phenomenon has been institutionalized in the seven inner city partnership committees. There are extensive links between regional office civil servants and local authority officers in servicing the partnership committees. There would appear to be considerable potential for regional office staff to afford higher priority to some projects than to others, and to influence what goes on the partnership committee agenda. Ultimately, though, partnership expenditure has to be compatible with the ideas of both the DOE and the local authorities.

There thus appears to be considerable scope for regional civil servants in the DOE to influence policy-making within local authorities on a variety of issues. This influence comes from knowing what the minister is likely to find acceptable. Often the informal response of civil servants might be 'The minister won't have that' or 'We can't get that through for you'. There may even be occasions when this approach is used to help in arguing a particular point of view with a specific local authority. This variety of attempts to influence local authority policy-making seems to be based largely on constraining the options that are available to a particular authority on a specific issue. The aim always seems to be to ensure that there are coherent links between policies and documents that are interrelated, matching HIPs with structure plans on housing land requirements, or major land release schemes for housing or industry with Regional Water Authorities capital programmes, for example.

The tentacles of central government appear to stretch farther into local authority decision-making processes than they did in the early 1970s. The extent to which this is a byproduct of what has happened as opposed to a conscious effort to achieve this outcome, is unclear. It might profitably be the subject of further research. It seems that particular individuals have sought to intervene more than others, contributing to a varied pattern across the country.

Assisting Local Authorities in the Lobbying Process

The process of attempting to persuade government departments and agencies to amend policies or devote more resources to particular authorities is enormously varied. It ranges from the emotional outburst to the highly sophisticated. On the one hand there is the telegram to the minister. Following the eruption of a serious local issue there may be a spontaneous all-party political outburst around a committee table or in the Council chamber. On the other hand, there is the appreciation of the fact that lobbying is a continuous process, and that there is a need not just to commit officer time to it within the authority, but to develop a dialogue with particular parts of government on a regular basis. The most sophisticated lobbyists regularly submit papers, develop informal links, and travel to London to meet ministers and senior civil servants.[18]

The most effective lobbying papers all seem to contain three elements. They analyse existing problems; they explain why government policies are misguided; and they suggest the most suitable government response.

What stands out from reading a range of lobbying papers from urban authorities is the overriding importance of statistics. An authority's ability to get a favourable response from government depends on its being able to make out a case showing how bad its problems are. The easiest way to prove a case to the satisfaction of central government is to produce detailed statistics illustrating the lobbying organization's deteriorating position both over time, and relative to other authorities.

There appear to be three main channels by which local authorities can seek to press central government. First, there is the contact between local authority officers and the chairmen of the main service committees, and the civil servants and ministers of central departments. If the reply from the centre disappoints local authority politicians and senior officers, it is liable to be 'taken onto the politican network'. This involves senior councillors using their political contacts within their national political party to try to further their authority's cause. The local MP may go and see the junior minister, for example, to ensure that ministers and not just civil servants see the files. Once the issue has been taken onto the political network local political leaders often press the idea of sending an all-party delegation to discuss the issues with the minister.

A wide variety of channels are used to supplement the direct approach: this might best be termed lobbying via third parties. Thus, for example, individual districts seek to persuade the county above them to voice the district's concern in the right places. Chambers of Commerce, Economic Planning Councils, and the local authority associations are examples of other third parties that become intimately involved in the lobbying processes.

The third channel that local authorities use to press central government is the regional office of the major departments, particularly Environment. Writers appear to have rather underestimated the influence of regional DOEs. The regional office in fact plays a classic middleman role having loyalties to the centre while developing loyalties to the region. When departments in Whitehall receive lobbying documents from local authorities asking to be a partnership authority in the inner city programme, or for more advanced factories or whatever, one of the first things they do is to ask the relevant regional office for its comments.

The advantage to a local authority of developing informal relationships, based on mutual trust and respect, with the Regional Office is twofold. First, it has an 'ear at court' and thus gets an inkling of what it is best to press for, and what it is pointless to ask for. Secondly, it is obviously a great help if the 'objective' regional office is arguing a particular authority's case within the system. If the local authority is of a different political complexion to the national government the regional office appears able to 'neutralize' the party difference by giving an impartial view.

Getting others, particularly from within the Regional Offices of government departments, to argue your case from inside the government machine, appears an indispensible lever that the more successful lobbying authorities need. In the late 1970s districts in the western parts of West Yorkshire County Council found it very hard to do any effective lobbying in the face of DOE and Department of Industry antipathy from the Leeds offices. By contrast in the early 1970s North-East Lancashire received considerable benefits from the Manchester Regional Offices' championing its cause.

The regional offices are in fact in an ambivalent position. They represent the region's interests to the centre, but try to retain a sense of balance and objectivity when arguing Marsham Street's views and ministers' arguments in the region. It seems that the most significant of the three channels of influence mentioned earlier in this section is the last: regional civil servants can, and frequently do, 'fight the centre'.

The 'eyes and ears' of Whitehall

The policy-making process in Britain lays great emphasis on consultations with all organizations. Regional offices regularly get consulted when new ideas are being considered in London. However, once policy has been made in a new area, Whitehall has a vested interest in maintaining it and not constantly changing it. But departments know they need detailed information about how new policies are working out at the sharp end—London civil servants are far removed from the problems of implementation. The last important function of the regional office is to provide confidential, accurate feedback to the centre so that policy can, if necessary, be amended to make it more effective.

The impact of feedback from the regional offices to Whitehall is erratic. Sometimes it appears to have no more impact than water on a stone. The Northern Regional Strategy Team's call for regional budgets got nowhere. It took the West Midlands DOE and DOI the best part of a decade to persuade Whitehall to remove the obstacles to indigenous growth posed by the need to acquire an Industrial Development Certificate for a new building or extension.[19] In the face of the evidence, the Government finally conceded that the process of preventing some industrial investment taking place did not necessarily lead to it going to a new town or assisted area. Stopping it often meant it did not take place at all.

The Community Land Act, though, was amended more swiftly.[20] One of its two main aims had been to enable local planning authorities to overcome the high cost of land so they could acquire sites for development at realistic prices. The regulations imposed at the start of the scheme in December 1976 proved so tight that the scheme became virtually unworkable. The main factor leading to the relaxation of those regulations appears to have been the DOE regional offices. Their day-to-day contact with local government officers actually trying to work the new system led to their learning a lot about the implementation problem that was fed back to London. The result was that Guidance Note 19 in November 1978 relaxed many of the controls and made it easier for local authorities to operate.

The feedback mechanism is to some extent formalized up and down. DOE regional civil servants have regular meetings with chief executives and planning officers of the major authorities, and go and visit the smaller districts to develop a dialogue with them too. Senior civil servants from different regions also have meetings with each other, and with ministers and headquarters civil servants in London. Whitehall expects to be briefed on all the relevant points that might be raised by a delegation going to see a minister, and to be alerted to unexpected developments in the region—a big closure or a controversial planning application that might need to be called in for example. Whitehall departments rely on their regional offices to ensure that they are never taken by surprise. In that sense they are the 'eyes and ears' of central government.

CONCLUSION

This analysis has illustrated the wide variety of roles that are played by regional offices, especially of the DOE. The DOE has probably gained influence from chairing the interdepartmental Economic Planning Board made up of the heads of each department in the region. There is considerable discretion available to senior civil servants in regional offices as over the

TPP and HIP allocations where ministers largely follow regional civil servants recommendations. In the housing field there is some evidence that money gets pushed at the most efficient spenders by regional civil servants. Individual senior civil servants develop different styles and approaches. The West Midlands DOE appears to have been very interventionist and apt to take the initiative on a variety of issues. The DOI in Birmingham has been more passive. In Leeds in the late 1970s the approach of these two departments was reversed. The DOE was comparatively cautious, while the DOI took a strong line about developing some parts of the region and not others. Thus Kirklees, Calderdale, and Bradford Metropolitan Districts in West Yorkshire for example were discriminated against when it came to steering offices or industry to those peripheral areas, to allocating EEC Regional Development Grants, and to building advance factories.

This development of different styles meant that differing amounts of discretion were used. One of the clearest examples in the 1970s was the willingness of the DOE in Manchester and Birmingham to stretch the availability of Derelict Land Grants to the limit, despite Whitehall's tight definition of the circumstances in which they could be allocated.[21] In the North West this included the demolition of derelict textile mills. However, the Leeds DOE was more conventional and consistently refused to approve applications to demolish similar structures in West Yorkshire. In other policy areas there was less scope for discretion because the regional offices did not make the final decisions. On priorities within the road programme and the HIPs each made recommendations to Marsham Street (the DOE headquarters): the argument was continued in the Cabinet, particularly over relating HIP allocations to the inner city programme authorities.

Analysing the different roles of the regional offices also shows the importance when discussing central-local relations of distinguishing between those acts of intervention which prevent local authorities from doing something, as opposed to those which seek to push and persuade local authorities into doing things they had not thought of doing. The attempts to control the development of structure plans are examples of the first, and the mothership heading provides examples of the second. It is usually argued that it is easier to stop local authorities from pursuing particular objects, than to cajole them into new lines of action. Further study of regional offices might well show that it is at this tier of government that central government departments are at their most positive in a creative way.

This is partly because of the links that are built between individual regional civil servants, and senior officers and committee chairmen within local authorities. It is always difficult to generalize about the 'corridor politics' part of any sphere of policy making, but the development of informal contacts must not be underrated. The phone, the working lunch, and the occasional drink on the way home lead to the development of relationships of trust and mutual respect between civil servants and important officials within local government. These relationships provide a climate in which the more interventionist regional offices can positively influence what local authorities decide to do. The first factor that influences the role of regional offices is the context within which it operates— the historical, economic, and industrial heritage which has left an outworn infrastructure demanding different degrees of reconstruction and investment. During the 1970s regional offices of the DOE in the more deprived and declining regions showed, in their attitudes to lobbying, how conscious they were of their legacies of outworn infrastructure. The expansion of the Assisted Areas, and the great variety of schemes that were introduced or extended also illustrate the competition between some of the regional DOE offices. The West Midlands appears to have become extremely conscious of its relative decline during the 1970s, for example.[22]

However, it is not just the legacy of decline that is important. Personalities have also been significant, although it would be invidious to single out individuals. An ambitious thrusting civil servant in his forties out to make a name for himself is liable to behave quite differently from someone of fifty-eight waiting for retirement. Further, some develop a loyalty to the region which challenges their loyalty to the centre. This is often expressed in a determination to see that authorities within the region spend all of what is available, and what can be fought for. Other civil servants see their duty as saving public funds rather than encouraging expenditure. At the micro-level where the nature of the relationship between central and local government is somewhat intangible, different personalities can be noted as the second factor that explains why different regional offices develop different styles.

The third factor is that there has been no attempt by Whitehall to lay down what the role of regional offices should be. The DOE is less centralized than the DOI. As a result different styles have evolved. Each regional office has a list of responsibilities. However, some have built on that minimum list as opportunities have arisen to develop their role and influence. More imaginative civil servants have seized the opportunity and taken the initiative.

The final factor that explains why the variety of styles and roles have developed is the fact that by contrast with Scotland and Wales, there is no Secretary of State for England in the Cabinet to provide overall leadership which civil servants can follow. In the midst of the Chrysler crisis for example in 1976, there was no minister to defend the Ryton plant at Coventry in the Cabinet, even though the cause of the Linwood plant was strongly advocated by the Secretary of State for Scotland. The fact that there has been no English Office has encouraged the evolution of offices for some of the more deprived English regions.

The experience of the regional DOEs during the 1970s with their roles developing in different ways in different regions, show the crucial ambiguities in their relationship with Whitehall. Are they agents of the centre, an intermediate tier, or some kind of *de facto* representative of the locality to the centre? In different places at different times there are elements of all three. It is not therefore surprising in a centralized state like Britain that some HQ civil servants were beginning to argue that some regional offices were ceasing to be as objective as they had been. By the late 1970s Marsham Street became aware that some regional offices were starting to become advocates of their regions, or the most deprived of them. During 1980 an internal committee chaired by Sir Derek Rayner, the Marks and Spencer executive seconded to the Prime Minister's office to examine waste and inefficiency in the civil service, undertook an examination of the role of regional offices of the Departments of the Environment and Transport.

The Rayner Report[23] was thus motivated by the search for savings. It analysed the work of regional offices and apparently emphasized their value to the centre in two particular ways. They were seen as being useful in interpreting and explaining central government decisions and circulars downwards to the local authorities. They were also seen as useful in alerting Whitehall to problems that were seen as significant within particular regions: this role has been discussed above under the heading 'The "eyes and ears" of Whitehall'.

The Rayner Report appears to have argued the case for retaining the system of regional offices. However, it recommended that the regional office could do the same work more cheaply if the boundaries were streamlined and rationalized. All of these recommendations were rejected by the Government in December 1980 with the exception of the transfer of Cumbria from the Northern to the North West regional office. However, the Secretary of State announced that in future there would be one regional director (at under-secretary level) for two pairs of regions: thus the West and East Midlands regions would have one regional director, as would the Northern and Yorkshire Humberside regions. The Rayner Report, and the Government reactions to it, thus appear to have emphasized the value of the regional offices to the DOE HQ in Marsham Street.

CHAPTER 5

The regional dimension of industrial policy administration

BRIAN W. HOGWOOD

INTRODUCTION

ENGLAND has a system of administering regional and industrial policy which differs from that in any other part of the United Kingdom. The evolution of this system stems not from a view that the problems of English regions had special features which require special administrative structures, but from the paradox that England is the only part of the United Kingdom for which special arrangements have not been developed and therefore has its own distinctive system by default.

This chapter outlines the system of administering regional policy in England, with a particular emphasis on the extent to which administration has taken place in the regions themselves. The administration of regional policy can vary from central determination of both policy framework and administration of individual cases through central determination of the policy framework with regional units having at least some discretion on implementation, to some regional involvement in the determination of the policy framework. Except in the case of industrial promotion, where industrial development associations have an important role to play (and local authorities also have a role), the policy framework in England—the institutional structure and statutory basis—is determined exclusively in Whitehall.

It should be noted that although the regional policy framework is defined in spatial terms, these spatial terms do not necessarily coincide with the boundaries of the areas for which regional offices are responsible. The various levels of assisted areas in England do not coincide with the regional offices of the Department of Industry (see Maps 5.1 and 5.2). Further,

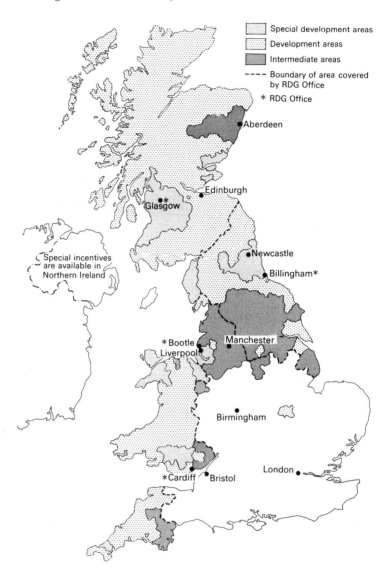

Map 5.1. Assisted areas and areas covered by RDG offices (assisted areas as at July 1980)

Map 5.2. Boundaries of Department of Industry regional offices and standard regions

despite the attempts since the mid 1960s and earlier to standardize administrative regions, no government department (including the Department of Industry) uses all the standard regions as the basis of its regional organization (see Chapter 2). For example, Barrow, which is in the post-1974 North standard region, comes under the Department of Industry's North West regional office.

These points all relate to specifically regional policies and arrangements for administering them. However, it is not possible to draw a neat line between regional policy and industrial policy. Centrally determined industrial policy outputs defined on a sectorial basis may also be spatially skewed in their distribution; this can arise because the spatial distribution of firms in the industry is uneven, because outputs are targeted in a spatial discriminatory way, or for a combination of both these reasons. The analysis in this chapter will therefore be concerned not simply with the administration of regional policy but will also deal more generally with industrial policy where its administration can be shown to have spatial implications.

Using the terminology of deconcentration outlined in the introductory chapter, we find that in the English regions we are dealing with a pattern of deconcentration of the administration of aspects of regional and industrial policy, with a greater degree of discretion accorded to the regions in the 1970s than in the 1950s and 1960s. At the level of England as a whole we are dealing with a department which originally was responsible for the administration of regional policy throughout Great Britain but which now (as the Department of Industry) is responsible for the actual administration of regional policy (as opposed to designing the policy) for England only. Thus it is correct to talk of responsibility for regional policy being decentralized within the UK. This may seem absurdly pedantic, since England contains over 82 per cent of the UK population. However, the perspective is rather different in terms of numbers unemployed in assisted area. Based on 1978/9 figures, England contained only 49 per cent of unemployed in development and special development areas in Great Britain (44 per cent in UK), and 65 per cent of unemployed in all assisted areas (60 per cent in UK). England's proportion will be reduced as a result of the reductions in coverage of assisted areas announced by the new Conservative government in 1979. Thus, the administration of regional policy in England is worth studying not because it continues to constitute the British 'norm', but because it is one of four distinct systems of regional policy administration in the United Kingdom, each of which are worth studying in their own right.[1] The system as it operates in England in 1980 is the product of evolution over a number of years and we now turn to examine that evolution.

DECONCENTRATION WITHOUT DISCRETION TO 1970

The earliest forms of regional policy, the Special Assistance Acts, were administered through two unpaid Commissions for the depressed areas, one for England plus Wales and one for Scotland, under the loose control of the Ministry of Labour.[2] The Second World War saw the establishment of regions for defence and production purposes, and a number of government departments adopted a pattern of regional administration. After the war some departments closed all their regional offices, though the Ministry of Labour and the Board of Trade retained theirs. Under the Distribution of Industry Act 1945 certain areas in which there was or was likely to be a special danger of unemployment were designated development areas, which were similar to the pre-war special areas but with enlarged boundaries. Responsibility for the distribution of industry was given to the Board of Trade. The administration of the Board of Trade's controls over the location of industry under the 1945 Act became the responsibility of the regional controllers. The decline in administrative regionalism in the 1950s—a 'policy off' period for regional policy in Great Britain—was illustrated by the reduction in Board of Trade regional staff from 521 in 1953/4 to 360 in 1960/1.[3] The Local Employment Act 1960 abolished the development areas and provided for the establishment of a larger number of smaller development districts.

While the stick part of regional policy, that is the regulation of industrial location through industrial development certificates (IDCs) was administered by the Board of Trade, the carrot was administered partly by the Board of Trade and partly by the Inland Revenue. In the 1950s and the first half of the 1960s, financial assistance was mainly in the form of depreciation allowances and investment allowances administered by the Inland Revenue. No special staffing structure was set up specifically to deal with investment allowances. Under the Local Employment Acts of 1960 and 1963, selective assistance could be made available, and was administered through the regional offices of the Board of Trade, though with approval being granted from the centre in all cases.

The election of a Labour government in 1964 saw a return to the idea of development areas. The 1966 Industrial Development Act provided for investment grants for the whole of Great Britain, but with higher rates applying in the development areas. There was therefore a need for machinery to cover the whole country and not just the development areas. The investment grant system was administered by five investment grant offices situated in Glasgow, Cardiff, Billingham, Bootle, and Southend, involving a total staff of 1,000. There were a number of reasons for this decision to deconcentrate the administration of the scheme on a regional basis:

(*a*) It would have been inconsistent with the government's policy of dispersal to have established a single unit in London.
(*b*) Industry had expressed a strong preference for local decisions.
(*c*) The need to inspect assets to determine eligibility and carry out subsequent monitoring made area offices desirable.[4]

However, because of the need for consistent treatment throughout Great Britain, there had to be frequent inter-office consultations. The investment grant division at departmental headquarters in London provided policy direction and gave guidance to the regional offices on procedures for dealing with applications. These were supplemented by instructions on particular matters raised by individual cases, though there was a continuing need for difficult cases to be submitted to headquarters.

The selective assistance available under the Local Employment Acts of 1960 and 1963 was modified by the Industrial Development Act 1966 and the Local Employment Act 1972.

The selective assistance available under these Acts took the form of loans on favourable terms, building grants, removal grants, and operational grants. In contrast to investment grants, these forms of assistance were normally negotiated case-by-case and linked to the provision of new employment, or in some cases the preservation of existing employment. The grants were standardized by statute or administrative decisions, but loans were more flexible. The administrative machinery for processing this assistance consisted of the departmental headquarters in London (initially the Board of Trade and later the Ministry of Technology), the departmental regional offices, and an advisory committee.[5] The regional offices were not authorized to approve assistance even in small cases. Both the investment grant offices and the regional offices dealing with selective assistance were limited to application processing and could therefore be described as deconcentrated units without discretion.

Another form of spatially discriminatory assistance introduced in the late 1960s was the regional employment premium (REP), which was payable on the basis of employees for whom Selective Employment Tax was payable and who worked in development areas. Although SET was abolished in 1973, these conditions governing eligibility still applied until REP itself was abolished at the beginning of 1977, and the administrative arrangements still reflected the REP's origins. Thus, the arrangements were carried out by the Department of Employment rather than the Department of Industry. Applications for REP were processed by twenty-two local offices of the Department of Employment.

In addition to these carrots, the stick of IDC control continued to exist. Distribution of industry functions remained with the Board of Trade until October 1969, when they were transferred to the Ministry of Technology. The discretion of controllers at the Board of Trade was in part expressed in terms of the size of factory or factory extension up to which they could decide on the issuing of IDCs. (It should be noted that the Board of Trade's regions did not necessarily coincide with planning regions—the controller for the Midlands covered both West and East Midlands planning regions.) However, regional discretion was exercised strictly in accordance with centrally determined policy. The large majority of industrial development applications were dealt with by regional controllers. Regional controllers in the Midlands, South East England, and Wales interviewed by Cross did not feel that they could or should exercise a wider range of discretion.[6] It was also felt that industry would view unfavourably the inconsistencies of treatment which a wider range of discretion at regional level would entail. This illustrates a much more general attitude about British ideas of territorial justice: the rather paradoxical view that spatially discriminatory policies should be determined and administered in such a way as to ensure equality or consistency of treatment. As we shall see below, this principle has been relaxed somewhat for selective industrial assistance (and, of course, never applied to Northern Ireland) but it is still reflected in government comments on the implication of devolution of central government functions, particularly to the English regions.

The machinery of regional economic planning is described in more detail in Chapter 8. In the context of the administration of regional policy in England, the point worth drawing attention to here is the minimal impact of 'regional economic planning' on the actual administration of regional policy. The establishment of the regional economic planning machinery and of a stronger regional policy in the mid 1960s both reflected a renewed interest in the regional dimension of the British economy. The Regional Economic Planning Councils (now abolished) provided an additional channel for the articulation of regional demands. However, as the description in this section of the chapter has shown, the lines of communication and decision-making were essentially vertical between the relevant regional offices and their Whitehall headquarters rather than horizontal within the 'planning' machinery at regional level.

DECONCENTRATION WITH DISCRETION FROM 1972

In 1970 the incoming Conservative government abolished investment grants, replacing them by a system of tax allowances, but there continued to be a need for administrative arrangements to process grants for contracts already signed. In 1972 the government, as part of its now more interventionist approach, introduced regional development grants and a system of selective financial assistance wider than the old Local Employment Act measures. Because the regional development grants were payable only in assisted areas, there was a need for grant offices only at Billingham, Bootle, Cardiff, and Glasgow. As with investment grants, there was a policy division at London headquarters. Because of the limited geographical coverage and the relative simplicity of the regional development grant system, the number of staff involved was cut considerably as the old investment grant system was wound up.

In contrast to the regional offices of the Department of Environment, described by Young, which carry out the same functions in all regions of England, there are two quite distinct types of regions in England as far as the administration of regional policy is concerned: those with substantial assisted areas within their boundaries, which have regional offices exercising discretion on regional selective assistance, and those without large assisted areas, which do not, of course, require special machinery for administering regional aid.

A distinction also has to be made between the area offices at Glasgow, Billingham, Bootle, and Cardiff, which administer regional development grants in specified areas (see Map 5.1), and the Department of Industry regional offices, which have a certain amount of discretion in allocating selective assistance in their regions (see Map 5.2). The four regional development grant offices administer the grants under policy instructions prepared in London. While the grants are automatic rather than selective, the department does have some discretion in determining the eligibility of applicants and assets and in imposing conditions. However, we should not expect any significant regional variation resulting from this discretion. Regional variations in outcome are likely to reflect variations in application rates, rather than differences in criteria used by the regional development grant offices, which are not strictly regional offices in any case.

The most interesting administrative innovations were those concerned with selective financial assistance under Section 7 of the Industry Act 1972. Within guidelines laid down by London departmental headquarters in consultation with the

Treasury, regional offices of the Department of Trade and Industry in the North West, Northern, and Yorkshire and Humberside regions (and in Scotland and Wales) were given authority to approve assistance in individual cases, initially of up to £0.5m. in loans, and by 1976 of up to £2m. Table 5.1 indicates for each region the maximum grant each regional office can authorize and the maximum size of project the regional office can appraise.

Table 5.1. Delegated authority of DOI regional offices in Section 7 cases

Regions	Maximum grant regional office can authorize	Maximum size of project regional office can approve
Northern		
North West	£2m	£10m
Yorkshire and Humberside		
South West		
East Midlands	£500,000	£2.5m
West Midlands	£50,000	£250,000

Source: *Industry Act 1972: Annual Report*, HC 772, Session 1979/80 (London: HMSO, 1980) p. 43.

The offices with substantial assisted areas were strengthened by the appointment of regional directors at Under-Secretary level and Regional Industrial Directors recruited from the private sector to help advise on industrial development and to appraise development projects put forward for selective assistance. The relationship between the Regional Director and the Regional Industrial Director was described by one Regional Director as that of joint managing directorship.[7] However, it would probably be more accurate to say that the Regional Director is the head of the administration and that the Industrial Director is seen as an expert who is given the title of assistant secretary to emphasize his status. The Industrial Director is largely concerned with processing cases whereas the Regional Director is more concerned with overall strategy and policy.

When an application is received, the detailed work on it is done by a team under the Regional Industrial Director. After this examination, on all but clear-cut cases, the Regional Director and the Industrial Director submit a joint application to non-statutory advisory bodies called Regional Industrial Development Boards. In the event of disagreement between the two directors, the matter would be referred to London. The approval of the RIDBs is not mandatory for assistance to be paid, but their view is invariably accepted.[8] The regional offices also examine applications for assistance beyond their delegated power to approve cases of assistance up to the limits shown in Table 5.1. and submit a report and recommendations on the case to London headquarters. In such cases the Industrial Development Advisory Board is generally, but not always consulted, and there have been cases where the minister has rejected the IDAB's advice. London headquarters also deals with cases outside the normal guidelines for Section 7 assistance and with projects which are part of the overall plan of a larger company.[9] The proportion of assistance which falls outside the normal guidelines varies considerably from year to year; in the year ended March 1976 it amounted to £25.2m. out of a total of £75.5m., while in the year ended March 1980 there was no assistance outside the guidelines.[10]

Thus, regional offices in regions with substantial assisted areas do have some autonomy in practice. They effectively take certain decisions about Section 7 assistance. This is monitored by London headquarters by reviewing decisions above the £2m. limit and by regional offices consulting headquarters about precedent-making cases. Regional offices are not given set budgets, nor has there been an effective budget limit for England as a whole (though the situation may change as a result of the tighter criteria for assistance announced in June 1979). Accordingly, no applications have been turned away by regional offices because of a shortage of funds. Even if the forecast limit were exceeded it would be expected that extra funds would be made available. Only if there were an investment boom would it be expected that the Treasury would start to put the squeeze on.

Regional offices in English assisted areas also effectively administer Section 8 selective assistance (i.e. non-regional assistance). The regional offices act as 'brokers', indicating to inquiring firms what the best source of assistance is. For example, they might point to Section 8 assistance where projects are capital intensive, since Section 7 has a cost-per-job limit. Formal decisions on Section 8 assistance are taken at London headquarters. In non-assisted regions the situation is rather different, since they lack the same administrative structure to analyse selective assistance questions as the assisted area regions. Accordingly, more Section 8 assistance is dealt with at headquarters for non-assisted regions.

In addition to these application processing and 'brokerage' roles, regional offices also have 'promotional', 'steering', 'monitoring', and 'co-ordinating' roles. Concern has from time to time been expressed at the extent to which businessmen are actually aware of the assistance for which they may be eligible; the official DOI approach is to encourage a promotional role for its regional offices:

We do go to them, we do not rely entirely on people coming to us. Regional directors and their staffs, especially in assisted areas, visit them frequently. We put a great deal of intensive effort into going to companies, talking about their problems, discussing their future prospects, how they are going to survive in an increasingly competitive world and displaying our wares to them. So they should be fully aware of the advantages they can obtain from these schemes.[11]

However, as Stephen Young has pointed out in Chapter 4, regional offices vary in the extent to which they play an activist role. It is often difficult to disentangle the influence of environment (regions with assisted areas offer more scope) from the impact of the personalities of individual regional directors.

Regional offices also play a role in steering industry within and between regions. Historically, as we have seen, regional offices have played a role in administering the 'stick' part of location policy—IDC control. The role of offices in regions without assisted areas was essentially the negative one of refusing IDCs for projects which could be located in assisted areas. This regionally-varying role emphasized the centralist role of the offices; they were acting against what might be perceived as the interests of their region. However, the 1970s saw a considerable decline in the significance of IDC control, reflecting a concern to secure industrial expansion almost anywhere during a period of recession. From 1972, IDCs were not required in development areas, but this simply removed a routine processing function, since they were automatically available in these areas. More significant was the decreased rigidity with which IDC control was applied in the non-assisted areas. By 1978, the DOI was almost trying to 'give away' IDCs; one witness told the Expenditure Committee in that year that since 1972/3:

> . . . we have had a very relaxed regime over IDCs, much more relaxed than in the period of the 1960s and early 1970s, simply because we are in a state of heavy recession and these negative controls are not suitable for a period of this kind. The number of IDCs that have been refused has gone down dramatically. . . .
> We can say to the manufacturers of the West Midlands, and we have said it, 'We have a very relaxed IDC policy, apply for them please'.[12]

However, regional offices also perform a steering role within their regions. For example, though all large inward investment cases are processed at London headquarters, the regional offices do have a role in showing intending visitors round potential sites within their region. Some regional offices may take a more directive role in this than others. Stephen Young in his chapter gives the example of the Yorkshire and Humberside regional office taking a strong line about developing some parts of the region and not others.

Regional offices also play a role in monitoring firms after assistance has been given, and indeed this is one of the main 'administrative convenience' reasons for the existence of regional offices. The degree of monitoring varies according to the case, with straightforward cases getting only statistical reviews and more difficult cases involving regular visits by regional officials.[13] Although monitoring may be considered a basically administrative task it is one with considerable potential political sensitivity.[14]

Finally, we have to note that DOI regional offices do not exist in splendid isolation from all the other activities of government, and it is of interest to consider how far co-ordination takes place at regional level with other government departments or other organizations. Certainly, some operational co-ordination does take place. Smaller cases of assistance, including rescue cases, are dealt with by consultation between DOI and Department of Employment officials; larger cases are dealt with in London, and in a case like the Chrysler rescue involve Ministerial consultation from the start.[15] In other matters, the Department of Industry does not always appear to feel obliged to take full account of the policies or plans of other organizations, such as county structure plans. Similarly the DOI has tended to pay lip-service to inner cities policy, taking the attitude that industry is more likely to expand if located in areas outside inner cities. This policy fragmentation at regional level is, of course, simply the spatial reflection of functional fragmentation at the centre, and emphasizes that DOI regional office links are essentially vertical to London rather than horizontal to other organizations at regional level or local level.

We thus have to put into persepctive the discretion accorded to regional offices, particularly in assisted areas. The discretion accorded to the regional offices leaves open the possibility that regional variations in expenditure may be due to differences in exercising that discretion. The Comptroller and Auditor General was sufficiently interested in the possibility of variations between regions to mention that the question of consistency between regions in the administration of selective regional assistance was one of the issues he might want to raise with the Department of Industry.[16] However, the extent to which politically interesting variations between regions (such as large rescue cases or a weaker application of commercial criteria) might be due to the exercise of regional discretion is reduced by the fact that in addition to the cases over £2m., and those with implications for more than one region, the regional offices also have to refer to London the 'exceptional' cases, for example, where there is an imminent risk of significant redundances in an assisted area unless help is provided. Further, in making decisions about Section 7 assistance and in carrying out the brokerage role, the regional offices have to take account of the DOI's sponsorship divisions at headquarters.

Ideally we should try to measure any effects of discretion in terms of regional variations in assistance. However, some reflection will indicate that such an analysis could be misleading. In the first place there are large cases and other applications referred to London headquarters which reflect central priorities rather than regional discretion. Secondly, variations in application rates arise from two different causes which it is difficult to untangle: autonomously generated applications from firms in the region and those which have been solicited or encouraged by the regional office. Application rates as recorded will also be affected by the extent of pre-vetting by regional offices to weed out cases which stood no chance of success. Because of the potential for variation in pre-vetting and other factors we are also unable simply to attribute variations in the success rate of applications to varying use of discretion by regional offices. Thirdly, it is misleading to aggregate total figures for assistance, since this is made up of a mixture of grants, loans, and interest relief grants, which can vary over time and between regions. Finally, there is the problem of the basis for comparison. It might seem obvious to use unemployment, or unemployment in development areas within each region. However, we should not assume that uniform exercise of discretion would be directly correlated with unemployment, as is indicated by the following exchange between an MP and a DOI official:

Do you see wide variations in the amount of business being generated by your various regional offices?—There are differences, yes.
Is there a correlation between that and the unemployment rates in that same area?—Not so much the unemployment rate but perhaps, referring back to something you raised a little earlier, the state of industry in that area which, of course, does have its repercussions ultimately on the employment rate. The fact is one of the chief problems of the assisted areas is their heavy concentration on certain types of heavy engineering, in particular steel, shipbuilding, textiles. These are declining industries, at least in terms of employment, and the industrial structure of a particular district or region does have an important part to play in determining how much assistance is offered because certain industries are expanding and others are not.[17]

Accordingly, rather than perform sophisticated statistical manipulations on the wealth of data presented in the annual reports on the Industry Act, summary figures are shown in Table 5.2 which do at least give us some idea of the varying volumes of activity which have passed through regional offices between the passage of the Industry Act 1972 and March 1980. To provide some basis for comparison with the economic problems of each region, Table 5.3 gives figures for unemployment

Table 5.2. Payments under Parts I and II of the Industry Act 1972 to March 1980 (£million)*

	Regional Develop- ment Grants	Section 7		Industry schemes	General schemes		Total	
		Grants	Loans/ Equity†	Grants	Grants	Loans/ Equity	Grants	Loans/ Equity
Scotland	585.7	48.7	41.5	8.9	2.0	—	645.3	41.5
Wales	350.4	20.8	21.4	1.7	2.0	—	374.9	21.4
Northern	751.0	31.7	19.6	7.7	6.6	0.5	797.0	20.1
Yorkshire and Humberside	130.8	25.6	8.7	28.7	6.0	—	191.1	8.7
East Midlands	13.4	3.7	0.8	17.3	3.7	—	38.1	0.8
South Eastern	—	—	—	20.6	11.5	0.4	32.1	0.4
South West	35.4	6.0	3.5	8.4	3.2	—	53.0	3.5
West Midlands	2.5	0.1	0.1	15.4	9.7	—	27.7	0.1
North West	332.6	71.0	31.6	13.4	6.2	—	433.2	31.6
Northern Ireland‡	—	—	—	0.5	0.1	—	0.6	—
Applications covering more than one area	—	71.3	—	7.0	14.3	4.9	92.6	4.9
Total	2,201.8	278.9	127.2	129.6	65.3	5.8	2,675.6	133.0

Source: Industry Act 1972 Annual Report, HC 772, Session 1979/80, (London: HMSO, 1980), p. 113.

* This table excludes assistance under the Offshore Supplies Interest Relief Grant Scheme, assistance resulting from individual applications under section 8 such as British Leyland and Chrysler, and special assistance to shipbuilding and associated industries.
† The figures do not take account of repayments and interest.
‡ Northern Ireland has its own separate system of industrial assistance, figures for which are not included here.

Table 5.3. Regional unemployment levels and rates 1979†

Area	Number ('000)		Per cent	
Scotland	181.5		8.0	
DAs & SDAs		176.6		8.5
Wales	87.1		8.0	
DAs & SDAs		77.7		8.3
North	119.0		8.5	
DAs & SDAs		119.0		8.5
York. & Humber	121.1		5.7	
DAs		29.9		7.9
East Midlands	75.3		4.7	
DAs		2.1		6.9
South West	95.4		5.7	
DAs		25.9		9.0
West Midlands	128.0		5.5	
North West	203.5		7.1	
DAs & SDAs		93.3		11.2
South East	282.2		3.7	
East Anglia	32.4		4.4	
All DAs and SDAs		524.5		8.8
Total Great Britain	1,325.5		5.6	

Source: *Industry Act 1972 Annual Report*, HC 772, Session 1979/80 (London: HMSO, 1980), p. 36.

† Monthly averages for calendar year, excluding adult students. Data are based on boundaries current at 31 December 1979. Note that regions do not in all cases correspond with DOI regions (see Map 5.2).

levels and rates. It can clearly be seen from the tables that there is a clear if crude relationship between scale of unemployment and volume of assistance, and that the greater regional assistance going to the assisted areas is not offset by non-regional assistance going elsewhere, though this reflects the overwhelming dominance in the total of automatic regional development grants rather than the selective assistance processed through regional offices.

DEVELOPMENTS IN OTHER ORGANIZATIONS

Although there are no regional development agencies in England corresponding to the Scottish and Welsh Development

Agencies set up in 1975 and 1976, the National Enterprise Board set up two regional boards in 1977 in the North and North West regions. These regional boards were given delegated authority to approve new investments of up to £0.5m.; they also make recommendations to the NEB on investments above that figure and generally advise the NEB on matters of importance within their regions. Occasionally, companies just over the borders of these regions are handled from Liverpool or Newcastle, rather than London, for reasons of administrative convenience. At the same time, a number of firms which are major NEB investments, such as BL, Ferranti, and Fairey have important plants in the North or North West regions, and these are handled from London Headquarters. The potential for overlap between the NEB and the administration of Section 7 assistance is reduced by the fact that Section 7 assistance comes mostly in the form of interest relief grants and soft loans. The NEB is mainly concerned with equity investment. By contrast, the role of Section 7 is not seen as including the provision of risk investment.

Factory construction within the English assisted areas is undertaken by the English Industrial Estates Corporation on behalf of the Development Commission; elsewhere in England factory construction is undertaken by the Council for Small Industries in Rural Areas (COSIRA). The Development Commission prefers to operate by securing consensus for its plans from both the Department of Industry and the Department of the Environment.[18] COSIRA also provides soft loans for building, plant and equipment, and working capital to small businesses in rural areas. Help is focused on the Development Commission's Special Investment Areas, the government's Assisted Areas, and other rural areas identified by COSIRA's Small Industries Committee as requiring special attention. Applications for loans are vetted by local loan panels before being forwarded to headquarters in Salisbury. COSIRA's work underwent considerable expansion in the late 1970s: in 1973/4 COSIRA received from the Development Commission £0.84m. in grants for advisory and instructional services, £0.87m. (gross) for loans, and other development grants of only £10,266; in 1978/9 COSIRA received £2.75m. in grants for the provision of factory premises, £3.1m. (gross) for loans, and £2.8m. in grants for advisory and instructional services (£2.4m. for administration and £0.4m. for construction of a new head-quarters building in Salisbury).[19]

There is one aspect of regional policy administration, mainly concerned with industrial promotion, where there is a considerable local role in the establishment of institutions, and that is in the formation of industrial development associations (IDAs). Before the 1960s a number of regional councils or associations had been established to promote industrial expansion through the co-operative effort of local authorities in the area, in some cases also involving employers' organizations, trade unions, and statutory agencies.[20] Naturally, the IDAs in areas with high unemployment, such as the North East and the North West, were more concerned with the attraction of new industry to the region, while those elsewhere were more concerned with relieving congestion and finding land to accommodate expansion. In addition to their industrial promotion role, the IDAs have also carried out research into the problems of their areas, have acted as a channel for pressure on and consultations with central government, and have been the forum for a degree of co-operation between the local authorities involved in development designed to affect regional prosperity. The renewed interest in regional matters in the mid 1960s helped to rejuvenate the IDAs, and government departments had to take more notice of IDA activity during the second half of the 1960s.[21]

Central government gave grants totalling around £750,000 in 1979 to four of the current IDAs: the North of England Development Council (NEDC), the Yorkshire and Humberside Development Association, the North West Industrial Development Association (NWIDA), and the Devon and Cornwall Development Bureau. As can be seen from Map 5.1, these coincide almost exactly with the areas in England designated as assisted areas up to 1980. The allocation of these grants gives central government a legitimate interest in scrutinizing the operation of the IDAs. In 1979 the Department of Industry commissioned Coopers and Lybrand Associates to undertake a review of the four IDAs receiving government grants. After receiving their (unpublished) report, which contained criticisms of the amount of money spent by the IDAs relative to the jobs they created, the government announced in March 1980 that government funds for the four agencies were to be cut by 14 per cent. The associations are discovering that the price of receiving government grants is a degree of answerability for their activities.

CONCLUSIONS

In focusing as this chapter does on the activities of offices at regional level there is a danger of failing to bring out adequately the centralized nature of the Department of Industry. The framework in which the regional offices operate is determined at the centre as are all important individual selective assistance cases; the bulk of funds are allocated automatically through separate offices. There is significant discretion available to regional offices, but this discretion has been accorded because it is functional for the centre to allow such discretion on details. That is not to say that this discretion is not important for the particular cases or areas to which it is applied.

Paradoxically, the spatial variations in the tasks facing the Department of Industry, in contrast to the relative spatial homogeneity of tasks faced by other departments, inevitably implies a high degree of centralization, though this can vary over time. In the regions with assisted areas we find important discretionary decision-making powers, a larger role in application-processing, and scope for active promotional and steering functions; the NEB subsidiaries, the Industrial Development Associations, and the English Industrial Estates Corporation are also active in these regions. In the non-assisted regions there is a much lower volume of activity (as evidenced by the fact that there is now one regional office for the whole of the South East and East Anglia regions); in the 1950s and 1960s these regional offices had an important 'negative' role in vetting applications for IDCs, but the significance of this activity had declined with the relaxation of IDC control in the 1970s. Although these non-assisted regions do benefit from non-regional selective assistance, headquarters plays a bigger role in processing applications than for the assisted regions. The expanded activities of COSIRA provide only a modest offset to the concentration of other industrial policy organizations in the assisted areas. In the context of this spatial variation of tasks it is by no means clear how 'industrial policy functions' would be allocated to devolved regional assemblies in different regions.

This chapter has shown a distinctively English pattern of administration of regional policy had emerged by the late 1970s. This pattern was only to a limited extent designed to meet distinctively English needs but emerged largely as a consequence of Scotland and Wales opting out to establish special arrangements. The Department of Industry now has an ambiguous role in terms of its territorial jurisdiction. On the one hand it is still the 'lead' department in the UK in the formulation and administration of industrial policy (the other three industry departments being the Scottish Economic Planning Department, the Welsh Office Industry Department, and the Northern Ireland Department of Commerce). On the other hand, as far as the administration of selective regional assistance is concerned, it is responsible only for the English regions and has a special role to 'speak for England'.

The pattern of administration of industrial policy described in this chapter has emerged as a result of changes in regional policy instruments and in the coverage of designated areas. Accordingly, we should expect further changes in the structure and process of regional policy administration in response either to the reductions in the coverage of assisted areas announced in 1979 or to other developments in the future.

CHAPTER 6

Regional Health Authorities: Regional Government or Central Agencies?

S. C. HAYWOOD and H. J. ELCOCK

INTRODUCTION

THE National Health Service (NHS) has had a regional tier of administration since its inception in 1948. On grounds of experience alone Regional Health Authorities (RHAs) and their predecessors, Regional Hospital Boards (RHBs) merit a central place in a discussion of regional government in England. The relevance of NHS experience has been further highlighted by the retention of regional authorities in two recent far-reaching reorganizations of the service. In the initial stages of the 1974 reorganization process the Government suggested that the regional tier might be abolished:[1] as the debate progressed, however, the regional tier re-emerged, first as a council without responsibilities for the supervision or control of Area Health Authorities (AHAs),[2] and finally rehabilitated as an important link in the hierarchical chain of command.[3] Similarly, RHAs have emerged unscathed, indeed perhaps strengthened, from changes planned for 1980-2 by a government committed to reduce public 'bureaucracy', though a later 'review' of their role is promised.[4] Regionalism in the NHS is, therefore, much more than the product of administrative inertia: the principle has survived re-examination of its utility. Its tenacity—or indispensibility—thus suggests a phenomenon that merits considerably more attention than it has so far received from students of British government.

This paper, however, is concerned with more than the description of neglected institutions. It is primarily concerned with the implications of this form of regional administration for the public accountability of Ministers, who retain statutory responsibility for the provision of the Service. The discussion accordingly centres on the sensitivity of RHAs to government preferences and priorities as a necessary condition of effective public accountability.

Two tests of RHA sensitivity are used. The first is the impact of members of RHAs on regional policy-making on the ground that, although not elected, they fall into the category of public persons to whom pre-eminence is accorded in theories of government in liberal societies. Members of RHAs were appointed for three reasons. The original intention seems to have been to appoint members who were capable of making a managerial contribution to the government of the NHS but some members were expected to act as representatives of the professions concerned with the provision of health care. Others were members of local authorities with an indirect mandate from the people through their election to the local authorities which in turn nominate them to membership of the RHA. A prominent role for RHA members would thus imply acceptance of the view that RHAs should administer the Health Service in ways that are sensitive to the views and interests of those members' constituents, to use that term in a loose sense. Conversely, a nominal member role would indicate that sensitiveness to local or regional interests was not regarded as important. The second test relates to the relationship between RHAs and the central government. If RHAs are not to be responsive to regional views and interests they may be expected to act as the agents of the Secretary of State for Social Service who has ultimate responsibility to Parliament for the affairs of the NHS. The NHS is also financed almost entirely from the central Exchequer. We test this second proposition by examining RHAs' response to Government attempts to equalize the resources distributed to health authorities.

The paper ends with a discussion of the implications for ministerial accountability for the NHS of RHA performance in the light of these tests. It begins, however, with a scene setting description of the organization and function of RHAs.

REGIONAL HEALTH AUTHORITIES IN ENGLAND

The administration of the NHS was originally divided into three parts. Community health services were provided by local authorities, family practitioner services were administered by executive councils, and the hospital services were the responsibility of hospital management committees and RHBs. The regional dimension was confined to the latter. Thirteen RHBs were established in 1948 and a fourteenth (Wessex) in 1959. Their successors, the fourteen English RHAs, are different in two important respects as a result of the 1974 reorganization of the service. Boundaries have been changed and responsibilities have been extended to embrace community and family practitioner services.

Why regions?
The function of RHAs is essentially strategic. The blueprints for the reorganized service said that the job of the RHAs was to 'establish planning guidelines for AHAs on priorities and available resources . . . review objectives, plans and budgets submitted to (them) annually by AHAs and the RTP [The Regional Team of Officers (an administrator, medical officer, nurse, treasurer, and works officer)], . . . resolved competing claims for resources between AHAs and agreed targets with AHAs against which their performance can be assessed.'[5] The planning function also extends to the appointment of hospital consultants who are employed by RHAs rather than field authorities, and to preparation, design, and management of major capital projects. They also have some operational responsibilities for services most conveniently run at regional level: blood transfusion, management services, and ambulances (for metropolitan districts but not Shire Counties) fall into this category. Their main functions, however, remain the preparation of regional plans and securing their implementation, the allocation of resources within their regions, and the monitoring of the performance of health authorities.

Operational factors and planning considerations are not the only explanations for a regional level of activity in the NHS. The control of the service by the centre has perhaps been a more important factor in recent years. Levitt suggests that this consideration partially accounted for the rehabilitation of the regional tier in the run-up to the 1974 reorganization. During that period she noted a 'growing conviction of ministers and their expert advisors . . . (of the) need for a co-ordination body

Map 6.1. Regional Health Authorities

between the DHSS and the area administration . . . to reduce the Department's span of control.'[6] This reasoning will have become stronger in the context of the 1980-2 reorganization which is likely to more than double the number of field authorities.[7]

The notion of a 'supervisory' role for RHAs (and their predecessors, RHBs) has, nevertheless, proved to be a problem area in the NHS. RHBs were criticized for encroaching on the day to day management responsibilities of Hospital Management Committees before 1974, but Richard Crossman, when Secretary of State, also criticized them for being insufficiently involved in the standards of care in long-stay hospitals, in which there had been a number of scandals. The nature of the 'monitoring role' of RHAs in respect of AHAs, and between officers of different authorities was given considerable attention in the blueprints for the post-1974 NHS but the problems have not been resolved. Relations between the DHSS and RHAs were sufficiently problematical to be the subject of an inquiry and report by three regional chairmen in 1976:[8] the relationship and respective responsibilities of RHAs and AHAs also became an issue during the debate on the Government's proposals for change made in 1979. It will remain a problem area while the centre tries to exercise its responsibility for the provision of services through familiar hierarchical mechanisms.

Why Health Authorities?

The reasons for the creation of regions do not, however, necessarily explain the establishment of *authorities*. There is always the option of a strong regional office on the lines of those, for example, developed by the Department of Environment. The reason for the continued preference for authorities naturally received a mention (but little more) in the blueprints for the 1974 reorganization of the NHS. The regional office option was rejected because it 'would result in over-centralization and delay' and separate authorities were also said to have the positive advantages of 'a body of local people knowledgeable about their region's needs.'[9] The preference for authorities rather than regional offices also carries with it the implication that RHAs are more than servants of the centre: they have some scope for regional initiative.

The academic literature on the development of autonomous governmental organizations, a category which could be held to embrace RHAs suggests, however, the possibility of more general factors at work. Hague has pointed to five common arguments of which the first is the need to protect certain activities from political interference, like broadcasting or university research; the autonomous organization acts as a 'buffer' against such interference. Second, there is the need to insulate some activities from the characteristic defects of government departments; nationalized industries, for example, need freedom to take commercial risks without immediately bringing down a shower of Parliamentary questions on their heads. Third, there is a need for organizations which provide more scope for the exercise of creativity than can exist in a government department preoccupied above all with keeping itself and its minister out of trouble. Fourthly, there is what W. J. M. MacKenzie has called the 'back-double theory', by which governments establish autonomous organizations to carry out activities which cannot be carried out within the existing administrative structure; and lastly, governments are frequently attacked for employing too many bureaucrats, and the establishment of independent organizations may provide a means to expand government activity without increasing the number of people employed in the regular civil service.[10]

The buffer explanation, while superficially consistent with the official reasons for the preference for authorities, is, nevertheless, not a particularly persuasive explanation in the case of RHAs. The constitutional duty to provide health services 'to such an extent as he considers necessary to meet all reasonable requirements', remains with the Secretary of State. The idea of a buffer between the political system and the NHS, in the shape of a national commission was also firmly dismissed by the Royal Commission on the NHS:

Some critics of present arrangements suggest that the creation of a public corporation or health commission would 'take the NHS out of politics'. We do not believe that this is in any wider sense desirable. We believe it is both inevitable and right that the affairs of the NHS should be kept firmly at the centre of public debate.[11]

The other reasons for the creation of autonomous authorities similarly do not offer convincing explanations for the preference for regional authorities in the health services. The responsibility of the centre means that the NHS has to be directly exposed to the so-called defects of government departments; the need for creativity at the periphery is obvious but it is not obvious why this should be linked with a regional, as well as a local health authority: similarly, while the existing governmental administrative structures might originally have been unable to cope with running health services, it has not stopped the centre becoming involved in minor details of administration (particularly pay and conditions of service) at local level: and the final presentational reason, to expand government activity without increasing the number of civil servants, has less force when applied to such a large and visible service.

The reasons for the preference for regional authorities in the NHS thus seem to stand apart from the explanations for the creation of autonomous government agencies. The specific context of the service (including perhaps the long tradition of lay involvement) is probably the major factor. The authority solution, in theory, should make it possible for RHAs to have sufficient discretion to avoid the delays supposedly inherent in a more centralized system and to respond to local factors without undue loss of central control.

RHAs: a brief profile

The number of regional authorities outside London was originally determined by the location of medical schools. Each provincial RHB was to have a medical school within its boundaries. This principle was eventually breached by the creation of Wessex RHB, since it preceded the establishment of a medical school at Southampton University. Also, in another region (Sheffield), a second teaching hospital (Nottingham) was developed. Nevertheless, in the White Paper setting out the post-1974 arrangements this principle received first mention as one of the factors determining the location and size of health regions. Other factors identified were a 'size . . . sufficient for satisfactory planning but not too large for the coordination and supervision of the AHAs . . . suitable for the exercise of regional executive function' and the need 'to avoid disturbing the forward planning of the hospital service'.[12] The latter factors were presumably the operative ones for the division of London (where there were many teaching hospitals) and the home counties into four regions.

The result has been regions of widely differing size. At the time of writing the West Midlands region, for example, has eleven AHAs within its boundaries: in contrast the East Anglian RHA has only three. Similarly, there are (inevitably) considerable differences in the geographical spread of the regions. While Mersey is relatively well-contained (Cheshire and Merseyside), the South West embraces an area stretching from Gloucestershire to Cornwall and the Isles of Scilly. There are also considerable differences in the scale of operations. In 1980/1, for example, the revenue allocations to regions varied from £680m. (West Midlands) to £243m. (East Anglia). The disparities between regional resources not only reflect differences in scale of operation. They also reflect the unequal spread of facilities inherited by the hospital service in 1948, perpetuated by the budgetary policies of the first two decades of the service, and only partly rectified in recent years (of which more later).

The authorities themselves are composed of a chairman appointed by the Secretary of State; four members representing professional interests in the NHS (a hospital consultant, a GP, a nurse, and a psychiatrist); one-third of the total is nominated by local authorities in the Region, usually amounting to five or six members; and the remainder are appointed by the Secretary of State from among people appearing to him to have knowledge and experience of the NHS, management, or industrial relations, making a total of around seventeen members.

The original intention was that members should be appointed by the Secretary of State on the basis of their ability to play an effective part in the NHS management, and the notion of appointing members to represent the people and interests of the region or area was at best secondary, or arguably completely absent. In the event, the emphasis was changed, during the process of consultation and discussion from 'management ability' in 1971 to 'general ability and personality' in 1972.[13] The change of government in 1974 led to further changes: the proportion of places available to local authorities was increased.[14]

Finally, the RHA organization represents only a small part of the total activity in the region. In the West Midlands, for example, of the 75,400 staff (whole-time equivalents) employed in the NHS, in 1978/9, fewer than 3500 held contracts with the RHA. Of these, 2000 were involved in the *direct* provision of patient services as medical consultants, professional and technical staff, and ambulance men. Headquarter groups (administrative, clerical, building, and engineering) numbered about 1100—about one-tenth of the numbers of such staff in the region. The direct expenditure of RHAs is thus only a very small part of NHS spending in the West Midlands. The revenue allocation to RHA services (including consultants, ambulance, etc.) in 1978/9 was only £27m. out of a regional total of £425m.

RHAs IN ACTION: AGENTS OR GOVERNORS?

The summary of the formal management arrangements points to two organizational imperatives for RHAs. First, they must be sensitive to governmental processes and preferences since otherwise, the public accountability of ministers will be undermined from within the service. Second, they must use their discretion in ways sufficiently substantive to justify the existence of separate authorities. One test of utility of this model of regional administration is the success with which the balance between the two imperatives is struck in practice. Too great a sensitivity to the central government will reduce them to the status of mere agents and undermine the case for regional authorities: too great a show of independence would impose (even more) strains on the principle of public accountability.

We examine two areas of RHA activity to see how this balance has been struck in practice. Both are areas in which sensitivity to government could be expected to be an important consideration: a choice of more mundane areas of activity, with little political content, was avoided on the grounds that it would have exaggerated regional independence and would not have been germane to the issue with which all are concerned.

The first area of activity is the role of members of the regional authority. This 'oblique' test of RHAs was chosen because the 'public person' (even if appointed rather than elected) remains a significant element in our system of government. We reasoned that a significant role for members would, therefore, suggest a regional authority sensitive to the requirements of democratic self-government: a limited role, on the other hand, could be taken as an indication of a low valuation.

The second area of activity is the response of RHAs to governmental policy on the equalization of allocations between health authorities. The RHAs, as will be seen, were given considerable discretion in questions of implementation of this policy. It therefore makes a very suitable area to examine the way local discretion was used to balance central governmental preferences with other regional considerations. We reasoned that a higher priority for governmental preferences, when these clashed with other aspirations, would be indicative of authorities sensitive to the governmental system: a low priority would suggest the reverse.

The empirical material comes from studies of two of the fourteen RHAs in England.[15] The period of the research spanned the years 1975-9 when health authorities were beginning to settle down after the 1974 reorganization. There is no reason to think the nature of these two authorities, or the period of enquiry, is in any way untypical, and supporting evidence from other studies is also cited.

Members of RHAs

The blueprints for the 1974 reorganization had a lot to say about member roles: what was said indicated that they would have a prominent role in NHS affairs. They were expected 'to focus their limited time . . . on the critical policy, planning and resource allocation decisions which will shape the services to be provided . . . (and) control the performance of its officers.'[16] There was also considerable emphasis on the need for extensive delegation to officers. Members were 'not there to do the work that their officers are trained to do . . .'.[17] The echoes of the venerable (but questionable) distinction between policy-making and its execution was thus made obvious in the delineation of member and officer roles in the NHS.

The emphasis on major issues was to be facilitated by arrangements for their manner of operation. Members were to behave as 'a corporate body, the decisions being made collectively' and 'to judge as a group whether they are satisfied with what is being done'. Members were not, therefore, to speak at RHA or AHA meetings as representatives of particular localities or interests, and decisions were to be reached on the basis of a consensus among all the members rather than by majority votes. A further implication to be drawn from this specification of members' roles is that decisions should usually be made by all members in the full meeting of the Authority and not by sub-committees on which a few members with particular interests or knowledge sit; in particular, 'decisions on planning and resource allocation which will be the main function of members should be the concern of the whole membership.'[18]

In matters which fell within their remit, members were accorded primacy over officers. This perspective on the respective roles has also held good in official comments on the subject. In 1979 the DHSS in a circular on appointments to Area Health Authorities said that 'the authority as a whole is expected to *lead* and *direct* the officers of the AHA . . .'[19] [emphasis added].

These brief references are sufficient to establish the consistency between the formal arrangements for members and the prominent role one would expect for them in governmental organizations. The salience of this 'test' to the sensitivity of RHAs to governmental ways of working was further enhanced by the lines of accountability drawn in the 1974 blueprints for the management of the NHS; the line of accountability was to run between the statutory authorities.[20] Officers of the RHA were not to be accountable for officers of AHAs: this was the task of the AHAs' own members. The realization of accountability to the centre was thus also dependent on a strong member role.

How have members fared in practice? In the two RHAs in our study, the impact of members on decisions was minimal. The evidence for this judgement came from observations at meetings and discussions with members. In one RHA, for example, discussion was largely confined to questions and answers: general debate was infrequent. In the other, the debate was more lively but did not deflect the 'common front' of the chairman and officers. In both cases, the research team found it safe to proceed on the assumption that the reports prepared by officers represented authority policy. The comment by one of the research team on both RHA meetings makes the point emphatically.

Each agenda consists of between twenty and thirty-five items on average which must be dealt with at a monthly meeting of three to four hours duration and only a small proportion of the items can therefore be debated at any length. It is even more important than it is at local council meetings that most items should be passed 'on the nod' and this increases the need for the officers to agree their recommendations, or be persuaded to do so by the chairman and vice-chairman, before they are presented to the members, especially as little of the RHA members' work is done in committees and sub-committees.[21]

The minimal impact of members at formal meetings of the authority was, perhaps, understandable. The formal meeting was the end, or only one part, of a very long process; it was possible that members did influence other steps in the process. The very limited involvement of the members, in our sample —2½ days per month—however, made this unlikely. The infrequent interaction between members and officers would constrain the operation of the law of anticipated reactions: views of members, tested and developed in intensive discussion, would not be easily ascertainable. These constraints were further reinforced by other features of the management arrangements. Health Authorities were advised not to establish standing sub-committees, (although some have done so, calling them by different names) and members were told to keep clear of detail: they were also expected not to pursue and raise constituency issues. One RHA chairman told members on a number of occasions that their brief was to look at the service as a whole, and a councillor was rebuked in open meeting for behaving seemingly as a representative of a locality. The net effect of these requirements has been to limit the involvement of members mainly to preparation for and attendance at monthly formal meetings, and discussion of general issues on which considerable preparatory work had already been done. In these circumstances, it was not surprising that the members had an insignificant impact on officer thinking.

Evidence from other studies suggests that these two sets of RHA members are typical. In a report prepared for the Royal Commission on the NHS, Professor Kogan and his team said the impact of members 'was felt to be slim'.[22] This judgement was based on enquiries into a larger number of authorities and regions than was involved in our own research. Another of their observations—that 'the great majority of respondents at all levels either felt the impact was weak or recorded no comment at all about members' also echoed our own experience. In interviews with thirty-eight senior officers in 1978 on how the new structure was working, very few mentioned members. We took this as a further indication of the marginality of members of health authorities.[23]

There is other, though more indirect, evidence to support this view. The National Association of Health Authorities' discussion paper on the authority member (1979), observed that 'it was evident from the seminar (on the role of members), and elsewhere, that many members do not feel involved enough in the work of their authority . . . Planning and management tend to become abstractions in the absence of close contact with the service at patient level.'[24] The arrangement of seminars to discuss the role of members (by the National Association and others) is an indication of the difficulties members having in making an impact on local policy-making.

The mismatch between prescription and reality does not necessarily mean that a low value is attached to the contribution of the member to major decisions. It might be argued that 'technical' factors prevent its realization. However, there is little evidence that this is so. Members of authorities are drawn disproportionately from those groups in society that have been found in studies of councillors to be particularly interested in policy-making functions rather than specific, constituency cases.[25] They are well-qualified to operate at the rather abstract, detached level described in the blueprints by reason of education, expertise, and experience. It is hard to imagine a selection process that could produce a more suitable group of people.

The more plausible explanation for the lack of impact is a mismatch between the theory of the role of members and the facts of life within RHAs. Decision-making is dominated by expert opinion. The widely acknowledged considerable influence of chairmen of authorities does not undermine this view, since they are in a very different position to that of the ordinary member. They receive an honorarium for their duties which are officially supposed to require two days per week. In fact, the two chairmen in our study estimated their time commitment at eleven days per month, in contrast to the two and a half days of the ordinary members. The job also seemed to exclude other public roles, though they estimated that two days per month were devoted to voluntary work: the comparable figure for ordinary members was eleven days.

The position of chairmen of health authorities is, however, different from that of chairmen of committees of local authorities. Health authority chairmen are appointed by the Secretary of State and *not* elected by the members: their primary line of accountability is, therefore, upwards to him rather than to the members of their authorities. Observations of meetings and discussions with officers reinforced our view that chairmen were not extensions of member interest: rather, chairmen often saw their role in terms of helping managers to get business through the authority meeting. No doubt widespread disquiet among members would undermine the position of chairmen but they still do not owe their security of tenure to members: the confidence of the Secretary of State and of senior personnel in the authority is more important. Members thus do not have a senior 'represenative' (as do councillors) to do business on *their* behalf with officers and other agencies.

The negligible influence of ordinary members is thus much more likely to be a reflection of the nature of the decision-making process within RHAs. Technical problems (poor selection, no standing sub-committees) are not adequate explanations for their marginality: nor does the power of the chairman compensate for their weakness, since his authority does not come from the members. It is an indication of a system insensitive to the governmental value of an influential role for public persons. The power of the chairmen, as an appointee of the Secretary of State might, nevertheless, serve to realize another governmental value—sensitivity to the preferences of ministers in major decisions. In the next section we examine this second issue.

Priorities in the NHS

The 1974 reorganization of the NHS was at least partly designed to make authorities more responsive to central views about the 'correct' distribution of resources. Richard Crossman, when Secretary of State, had been infuriated by the attitudes of RHB chairmen: he felt that they had not shared his enthusiasm for giving a higher priority to services for the mentally handicapped. His own Green Paper setting out the case for reorganization reflected this view. It said that the principle of 'the same high quality of service . . . in every part of the country' had not been sufficiently realized since 1948:

Considerable differences in standards still remain. Further levelling up of resources, particularly of trained staff, is needed—especially in the Midlands and the North—to provide the same high quality of service all over England. There are also unustifiable differences between the average standards of care provided for long stay hospital patients—the elderly, the mentally ill and handicapped—and the standards of care provided for short stay hospital patients.[26]

Social criteria in decisions on allocations were accordingly to be injected more forcefully than hitherto into a system that had been incorrigibly incremental. Allocations had been based on previous budgets (thus reflecting the existing distribution of services), plus a 'fair' share of growth monies and additions for specified large developments. The pre-eminent criteria were thus *non*-redistributive, either between different parts of the county or different patient groups, particularly as decisions on major capital developments were seemingly unrelated to such considerations. The old criteria could also be seen as reflecting professional, managerial and technical assessment of priorities.

In the reorganized service a new planning system, informed by a statement of priorities by the Secretary of State, got under way in 1976. Although the system is still in its infancy, there are already signs in practice that central preferences are not being accorded a high ranking when they run counter to the interests of the powerful groups within the Service.[27] However, we confine our attention to the attack on the geographical maldistribution of resources since RHAs had a prominent place in this particular process.

We avoid any discussion of the merits of the instrument of this policy—the so-called RAWP formula—as a fair basis for allocating monies though it has been a matter of considerable controversy. (RAWP is taken from the initial letters of the

Resource Allocation Working Party which recommended the formula. The formula was used to calculate 'target' allocations based on population and mortality criteria rather than past expenditure.) Analysis of its defects and impact now constitute one of the few growth areas in the NHS and figured prominently in the work and report of the Royal Commission. While views about its utility, usually directly related to its impact on the authorities concerned, must have had some impact, it remained a policy to which the government was heavily committed during the period of our research.

The new method of allocating monies was applied cautiously.[28] Although comparisons of RAWP target and present allocations showed considerable regional 'surpluses' and 'deficits', the Secretary of State ensured that each RHA should receive at least the same amount of money (in real terms) as in the previous year. For the financial year 1976/7 he also set a ceiling of four per cent in any one year on progress towards each RHA's RAWP target figure. In the following year, when a modified, 'final' version of the formula was used, the Secretary of State acknowledged that some growth monies were needed by all health authorities (including those with more than their target) to meet the demands from the growing number of elderly people; a static budget would, in effect, have meant a *reduction* in service since there would be more demands on it purely because of demographic changes. The implication in the RAWP reports that some 'excess' regions might have their budgets cut was rejected in favour of a policy of differential expansion. The other consequence of this cautious policy, coupled with continuing financial restraint, was lower 'ceilings' on the additional monies that could be made available to deprive regions. thus lengthening the process of equalization. In 1979 the RHAs were told that it was intended to achieve 'equity' between regions by the mid-1980s but a longer period would be required for the redistribution process between AHAs. In promoting the criterion of territorial justice in regional (and area) decisions, ministers were not, therefore, asking for a radical change in the allocation of monies.

RHAs were also accorded considerable freedom of action since there were few 'earmarked' allocations. These were confined to finance for joint AHA/Social Service Department schemes, an extra allocation in recognition of the additional costs associated with training medical students, and an injection of funds for secure units in psychiatric hospitals. This last attempt at earmarking has however, been largely ineffective. Few regional secure units have been built and some RHAs have absorbed this allocation into their general budgets. There was also a requirement that a minimum sum from the capital allocation be spent on health centre projects. Also, expensive capital projects had to receive the specific approval of the DHSS. The overwhelming proportion of monies are, however, accounted for by the general allocation (with occasional special additions) and health authorities were given limited powers to carry forward under- and over-spendings (within limits) to the next financial year and effect transfers between capital and revenue budgets.

RHAs were expected to apply the RAWP principles to intra-regional allocations. While it was accepted that some authorities would not be able to work through the full procedure recommended by the working party for allocations in 1977/8, the Secretary of State advocated attempts to produce measures of relative need within regions, and if possible within areas. He, nevertheless, asked that full regard be paid to a number of other factors when allocations were finally made. These included, *inter alia*, uneven distribution of specialist units, teaching facilities for nurses and professions supplementary to medicine, and the incidence of capital schemes and 'other relevant local circumstances'. While judgements about the appropriate pace of movement towards equalization within regions was left to RHAs, it was made clear that redistributions of revenue resources were, nevertheless, expected: RHAs were asked for reports on their allocations, and explanations of why redistribution was impossible in particular circumstances.

The two RHAs in our study benefited by this change since both had existing resource allocations below their targets; the policy of equalization between AHAs could thus be pursued by differential allocations of growth monies. The application of the policy to their constituent AHAs (among which there was a wide range from those considerably below to those above targets) was none the less very cautious. North RHA opted for a policy of separate funding of the additional revenue costs arising from developments in the pipeline, and guaranteeing minimum allocations to all AHAs. Each was allocated an amount necessary to cover the costs of the previous year's services, updated for inflation, and compensated for the full additional revenue costs of major developments. In 1976/7 this meant that the remaining balance after these allowances had been made was only ¼ per cent of the total, and this minute sum was distributed in relation to the AHA's distance from its target allocation. In the following year, a larger increment allowed a larger sum to be so allocated: but one half of the growth monies was still earmarked for special funding of revenue costs of major developments. Since in many cases these had been conceived many years previously, there was no relation between them and the beneficiaries' distance from their target allocations.

South RHA was similarly cautious. In 1976 it decided to allocate funds for development to *all* AHAs except the one that was already substantially above its target figure in the period 1977-80 and fund 50 per cent of the revenue consequences of large capital schemes, in spite of the projected exclusion of specific monies for this purpose by the DHSS in allocations for 1977/8. It also sought to give special help to the two areas whose allocations were already near or above their target allocations to facilitate readjustment. In their *plans* (not their actual allocations) for future revenue allocations the RHA also agreed to make *additional* 'non-recurring' sums available to these AHAs. In this way, rates of growth for both 'surplus' AHAs could be *increased* for 1977-9 and one was also to be allocated a further £250,000 in 1978/9 to help with 'the difficult problem of adjustment (i.e. to low growth rates) during the course of the next few years'. Since the allocations (if they materialized) would not be made on a *recurring* basis, they could eventually become available for other purposes and for other authorities at some future date. One possible purpose, as noted above, was to speed up progress towards equality in allocations between AHAs—a development which would divert these non-recurring allocations from these two AHAs, but such a development was relegated to the distant future.

A change in the RHA's RAWP target and general financial restraint meant that the increase in revenue monies (over that required for higher pay and prices) was £2,500,000 *less* than expected in 1977/8. The previous strategy for equalization was, therefore, no longer considered to be practicable. The RHA, in the light of these changed circumstances, decided to maintain its policy of funding 50 per cent of revenue consequences of large schemes and certain others at a higher rate: and give *all* authorities an increase of ¾ per cent on their basic allocation (last year's expenditure updated for higher pay and prices) before 'any process of equalisation is introduced'.

These two decisions pre-empted a significant proportion of the increase in revenue monies and left a balance of less than 1 per cent of total funds to be distributed to AHAs on the basis of distance from their target allocation. The net result of these decisions was to ensure a minimum increase in funds of just over 1 per cent and a maximum of 2.3 per cent for AHAs in the region.

*Implementation of the RAWP policy in allocations to
Heath Authorities: comment*

The description of the response of two RHAs to the centre's policy on financial allocations underlines the extent of freedom at that level of decision-making. The guidance on the application of the policy made it clear that it was not to be applied mechanistically: RHAs were expected to vary the pace of implementation and its impact. It would be misleading, however, to see the extent of freedom of action determined by positive decisions by the centre on the 'appropriate' delegation to regional level. There are other (more) important factors at work.

First, there is the need to operate with the consent of the powerful interests within the NHS. The precedence accorded by the two RHAs to service maintenance over equalization of allocations reflected the broad base of consensus within the service. Even if the centre had played a more directive role in intra-regional and area allocations, it was hard to see any acceptable alternative strategy emerging—even if it wanted to accord the principle of territorial justice a higher ranking. The counter pressures would have been far too daunting. The freedom of RHAs is, however, grounded not only on the power of opinion with the NHS but also on the impossibility of any central department, regardless of the support it could command from the NHS, producing a rank order of objectives that would apply at all times and in all places. There is insufficient consensus for various reasons, including disparate interests and ideologies between groups in the NHS, for that. Given, therefore, that objectives are various and unranked, the balancing judgement will be made 'down the line' in health authorities themselves. In other words, where there is uncertainty about objectives and their ranking (i.e. the 'normal' condition in life), then there will be considerable freedom of action for the agencies and personnel who delivery the service.

The important question for the argument here, however, is the *way* the freedom is used. Are regional decision-makers sufficiently sensitive to the preferences emanating from government? Or are they unduly sensitive to the preferences from within the system, thus posing problems for the realization of ministerial responsibility and accountability? The judgement on the relative sensitivities to competing preferences has inevitably to be subjective, though we have earlier referred to other evidence of the centre's inability to effect changes in priorities. In the case of our two RHAs there were examples of them being more cautious than the DHSS in working towards a policy of equalizing allocations between areas. Both, for example, continued to place considerable emphasis on separate allocations for the additional revenue costs associated with development, although the DHSS was phasing out this element in allocations to RHAs. Since the developments were not directly related to measures of deprivation or surplus (as measured by RAWP formulae), these decisions were a significant constraint on the policy of equalization. There were also special attempts to protect the position of the surplus AHAs. In taking this line, RHAs, as we have said, were reflecting the opinions of powerful groups within the NHS, particularly those whose interests were adversely affected by the policy. The strength of these interests is considerable and pervasive. Nationally, they had already had some impact before RHAs were involved: the protests of the powerful London Teaching Hospitals whose interests were adversely affected by the RAWP system of allocation had produced an increasingly cautious response from ministers.

This considerable sensitivity to internal views is, of course, not surprising. It would be an odd organization that was *in-sensitive* to such pressures, since management has to be based increasingly on consent. Rather, the point of the observation is the *relative* sensitivities to internal and external pressures, opinions and values in the determination of policy. The RAWP example underlines the considerable sensitivity to internal views where these constrain or conflict with the preferences of governments. This view is also supported by other examples since the 1974 reorganization where health authorities have not been particularly zestful in applying central priorities. We have already referred to the allocation of earmarked sums for Regional Secure Units in psychiatric hospitals for which four RHAs had not even submitted firm proposals four years after the event. One explanation given by the RHAs—the opposition or reluctance of staff—also supports the thesis of greater sensitivity to 'internal' than to 'external' preferences where there is a conflict.

The emerging impression of RHAs as extensions of interests within the NHS rather than the representatives of central policy is reinforced by a brief examination of their structure. The arrangements for management mirror those of AHAs: the composition of officer teams is similar: officers belong to the same professional associations and have common conditions of service: and much of the advisory committee structure has many common features. In other words, RHAs mirror AHAs in form rather than the DHSS, and this is a significant pointer to the nature of their activity.

REGIONAL AUTHORITIES IN THE NHS: WHAT KIND OF FUTURE?

The behaviour of the two RHAs in these two respects suggests organizations relatively insensitive to government: where there is a conflict, the interests of powerful staff are more important. If this is also true of other activities and authorities, it diminishes the effective public accountability of Ministers. It is not a problem that is likely to go away although the position of RHAs is not absolutely secure. In particular the Government seems to have doubts about the extent of their responsibility for 'monitoring' the performance of constituent health authorities, and about whether region is the right level for the provision of some of the non-clinical support services. The Outer Circle Policy Unit has already suggested that RHAs be replaced by a 'regional presence comprising central and local interests'. In this scheme, regions would be 'co-ordinating and negotiating forums' and not a link in the hierarchical chain of command. Additionally 'they would provide specific supra-district services on an agency basis . . . and advise the DHSS on resource allocation and policy.[29]

Developments along these rather radical lines, however, are unlikely. RHAs have proved to be resilient organizations in the face of attack. They were scheduled for oblivion in the early stages of the 1974 reorganization of the NHS but emerged stronger than ever from the consultative and legislative process. There is also a strong body of opinion within the DHSS which favours their retention on the grounds that they make it possible to control the services: the DHSS would find it even more difficult to control 200 plus authorities. The likelihood is, therefore, the RHAs will continue to exist, have considerable discretion, and represent, perhaps to an increasing extent, the 'internal' interests of the service.

The Royal Commission recognized the problems caused by the present position of RHAs, referring to 'the inconsistency between the theoretical responsibilities for the NHS carried by health ministers, permanent secretaries and health departments, and the practical realities'. Its suggestions, however, assumed the retention of RHAs, recommending that they 'become accountable to Parliament for matters within their competence'. This arrangement would have the advantage of transferring 'formal responsibility to the authorities responsible in fact for running the services'.[30] Although not presented in such terms, the change could also have had some impact on the behaviour of RHAs by strengthening the links to the political system. Closer links may have had the effect of making RHAs more sensitive to preferences and priorities emanating from Parliament and ministers. Such a change could not have weakened RHAs since authorities made directly accountable to Parliament are more likely to gain than lose in stature. However, this 'radical' possibility was rejected by the government because it was held to be inconsistent with the statutory responsibility, and accountability to Parliament which the Secretary of State felt he must retain.[31]

The tenor of the latest reorganization might, nevertheless, diminish the problem for a time. The present ministers, like many before them, 'are determined to see that as many decisions as possible are taken at the local level . . . the service must be managed in such a way that it enables those with prime responsibility for providing the services to patients to get on with the job.'[32] The removal of a tier of management in some areas, the thinning out of the management structure within Districts, and the possible 'demotion' of RHAs flow naturally from these aspirations. If the policy is, in fact, put into operation (some ministerial decisions on small hospitals have already been made which are incompatible with it) the problems and tensions associated with public accountability could be lessened. Ministers could argue that their responsibilities in practice do not extent to *all* activities but are confined to the minimal requirements of accountability—that money is spent honestly and properly, efficiently and with economy.

Success assumes that future, or even the present administration, will want to confine their accountability in this way. There is, however, continuing concern among ministers and civil servants with the total impact of services, for example about whether there is a link between increased spending on education and improved levels of literary and numeracy. It is hard to imagine that ministers and civil servants will easily withdraw from involving themselves in such programmatic issues particularly as continuing constraints on public expenditure will increasingly turn people's attention to value for money and the ordering and realization of objectives. The growing gap between available resources and what is technically possible will also maintain the pressures (through parliament, the media, pressure groups, and parties) on ministers to intervene in programmes. In the highly probable event of continuing responses to these pressures, ministers will almost certainly want to retain their *full* formal public accountability for the service, rather than sharing it with RHAs, thus posing a real threat to the intention to give even more freedom to health authorities. It will also highlight again the inability of government to realize its responsibilities through RHAs, relatively insensitive as they are to the preferences mediated through the 'external', political system. If the pressures to respond are resisted by ministers, it will create an even more anomalous situation: RHAs will be seen to be even less publicly accountable than they are now.

The regional government model, at least in the NHS, has served to protect the interests of the traditional holders of power and prestige in the provision of health care: the medical profession and above all the hospital consultants. The 1974 reorganization of the NHS was intended to increase the status of other health care professions relative to that enjoyed by the consultants by ensuring that general practice, nursing, and ancillary workers were given parity of representation with the consultants on the Service's governing bodies. Reorganization was also intended to ensure the retention of the Services's sensitivity to local opinion and interests while increasing the centre's ability to secure implementation of its policy objectives. It achieved neither of these goals. The consultants have succeeded in maintaining the traditional high priority accorded to the hospital service in general and to acute high technology medicine in particular, in the face of attempts by the DHSS to secure re-allocation of resources in favour of the relatively deprived areas and services. RHA members have also provided no effective impediment to the pursuit by the NHS's traditional power-holders of their traditional policies and priorities which have not been displaced by the views of members or Ministers who might claim to represent the wider public interest.

The inherent tensions within RHAs and within the management structure of the NHS more generally will become harder to manage if and when the central Department becomes still more concerned about the performance of the Service—assuming, of course, that the government remains responsible for the provision of health services in Britain. In that event, the solution of the problem lies in the direction of removing RHAs from the chain of command and making regional organization (not RHAs) service agencies; or, following the recommendations of the Royal Commission, creating *additional* lines of accountability to the political system to 'sensitize' RHAs without diminishing their position.

CHAPTER 7

The Regional Water Authorities

CLIVE GRAY

THE reorganization of the water industry in England and Wales in 1974, as a result of the implementation of the Water Act 1973, led to a radical restructuring of the organizations responsible for the management and planning of water resources. Water organizations were removed from their predominantly local base and reorganized as regional bodies. The importance of this regionalization was felt to lie in the opportunities that it provided for improving the operational and financial management of the complete range of water services: benefits of scale and professional criteria for 'good' water management were felt to be obtainable through regional organization.[1]

The ten new Water Authorities (WAs) have overall responsibility for every aspect of water usage in England and Wales: the conservation, supply, and distribution of water; sewerage and sewage disposal; land drainage; water pollution control; and water-based recreation and amenity. Before reorganization these functions, where undertaken, had been divided amongst a number of organizations: water supply had been managed by 187 water supply undertakers; sewerage and sewage disposal by 1393 county boroughs and county district councils; and water conservation and land drainage by 29 River Authorities.[2] The WAs, while being considerably larger than the pre-reorganization bodies still vary considerably in size and in their command of resources (see Table 7.1 and Map 7.1).

The purpose of reorganization—to 'managerialize' the water industry[3]—has led to major changes: concern for the inter-related nature of the functions of the WAs has led to the replacement of locally based, fragmented, and often conflicting policies for water resources with an approach based upon

Table 7.1. Regional Variations between Water Authorities: 1978/9

	Thames	Severn-Trent	North West	Anglian	Yorkshire	Southern	Welsh	Northumbrian	Wessex	South West
Population (millions)	11.660	8.182	7.010	4.730	4.526	3.779	3.009	2.669	2.250	1.369
Population Density (per km^2)	890	376	472	184	335	354	141	290	234	126
Manpower*	12125	11073	9103	6823	6273	4122	5534	2385	2363	2491
Revenue Expenditure (£million)	258.158	211.717	173.454	157.777	124.989	88.402	106.933	51.539	55.535	44.503
Capital Expenditure† (£million)	59.191	76.235	66.679	61.818	54.103	36.506	33.964	53.667	24.475	17.189
Water Supply/ Sewerage Charges (pence per house per week)	56	68	61	88	64	77	92	59	87	93
Measured Water Charges (pence per 1000 gallons)	51	58	53	70	60	56	64	56	63	70

Source: Water Authority and National Water Council Annual Reports.

* Employed by Water Authorities. An additional 15800 are employed on water service functions by local authorities and Water Companies.

† Net of grants and other contributions.

hydrological and regional factors. This change has been supported by the movement towards an industry that utilizes

Map 7.1. Regional Water Authorities

multifunctionalism, corporate planning, and managerial members, in contradistinction to the pre-reorganization period. The acceptance of this managerial approach to water resource management has also led, however, to a separation of responsibility for water planning from responsibility for development planning, and to a reduction in the ability of communities to control their own water resources.[4]

The role played in the reorganization process by water industry professionals cannot be overlooked in this respect. The major impetus for reform came from within the industry, once the idea had been proposed.[5] This impetus was given shape by the values and expectations of the professionals within the industry. Water industry professionals are predominantly engineers who favour technological solutions to problems and who tend to see their work as a subject for the use of engineering and technical criteria rather than for political and social ones.[6] The shape of the Water Act, as originally envisaged, embodied the ethos of these professionals,[7] while the Ogden Report[8] clearly reflected a bias towards officers in the planning and decision-making processes of the new WAs at the expense of members. The shape of the reorganized industry was determined primarily by the concern of water professionals for a technically efficient industry, in terms of engineering and hydrological criteria, rather than for an industry that was open to participation from outside.

Reorganization thus led to a number of functional and managerial principles assuming a far greater importance than had previously been the case, this increase in importance being a consequence of the regionalization of water services. The nature of these principles, and the combination within the water industry of elements from both local government and the nationalized industries, have led to the WAs becoming a unique element within the administrative system of Britain. The retention of close links with local government through the operational activities and the membership of the WAs, and the organizational similarities with other public corporations makes the water industry a distinctive form of organization within the public sector: a form of quasi-nationalized industry.

THE FUNCTIONAL AND MANAGERIAL IMPLICATIONS OF REORGANIZATION

The development of certain distinctive principles within the water industry since reorganization has had important effects upon the operations of the WAs and upon their relationships with other branches of government. These principles can be divided into two groups: those related to the functions of the

WAs and those related to the management and planning of water resources. These two groups reflect different aspects of the managerial approach to water resources management, emphasizing efficiency and rationality, and indicating a willingness to solve problems, and resolve conflict, on the basis of technical, rather than political, criteria, with a subsequently greater role for WA officers in planning and decision-making, as a consequence of their technical knowledge and expertise, then they had prior to reorganization.[9]

Three principles are of particular importance in the functional group:[10] the water cycle; catchment areas; and multifunctionalism. All three have important implications both for the areal distribution of the WAs and for the organization of their operational activities. The water cycle and catchment area principles are directly related to the hydrological processes determining the availability of water in a particular place at any time.[11] The water cycle is the natural system wherein water circulates between land, air, and sea, while catchment areas are those areas of land that drain to a particular river. The importance of the utilization of these principles lies in the fact that the regional boundaries of the WAs are determined by catchment areas, and that each WA therefore deals with self-contained water cycles. The WAs can thus manage and plan water resources as a totality, and can assess conflicting water uses in terms of demands and activities elsewhere in the catchment area. The previously fragmented system, based predominantly on administrative rather than hydrological boundaries, was usually concerned with only one part of the water-cycle—either water supply, sewerage, or land drainage—and with one part of a catchment area. This geographical and functional separation of responsibilities for water resources had led to concern over the ability of the water industry to meet future demands and to resolve conflicts over different uses of water, and was a motivating force behind reorganization.[12]

Multifunctionalism forms an operational dimension of these hydrological factors and has two aspects. The first of these relates to the WAs themselves which are multifunctional in that they have responsibility for all functions relating to water. The second aspect refers to the operational divisions of the WAs, and is the more important. The extent to which these divisions are also responsible for all water functions indicates how far the industry has actually adopted the managerial approach to water resources management, and how far the catchment area and water cycle principles have been taken by the WAs. Nine of the ten WAs have some form of multi-functional divisional structure, the divisions having control of more than one activity.[13] This multifunctional approach in the WAs pursues the logic of reorganization at a sub-regional level, and emphasizes the movement of the industry from administrative to technical criteria as the decisive factors in operational decision-making.[14]

The principles related to the management and planning of water resources are directly related to the emphasis of the managerial approach on rationality, efficiency, and technical criteria, and to the regional nature of the WAs. The desire to operationalize these principles has been met in the WAs by a commitment to detailed planning. The WAs have a statutory duty to prepare annual and medium-term plans and the industry has, in general, adopted corporate planning on the recommendation of the Ogden and the Jukes Reports.[15] The reorganization of the industry on the basis of catchment areas allows the WAs to plan on a regional basis, transcending the generally local planning of the pre-reorganization system, while the multi-functional nature of the WAs permits an integrated approach to the planning of water resources. A concomitant of regionalization lies in the changing role of the member. Reorganization reduced the number of members concerned with the industry, and the movement to a regional basis necessitated a move away from the use of participation and political criteria in planning for a locality towards a consideration of efficiency and technical criteria for the region. The regional and water industry viewpoint has been strengthened by the appointment of non-local government members with knowledge of, or expertise in, the functions of the WAs, and by the emphasis placed upon the managerial, rather than the representative, role of the member.

WATER AUTHORITY BOUNDARIES

The regional boundaries of the WAs, based upon hydrological catchment areas, are of greatest utility for the overall, regional planning of water industry activities. For operational purposes, however, these regional boundaries are of lesser importance. The movement towards multifunctional divisions has been considerably complicated by the continued existence of water supply companies and by the presence of local authority sewerage agencies:[16] these remainders from the pre-reorganization system have also had an effect on the operational boundaries of these divisions. While multi-functional divisions exist in the majority of the WAs there are differences in the factors determining the geographical distribution of these divisions. The functional unity of the WAs at the regional level has not been completely maintained at the sub-regional level: the degree of acceptance of the managerial approach and the particular circumstances of the WAs have led to a variety of divisional, and divisional boundary, types being utilized. The general acceptance of the catchment area principle has led however to divisional boundaries which only rarely have any agreement with those of the WAs' constituent local authorities. This emphasizes both the movement away from a local government base to the industry, and the importance that the WAs attach to regional and hydrological factors in planning, rather than local, political, and administrative considerations. For example, while all of the divisional boundaries are influenced by catchment area principles, three different types of divisional boundary can be discerned in the WAs, each of which has implications for the relationships of the WAs with the local authorities in their region. These three types of boundary are the 'pure' catchment, the administrative, and the historical.

Five of the WAs—the South West, Yorkshire, Wessex, Northumbrian, and Welsh—have extended the catchment area principle downwards to a sub-regional level. The divisions in these WAs each cover an individual catchment area, or group of catchments, enabling water resource management on the basis of the hydrological cycle to be undertaken at the local level. This choice of boundaries accepts the functional and the hydrological principles adopted at reorganization[17] but has, inevitably, led to a considerable overlapping of boundaries with local authorities, some of which are split between two or three divisions.

Three WAs—the North West, Severn-Trent and Anglian—have arranged their divisional boundaries on administrative considerations. The North West has attempted to preserve an equality of population size between divisions as far as is practicable, while also making use of catchment principles, again leading to boundary overlaps with local authorities. The Severn-Trent WA has attempted to reconcile divisional catchment boundaries with those of the local authorities in its region, and while this has not proved entirely feasible there is a large degree of agreement between the two sets of boundaries, making WA-local authority co-ordination more coherent and unified at the operational level. The Anglian WA is anomalous in that it is the sole WA not to have formed multifunctional divisions; the major functions—water supply, sewerage, and land drainage—are managed on the basis of single-purpose divisions, with different boundaries for each service. Sceptisism about the benefits of multifunctional operation, and recognition of the particular resource problems in the region have led to this administrative division of functions,[18] and while land drainage is based on catchment areas, water supply and sewerage are based on groupings of pre-organization undertakings, leading to a complex set of overlapping boundaries both within the WA and in relation to local authorities.

The two remaining WAs—the Southern and the Thames—have been the most affected in their choice of divisional boundaries by the continued existence of the Water Companies. Both WAs have been limited in the extent to which they have been able to establish multifunctional divisions, and have made great use of pre-reorganization boundaries in choosing their own: the Southern WA has made use, where possible, of River Authority boundaries and the Thames WA has used groups of water supply undertakers. Both WAs have given greater emphasis to the principles of water cycle and catchment area management than to co-ordination with local authority boundaries without, however, being able to achieve either fully catchment area based or multifunctional divisions.

THE WATER INDUSTRY AT THE CENTRE

The interest shown by central government departments in the water industry is principally determined by two factors: the strategic planning role, at the regional level, of the WAs, and the capital intensive nature of the industry. The importance of WA regional strategies for providing services for domestic, industrial, and agricultural uses was clearly demonstrated during the drought of 1976, when it was the ability of the WAs to control *regional* water resources that enabled fewer restrictions on water use to be imposed than would otherwise have been the case.[19] The ability of the WAs to carry out their functions depends, however, upon the existence of adequate pipes, pumps, storage facilities, and purification plant, and the construction of defences against possible floods.[20] This dependence on capital works leaves the industry particularly open to government intervention when the control of public expenditure is a government priority.

The Water Act of 1973 had, as a central purpose, the promotion of a national policy for water resources. Responsibility for this was to be primarily a matter for the Department of the Environment (DOE) and the Welsh Office (WO)—for water supply, sewerage, pollution control, and amenity—and the Ministry of Agriculture, Fisheries and Food (MAFF)—land drainage, flood protection, and fisheries.[21] This intention was not, and has not since been, supported by the establishment of any centralized machinery to undertake detailed planning for water resources. The establishment of autonomous and executive WAs with clearly defined statutory duties and powers led to some changes in the relationships between central government and water industry organizations, increasing the independence of the WAs from detailed central control, and emphasizing their regional planning role rather than the role of government in national planning for water. The role of government departments in water industry planning is limited by the autonomy of the WAs and the lack of executive power at the centre. Both the DOE and the MAFF have, however, produced memoranda detailing the information that they expect to be included in the statutory plans of the WAs.[22]

The anomalous position of land drainage in the WAs and the special role of MAFF with regard to this function—stemming from the reorganization process—has inevitably led to a greater control of this function by the centre than is the case with those functions for which the DOE and the WO are responsible. In particular the attraction of grant-aid for land drainage schemes from MAFF has led to a greater involvement from the Ministry in the work of the WAs than is possible for the DOE to achieve.[23]

To provide advice to ministers and to co-ordinate the work of the WAs a number of national agencies have been established, none of which, however, has been given executive powers over the activities of the WAs.

The National Water Council (NWC) is the major such statutory body and acts as a consultative forum for the WAs and government:[24] it also possesses advisory functions for national water resources planning, and has special duties related to training, water fittings, and the promotion of the efficient performance of the WAs. The NWC, in the light of the importance of the functional activities that it is concerned with, has been subject to criticism since reorganization, principally because of its lack of executive powers and the fact that neither the government nor the WAs are obliged to accept the advice that it offers.[25] It does, however, perform a vital buffer role between the WAs and the government, and as the chairmen of all ten WAs are members of the NWC, provides a coherent voice for the water industry at the national level.

In practice, the central government departments concerned with the water industry have little say in the planning of the WAs: little of the discussion that takes place between the DOE and local authorities over structure and local plans is repeated with the WA corporate plans. While a centrally-determined national policy for water has not been forthcoming, government departments do have some control over the work of the WAs, if at 'arms-length' and in a negative form, through the determination of capital expenditure ceilings for both the industry as a whole and for individual WAs.[26] The structure of the financing of the WAs that reorganization created increased the freedom of the WAs from central control of charging, removed the loan consent procedures previously in force, and substituted capital ceilings in the latters' place. This change has led to increased *overall* government control of capital expenditure by the WAs, and has frequently been used as part of overall government strategy with regard to public sector expenditure: the first capital budgets drawn up by the WAs for 1974/5 were reduced by 60 per cent, and further cuts of 11.2 per cent were made in 1979/80.[27] These reductions have inevitably affected the development of some capital schemes and, consequently, the plans of the WAs. Apart from the manipulation of the cash limits set on WA expenditure there is little government can do to influence the WAs directly—the favoured approach consisting of exhortation and persuasion. Recent events have, indeed, shown how reliant government is on the WAs' co-operation. Attempts to reduce proposed rate increases from an average of 19.4 per cent involved the sending of teams of accountants around the WAs to look for waste and extravagence in their budgets. The failure to uncover such waste led to the government altering the cash limits of individual WAs within the same overall sum, and to requests for further savings to be made. The WAs co-operated by making further cuts and the average increase in rates fell to 13.3 per cent. Without the acquiescence of the WAs, however, there was only a limited amount that government could achieve. The result has been the postponement of some capital projects, criticisms of 'financial manipulation' and warnings that this form of intervention is likely to lead to increased costs in the future.[28] While the actual plans of the WAs are free from detailed central control and co-ordination the implementation of these plans is subject to governmental economic policies and priorities that can have serious effects on future WA activities.

WATER AUTHORITIES AND LOCAL AUTHORITIES

The concern of the centre with the strategic planning of the WAs indicates a desire to formulate a national policy for the industry, even if this desire has yet to be consummated. The local authorities, however, are more immediately concerned with the operations of the WAs, and the effect of regional plans on local developments. As with central government the WA corporate plans play a major role in the relationships between WAs and local authorities. The existence of local authority sewerage agencies further strengthens the local links of the industry, these agencies being undertaken with WA 'approval', although it is the responsibility of the districts involved to actually initiate and execute plans for sewerage schemes.[29] The regional nature of the WAs, however, and the functional unity of their operations extend the impact of the industry beyond the boundaries of any one local authority and have a major effect upon the plans produced at both County and District levels. Moreover, this supra-local orientation of the WAs has consequences for the strategies produced at the regional level. The problem of overlapping boundaries between WAs and local authorities is reproduced at the regional level where there is little relationship between the boundaries of the WAs and the Standard Planning Regions.[30] The lack of agreement between these boundaries can produce conflict when preferred regional water strategies fail to agree with regional strategies that are concerned with areas that are split between two or more WAs. Thus the existence and the geographical distribution of the WAs affect local authorities both in localized and in regional terms.

The importance of WA planning for the local level was recognized before reorganization, and the development of integrative machinery for local authority and WA planning has been a major task for the WAs since that time.[31] The WAs have a statutory obligation to consult with the local authorities in their area during their respective planning processes, and a further duty to 'have regard to' structure and local plans. The regional focus of the WAs, however, means that they actually play a major role in the production of these plans: firstly, they are in a position to ensure that the summation of district requirements and needs is consistent with county forecasts, and, secondly, that the summation of county requirements is consistent with their own, regional, forecasts. The WAs are thus in a position to influence the nature of the plans produced by the local authorities and, through these, are able to determine to some extent the feasibility of large-scale industrial and housing development proposals and small-scale rural housing schemes.[32] In this respect the different objectives underlying WA and local authority planning play an important part in the planning process. The task of the WAs in providing the essential infrastructure for development forms only a part of their planning objectives: the WAs also have a responsibility to maintain and improve their existing facilities and plant, while they also need to plan for the increased use of water from existing consumers, both domestic and commercial, while having 'due regard' to the protection of the environment and the need to be financially self-sufficient.[33] These requirements and needs, stemming from the functional nature of the industry, stand in contradistinction to those of local authorities, which are more concerned with the role of the WAs in providing the infrastructure for their own planned developments.

The WAs have argued that, apart from these differences of planning aims, a lack of investment in water services by local authorities before reorganization has further hindered their ability to provide development infrastructure. The inheritance received by the WAs in terms of the quality of plant varied considerably, especially in the case of sewage treatment works. The water industry severely criticized local authority investment as being inadequate due to a combination of local political apathy—the claim that there are 'no votes in sewage'—the localized nature of planning and the system of grant-aiding for water schemes before reorganization.[34]

Liaison between the WAs and local authorities is divided between WA headquarters and the operational divisions; liaison with county councils generally taking place through the former, and with district councils through the latter. This division is the result of both the localized nature of much of the planning of the districts, and the operational nature of the divisions. The divisions of the WAs are felt to have a greater understanding of the issues and needs that are involved at the local level than is present at regional headquarters, while the delegation of authority to divisions, enabling minor works to be undertaken without constant reference to headquarters, recognizes the essentially local nature of some schemes. Overall planning for the WAs, however, is undertaken at the regional level and while the divisions, and through them the districts, make a contribution to this planning their effort is severely limited by the perceptions of regional need that are held at the WA headquarters.

The operation of sewage agencies by district councils necessitates the development of close links between WA divisions and districts. Under these agency agreements the districts initiate and execute plans for sewerage for the locality, and operate and maintain sewers, being reimbursed by the WAs for the work undertaken. These agreements leave a limited control over water services functions with the districts, including the power to requisition sewerage facilities for domestic purposes, but there have been severe criticisms made of these agreements by the WAs. The most important of these criticisms concentrate on the problems that the WAs face in securing effective budgetary control over the sewerage function, and the effect that these agencies have on the role of the WAs in managing the whole of the water cycle, and are mainly directed at the small districts that did not inherit effective administrative machinery to manage the sewerage function at reorganization. The local authorities have replied to these criticisms by pointing out that the agency agreements enable them to organize the provision of some, at least, of the infrastructure essential for development alongside the other services that they have responsibility for, that this obviates the need to consult the WAs at all stages of development and prevents the obstruction of their local policies by the regional WAs. The focus of the WAs on the control and management of water resources rather than on the interrelationships that exist between WA and local authority services is seen by the latter as entailing a severe constraint on their own decisions and plans.[35]

The decision to remove water supply and sewerage functions from the local authorities led to problems even before reorganization,[36] and the concessions gained over membership of the WAs and sewerage agencies by no means placated them. The combined role of water industry professionals and land drainage interests in the reorganization process was seen as an attempt to produce an industry that would be dominated by these same groups, and that this would lead to a situation where local political choices would be overridden by appeals to technical factors. The results of the reorganization of the water industry lend partial credence to this fear: decision-making is effectively concentrated in the hands of WA officers and vested interests with little scope existing for participation from outside. The number of small schemes that the WAs can halt by means of appeals to technical criteria does act as a considerable constraint on both the development and implementation of local authority plans.[37]

However, while relationships between the WAs and local authorities are sometimes acrimonious they are generally satisfactory: the co-operation required between the two for both operational and planning purposes has led to the development of close links at divisional and regional levels within the WAs.[38] Since reorganization the focus of debate has shifted from the movement of water services out of local government to the role of members in WA decision-making, the, alleged, non-representative nature of the WAs, and the accountability of the WAs to the public.

WATER AUTHORITY ACCOUNTABILITY AND MEMBERSHIP

It is possible to identify three distinct forms of accountability in the public sector—political, legal, and ministerial[39]—and to identify two areas where accountability of different types to these is involved—intermediate *administration* and technical *expertise*.[40] The first three forms refer directly to the relationship between an organization and a group, body, or individual external to it but to which the organization must justify its activities. The last two—administration and expertise—refer to accountability in the sense of justifying the procedures utilized within an organization in undertaking its activities. In general, public organizations are predominantly orientated to one of the forms of accountability related to activities, although an element of procedural accountability is also generally present: local authorities are predominantly orientated to political accountability to an electorate, nationalized industries are orientated towards ministerial accountability in Parliament; for their activities both are also responsible to ombudsmen for the administrative or procedural element of these activities.[41] The question of which form of accountability —activity, or procedure-based—the WAs are primarily involved

with is considerably confused both by their hybrid constitutional arrangements and by their perceptions of their own
accountability.

The pattern of the WAs membership and accountability
that arose from the reorganization process illustrates this confusion as well as showing an ambiguity over the extent to which
the water industry should have been made managerial in orientation. The questions that arise concerning membership and
accountability in the water industry can only be answered by
reference to the assumptions that were made at reorganization
about the role and nature of the industry as a whole in England
and Wales. The movement of the industry to a regional base
provided support for the proponents of a managerial approach
to water industry management and planning, who argued that
a managerial approach makes local representation on the management boards of the WAs anomalous: accountability should
lie, for lack of a regional level of government,[42] at the centre,
as is the case with the nationalized industries. This argument
was countered by the view that the close links between the
work of the local authorities and the WAs was made local
accountability essential:[43] this argument can be seen as being
one between the ministerial and political forms of accountability. The development of organizational accountability in
the WAs shows that this argument is still active, although the
WAs themselves are convinced that this is now a non-issue,
and that their accountability is towards ministers in Parliament, with their procedures being checked by investigations
from the local ombudsman.

The original proposals made in relation to WA membership would, indeed, have supported this central form of accountability: WA management boards would have been small
with only a limited representation from local authorities.[44]
The proposal to include a majority of local authority members
on the WA boards was in opposition to the idea of a truly
'managerial' membership, and has been seen as a negotiating
stance for the DOE in the light of the decision to take water
services out of local government hands.[45] The outcome of the
consultative process was a much larger membership than had
originally been envisaged, with local authorities providing a
majority of members.

The appointment of members to the WAs provides a further illustration of the confusions and conflict that surrounds the subject of WA accountability. Local authorities appoint members on the basis of a simple formula: one member for each non-metropolitan county and one member to represent all the districts within a county, and two members for each metropolitan county with a further two members representing the districts within each county. Exceptions are made for the Thames WA, where the GLC appoints ten members and the London Boroughs a further ten, and for the South West WA, where the Devon and Cornwall County Councils appoint two members each, and their constituent Districts a further two members each.[46] This method of selection was criticized, however, as not being sufficient to ensure the adequate representation of the districts. Consequently an increase of almost 30 per cent in district representation was made for the nine English WAs, with certain seats being reserved for the major cities—Birmingham, Leeds, Sheffield, Liverpool, Manchester, and Bristol—the intention being to increase the accountability of the WAs and to 'tidy up some of the difficulties' arising from reorganization,[47] implying, at the least, a commitment to some form of *local* accountability.

The Ministerial appointments to the WAs are made by the Secretary of State for the Environment and the Minister for Agriculture, Fisheries and Food, with the Secretary of State for Wales appointing members, other than MAFF nominees, for the Welsh WA. The basis for appointment for these members lies in their having knowledge or expertise that is relevant to the activities of the WAs, or in their representation of particular groups, such as anglers or industrialists. The larger WAs also have a member appointed to represent consumer interests, although such an appointment is not statutorily required. The MAFF members form a minority—between two and four in each WA—and are appointed for their knowledge of agriculture, fisheries, or land drainage. These appointments indicate a commitment to a ministerial form of accountability, as distinct from the local, political accountability of the local authority members of the WAs and serves to illustrate the hybrid nature of the membership and accountability of the WAs.

This hybrid membership has been criticized as being neither

adequately representative of the public, nor completely based upon the criteria of managerial expertise: the belief that the WAs require only small management boards to secure effective management is balanced by a desire to ensure that an element of political accountability is present in the industry.[48] The membership of the WAs combines both a local and a central perspective which has served to confuse, and obscure, where their accountability lies. The size of the WAs and the commitment to a managerial approach to water services precluded the appointment of as many members as would be needed to ensure the representativeness of the WAs, while the appointment of local authority members has inhibited the development within the water industry of the patterns of accountability that are present in the nationalized industries. The WAs are, therefore, in the situation of facing both the local authorities in their areas and central government without the form of membership that is required to ensure either fully local or fully central accountability.

The problem of WA membership extends beyond the consideration of the accountability of the WAs: the role of the member within the industry has been considerably affected by reorganization. While the role of the ministerial appointees is clear—acting as an expert manager—that of the local authority appointee is less so. Local authority members have to fulfil a number of roles—managers, consumer representatives, and local authority delegates—while their attention is divided between the interests of the locality that they represent and the regional interests of the WAs. The regionalization of water services has reduced the importance of the traditions of local participation and democratic control that were inherent in the water industry before reorganization, replacing these with a concern for technical solutions and a belief in the apolitical nature of water services. The mixed forms of membership of the WAs, however, incorporates both the local, political, and regional, technical, perspectives. This fact, and the close relationship between the work of the WAs and that of the local authorities, has produced a confusion over which of the roles of the local authority is the most important.

The decision-making role of the local authority member has been limited by three factors: the insistence of the Ogden

Report on seeing their role as that of a delegate;[49] the demands on these members' time; and the problems of attempting to act independently of officer expertise and minister-appointed member knowledge. This is not to say that local authority members have no role at all in WA planning and decision-making: in the Northumbrian WA, for example, member-officer working parties are responsible for the formulation of Authority policy for all services, while in the Yorkshire WA members have developed close links with the divisions of the WA and utilize this local knowledge of water service operations when considering regional policy. The problem remains, however, of ensuring an effective role for local authority members as anything other than a delegate.

The hybrid constitutional arrangements of the WAs, with the subsequent confusion concerning the role of the member and the accountability of the WAs, indicates a much greater withdrawal from the managerial approach to water resource management than has generally been seen to be the case.[50] The commitment to local authority representation on the WAs has led to a confusion of responsibilities for local authority members between their roles of delegate and manager. The pattern of membership selection at the district level, while increasing, is still inadequate to ensure representation at this level,[51] while any substantial local authority representation counteracts the intention of managerializing the water industry. The seemingly innocuous question of WA membership thus raises serious questions concerning the extent of local authority involvement in policy-making, the role of members within the industry and whether the WAs are accountable to the local, political level or to the central, ministerial level, or whether they are accountable at all.

WATER INDUSTRY FINANCE

The water industry in England and Wales provides a wide range of services, the majority of which require a great deal of capital investment; the capital assets per employee for the industry in 1975 were £39,000, compared with totals of £14,000 in the gas industry, and £11,000 in ICI, while the total capital assets of the industry in 1977 amounted to approximately £3,300 million. Capital investment since reorganization has taken place on a large scale, both to provide new services and to replace aging assets (see Table 7.2).

Table 7.2. Water Authority Expenditure: 1974–80*

	Revenue (£million)	Capital† (£million)	Depreciation and Interest (as % of revenue)
1974/5	770.398	524.485	47.99
1975/6	804.623	505.043	45.42
1976/7	808.288	463.675	45.65
1977/8	839.307	388.805	46.57
1978/9	852.183	369.431	45.82
1979/80	883.152	350.736	43.68

Source: calculated from figures in *National Water Council Annual Reports, 1974/5–1979/80.*

* All figures at 1975/6 prices.

† Gross of grants and other contributions.

Changes in the financing of the industry have had marked effects at all levels from individual consumers to central government. The three major effects arising from these changes are: an increase in charges to the consumers, a greater involvement of government in overall WA expenditure, and changes in the financial policies pursued by the WAs. The removal of water services from local government had major implications for the methods of financing revenue expenditure in the WAs. Water supply and sewerage and sewage disposal account for 95 per cent of all water industry revenue expenditure[52] and while these were local government services the cost of their provision was subsidized through the Rate Support Grant (RSG) and, in the case of water supply, through precepts on the general rate funds. This subsidization had two results: everyone paid for these services, whether they received them or not, through the general rate, and the true cost of service provision was hidden—some areas in Wales, for example, received over 50 per cent of their running costs through rate support and precepts.[53] The Water Act removed these subsidies and charged the WAs with the following duties: at least to break even, taking one year with another; only to charge consumers for services actually received; and not to discriminate between different classes of consumers. The results of this were soon apparent, though apparently unforeseen by the government prior to reorganization: charges rose by an average of 41 per cent in 1974/5, and in 1975/6 at rates of between 25 and 90 per cent.[54] The duty to charge consumers only for those services actually received, led eventually to the WAs having to reimburse some £60m. to owners of unsewered properties, with subsequent rises in charges to other consumers.[55] The methods of raising revenue finance altered little as a result of reorganization but the effects of the removal of subsidy through grant support led to the uncovering of major regional disparities between the WAs: the reliance on government support, through the RSG, of the more rural WAs had effectively hidden the true cost of provision. The loss of this subsidization led to disproportionate increases between regions, with the Welsh WA levying the highest increases. The outcry against the size of these increases led to the appointment of the Daniel Committee, which recommended both the equalization of charges between areas within the Welsh WA and the return to some form of interregional subsidization to reduce regional disparities. The response of the government was to produce an interim Water Charges Equalisation Act as the first step towards a more equitable national system of charging. By the use of a self-balancing system of levies and grant payments the disparity between regions was considerably reduced, from a range of 17 per cent below to 44 per cent above the national average, charges were brought within a range of 12 per cent below to 21 per cent above the average.[56] This system is internal to the water industry, rather than government financed, and effectively subsidizes rural areas, where the costs of supply are high because of low population densities and high capital costs, at the expense of urban areas, even though the more 'rural' WAs still have higher charges than the 'urban' WAs (see Table 7.1).

Retaining the pre-reorganization method of raising revenue through rates on property values has been a major source of debate for some time. Apart from the regressive nature of this form of taxation it fails to act as a brake on the demand for water. Once the rate has been paid the quantity of water consumed, and wasted, is not important for the consumer.

Proposals to introduce a more equitable form of charging for water services, and, in particular, water supplies, have usually centred on domestic metering. Water supplies for commercial and industrial users are predominantly metered but few domestic consumers have metered supplies. The issues surrounding metering are complex but basically settle around those of the price elasticity of water demand and the effects of metering, to reduce demand, on public health.[57] Domestic metering is allowed for in the 1973 Water Act and most of the WAs are prepared to install meters as long as the consumer pays the installation costs. Despite evidence showing considerable reductions in demand when meters are introduced the WAs do not seem willing to force the issue, not wishing to stir up dispute and argument about their policies outside of the water industry.[58]

The changes in capital financing for the industry are of greater importance than changes in revenue financing, in that the former has considerable implications for the latter, and that these changes have led to an increasing involvement of central government in the regional planning of the WAs—the need to spend large sums on capital works in the water industry makes allocations for this purpose, and restrictions on this expenditure, of vital importance to the WAs. The areas of greatest capital expenditure in the water industry are water supply and sewage disposal, these accounting for 77 per cent of gross expenditure, with a further 20 per cent being accounted for by water resources development and land drainage.[59] The system of loan sanctions for capital projects that was used before reorganization has been replaced by the introduction of cash limits for the WAs. This change has given the WAs an opportunity to determine their own priorities to a far greater extent than had previously been possible, when each scheme was evaluated on its own merits, and not as part of a regional or national strategy. Within these cash limits the WAs finance their capital expenditure either through borrowing, from the National Loans Fund or overseas, or through self-financing from depreciation funds or profits. The functional integration and regional basis of the WAs allows them to determine priorities among their plans and schemes in a more effective and co-ordinated manner, in terms of the needs of the region, than the pre-reorganization system allowed. However these same factors enable central government to exert a greater influence on WA expenditure than had previously been possible: the local nature of pre-reorganization schemes, serving only a limited area within a catchment-basin, meant that while each scheme, when evaluated for loan sanction, could be seen as essential for the locality, regional advantages were lost through duplication of effort and separation from other catchment developments. The regionalization of the water industry and the introduction of cash limits for the WAs have had major effects on the nature, and number, of capital works actually undertaken since reorganization and provides examples of some of the economies of scale that have been forthcoming.

The practice of financing capital expenditure before re-organization almost entirely through loans rather than through a mixture of loans and revenue had wide implications once the WAs were established. Part of the inheritance from local government, in particular, was a debt of £2,200 million that had to be serviced from revenue. The low self-financing ratio of the industry, by means of depreciation and the use of revenue surpluses, in comparison with other public utilities, has placed a large burden on the WAs revenue account[60] (see Table 7.2). A movement away from financing capital expenditure through borrowing was recommended before reorganization,[61] and increasingly the WAs are moving towards the internal financing of such expenditure, although with considerable regional variations: WAs covering development areas are eligible for grants from the EEC for water services projects, and some grants are still available for rural water supply and sewerage schemes, although on a lesser scale than those available for land drainage,[62] with the consequent effect of reducing the borrowing requirements of these WAs.

Regional variations in borrowing requirements do not, however, depend purely upon the availability of grants: the age and condition of the physical assets of the WAs are also significant factors in this respect. WAs with aging assets may well have repaid the original loan raised to finance their construction but the need to renew or replace those assets requires that new sources of capital are found: loans at high interest rates, under present market conditions, will severely restrict the construction of new capital works in those areas with a need to replace aging assets serving existing consumers. Thus the possibility of providing development infrastructure is restricted not just by the role of the WAs as providers of services to existing consumers but also through the implications of increasing capital expenditure for consumer charges and the use, by government, of cash limits for the WAs which effectively restrict the availability of finance.

Reorganization has therefore had major consequences for the financing of the water industry: while under local government control water supply, sewerage, and sewage disposal were financed as services, and were subsidized through the RSG and by grant-aid; the WAs, with the managerial approach being extended to their finances—the need to break even in particular—have had to increase charges dramatically to fulfil their statutory duties. The size of the WAs and the introduction of equalization have, however, led to the internal subsidization of consumers—principally rural ones by urban—within the industry. The regionalization of water services and the emphasis arising from this on regional planning has, in conjunction with the introduction of cash limits, had an effect on the capital expenditure of the WAs: schemes are evaluated in terms of their regional, rather than local, significance, thus realizing some economies of scale through a co-ordination of hydrological and planning considerations. Finally, the movement towards self-financing capital investment in the WAs provides the basis fo the industry to reduce, relatively, its revenue requirements in relation to debt servicing in the future.

CONCLUSIONS

Since reorganization the water industry in England and Wales has assumed a new position of importance in the governmental system. The fragmented and predominantly localized system that had existed before 1974 had consistently undervalued water services and had been unable to exploit the operational advantages of catchment basin and water cycle management and planning. The regionalization of the water industry, and the unification of functionally related water services within a single organizational framework, has shown the importance of these services for development and has provided the opportunity to manage and plan water resources within the framework of hydrological interdependencies that exist between conflicting water uses.[63] The operational advantages of this change have enabled the WAs to continue to provide what is arguably the highest level of water services provision in the world, and concern with their control, accountability, and interrelationships with other branches of government must be seen in this light. The structural successes of reorganization need, however, to be balanced by a consideration of the behavioural consequences of the 1973 Water Act. Reorganization has had a major effect on the relationship between local authority and water industry planning, particularly with regard to the role of the member in this area. The unification of water services within an organizational framework that forms what is almost a 'closed' system to external considerations has led to an increasing reliance on the managerial premises of reorganization. This, in turn, has acted as a major limitation on the ability of local authority members to fashion an effective role for themselves in the decision-making and planning processes of the WAs. The socialization of WA members into the roles that water industry interests think most fitting has enabled the industry to remain closed to participatory pressures from outside the spheres of these same interests.

The importance of the WAs at both the local and the regional level has led to concern over their accountability and this has led to the development of a 'discursive' approach to the discharge of their functions: discussion takes place with local authorities for their operations and plans as they affect the locality, and with central government—both as individual WAs and through the NWC as a collective voice—for the regional and national implications of their activities. The utility of these approaches as long as the WA remain effectively closed to participation from outside the industry is open to question, but, without pressure for further reform, the importance and impact of the WAs as an 'unintentional' form of regional government can only be expected to grow with time.

West Midlands
County Council
Planning Department

CHAPTER 8

The framework of regional planning 1964–1980

P. D. LINDLEY*

SUMMARY

THIS chapter reviews the major landmarks in the development of regional planning during the past fifteen years. It examines the background to the creation of the Regional Economic Planning Councils and Boards and describes the tasks they were assigned. It offers an explanation of the alteration in the respective roles of the Councils and Boards which took place in March 1966. It suggests that a major change of direction became unavoidable after the collapse of the National Plan in July 1966, and shows how this was reflected in revised guidelines in which the Councils and Boards were asked to produce 'regional strategies' rather than 'regional plans'. It compares and contrasts the different ways in which the various Councils and Boards approached their task of preparing a 'regional strategy', and notes that the demise of the Department of Economic Affairs and the assumption of responsibility for regional planning by the Department of the Environment was followed by an emphasis on tripartite regional strategies commissioned by central and local government and the relevant Regional Economic Planning Council. The final section of the chapter reviews the regional strategies produced during the 1970s and considers the implications for the future of regional planning of the abolition of the Regional Economic Planning Councils by a newly elected Conservative Government midway through 1979.

* The views expressed in this chapter are those of the author and should not be attributed to the Civil Service College or the Civil Service Department.

THE DEVELOPMENT OF REGIONAL PLANNING BEFORE 1964

Until 1964 regional planning had developed along two separate paths, each with its own distinct objectives, measures and administrative machinery.[1] The first had its origins in the Special Areas legislation of the 1930s, and was mainly concerned with the relief of unemployment in the depressed areas; while the second began with the encouragement of town planning regions by the Ministry of Health in the early 1920s,[2] and was mainly concerned with the relief of overcrowding and the provision of better living conditions in the major cities. In 1940 the Report of the Royal Commission on the Distribution of the Industrial Population[3] made a strong case for bringing the two strands together. However its recommendation that a national authority—a dissenting Minority Report suggested a new government department--should be set up with responsibility for developing a unified national policy for achieving a regional balance of diversified industry and the decentralization of industry and population from congested areas was not implemented. Although the Ministry of Town and Country Planning was established as a central planning authority in 1943, it was only assigned land-use powers, and industrial location powers were assigned to the Board of Trade in 1945.

The shortcomings which resulted from this administrative separation of the two strands of regional planning were highlighted by a series of major regional planning reports which appeared during the early 1960s. The first of these, the Toothill Report on the Scottish Economy,[4] grew out of concern about the high level of unemployment in Scotland. It advocated a much more positive approach to the planning of regional development. Government acceptance of its thinking was marked by the setting up of the Scottish Development and Scottish Development Group in 1962,[5] the assignment of special responsibilities for the North East to Lord Hailsham in January 1963, and the initiation of special studies of Central Scotland and the North East.

White Papers on Central Scotland,[6] and the North East[7] were presented to Parliament in November 1963. The favoured treatment accorded to these areas led to pressures for similar studies from other regions, and in October 1963 Edward Heath was appointed Secretary of State for Trade, Industry and Regional Development, with responsibility for co-ordinating the central government input to regional development. A Regional Development Division was set up in the Board of Trade to supervise a programme of further studies of other regions.

In the meantime a separate study of the South East had been started in the Ministry of Housing and Local Government (MHLG) in 1961. This study had been occasioned by projections of major population growth in the South East, and was concerned with assessing land requirements and producing proposals for channelling the physical growth of the region into an orderly pattern. The report of the study[8] appeared in March 1964 and was accompanied by a White Paper[9] setting out the Government's response. It contained bold proposals for housing London's overspill by creating a second generation of new and expanded towns, but further away from London and on a much larger scale than the first round.

Not only did the study of the South East differ from the other regional studies in terms of its major theme—the physical problems of growth rather than the economic problems of decline—it also covered a much wider area: the study area contained approximately 40 per cent of the population and employment of England and Wales, and 30 per cent of the surface area. There was thus a clear risk that the proposals would be on such a large scale as to dwarf those for the other regions. The White Paper sought to obviate this difficulty with assurances that the study proposals would not prejudice growth in other parts of the country.[10]

A number of commentators challenged the wisdom of producing regional studies on a piecemeal basis in response to particular problems as they arose, and drew attention to the absence of a national dimension, and to the fact that the studies of the South East, Central Scotland, and the North East were self-contained, with no assessment of their repercussions on other regions.[11] These weaknesses highlighted the case for instituting more systematic arrangements for ensuring that regional proposals were in harmony both with each other and with national policies and priorities.

Other developments which contributed to the growing importance of regional planning in the early 1960s included the emphasis placed by the National Economic Development Council on regional balance as a key element of policies to stimulate economic growth,[12] and the recommendation in the *Buchanan Report on Traffic in Towns*[13] that regional development agencies should be set up to tackle the related problems of traffic growth and urban renewal highlighted in that report.

THE TASKS REMITTED TO THE REGIONAL ECONOMIC PLANNING COUNCILS AND BOARDS IN 1965

The Labour Manifesto at the 1964 General Election pledged a Labour Government to set up regional machinery to produce comprehensive plans for the regions of the UK within the framework of the National Plan; and this pledge was fulfilled between April 1965 and April 1966 by setting up a Regional Economic Planning Council and Board in each of eight newly defined English economic planning regions, and in Scotland and Wales. The Councils were drawn from both sides of industry, local government, and other walks of life in the regions, and the Boards comprised senior regional representatives of government departments concerned with regional planning.

On 10 December 1964 Mr George Brown, the Deputy Prime Minister and Secretary of State at the new Department of Economic Affairs (DEA), which had been set up with responsibility for national and regional planning, explained the role of the Councils and Boards in the following terms:

The purpose of the regional councils and boards which the Government intend to establish is to provide effective machinery for regional economic planning within the framework of the national plan for economic development. Regional economic planning has two main purposes: first, to provide for a full and balanced development of the country's economic and social resources; and, secondly, to ensure that the regional implications of growth are clearly understood and taken into account in the planning of land-use, of development—in particular, of industrial development—and of services.

The economic planning councils will be concerned with broad strategy on regional development and the best use of the region's resources. Their principal function will be to assist in the formulation of regional plans and to advise on their implementation. They will have no executive powers.

The economic planning boards, on the other hand, will provide the necessary machinery for co-ordinating the work of Government Departments concerned with regional planning and development, but their creation will not affect the existing powers and responsibilities of local authorities or existing ministerial responsibilities.[14]

The emphasis in the statement on the advisory status of the new regional bodies was intended to reassure local government interests that the Councils and Boards would not encroach upon their physical planning responsibilities. As the following passage from George Brown's autobiography shows, it was also for this reason that the prefix 'economic' was included in the formal titles of the Councils and Boards:

These Councils were formally called Regional Economic Planning Councils. We wanted them to be called simply Planning Councils, and the 'Economic' was put in to appease the local government people, who feared that their functions might be confused with physical planning, which was in local government hands. I always thought the two forms of planning went together, but I reckoned that by agreeing to have the word 'Economic' in their title we could leave enough ambiguity in the situation for our scheme to go ahead without too much fuss.[15]

Although Richard Crossman, the then Minister of Housing and Local Government, claimed in Volume One of his Diary that this concession had rendered the Councils and Boards 'inadequate and meaningless',[16] DEA Ministers still envisaged that whatever their starting point, the Councils and Boards would become increasingly involved in producing plans covering both the economic and physical development of their region.[17] It was also their intention that the new regional machinery would in due course be turned into elected regional authorities.[18]

Part of the thinking behind the Councils and the Boards was derived from ideas generated at a series of seminars arranged by William Rodgers, who became the DEA Junior Minister with day-to-day responsibility for setting up the new regional machinery before the Election. Certain of the ideas were clearly influenced by the system of regional planning in France. As with the DEA-sponsored regional plans that were now envisaged, French regional plans were prepared in the form of regional breakdowns of the National Plan by interdepartmental regional representatives of central government assisted by regional advisory bodies. Although the Chairmen of the Boards were not assigned executive powers of a kind exercised by the Regional Prefects in France, a move which would have run counter to the British tradition of strong local self-government, it was the intention that the Boards and Councils should provide machinery capable of producing comprehensive and systematic regional plans of a similar type to those produced in France.

The nature of the Boards was heavily influenced by the experience of the Board of Trade Regional Development Division (BOT RDD) which had pioneered the practice of relying on integrated regional arms of central government to prepare regional plans, including the bringing together of the regional offices of the various departments concerned in one building in a regional capital. It was possible to create the Boards simply by extending these practices to the country as a whole.

When the DEA was set up in October 1964 it assimilated the BOT RDD and assumed responsibility for its work on regional studies, including studies of the North West and West Midlands that were still in progress. The reports of these studies[19] were published in July 1965 with a disclaimer that they did not make recommendations for action, but simply presented and analysed the basic data on which future plans for their region should be based. The North West and West Midlands studies provided guidance on the scope and methods of a regional study for regions where such initial groundwork had yet to be undertaken such as Yorkshire and Humberside, the South West, and the East Midlands. Their findings were also fed into the National Plan, which appeared in September 1965.

The Plan emphasized that the Government viewed the achievement of a more balanced economic development throughout the country as an essential element in their overall strategy for achieving faster growth, and made it clear that 'radical changes in the structure of economic activity and many accompanying changes in the social and economic environment'[20] were envisaged. As background for working out regional plans the Plan provided new regional statistics of population, employment, incomes and earnings, output in manufacturing, labour supply and demand, and for the first time, government departments' forecast expenditure on new buildings and works. The latter figures in particular were seen as providing a starting point for the Councils, and Boards, own assessment of the needs of their regions.[21] The Plan also contained forecasts of likely trends in the major industrial sectors, and the Councils and Boards were expected to examine the implications for their region in the light of the Plan's proposed increase in national output of 25 per cent between 1965 and 1970.

More details of the tasks of the Councils and Boards emerged in a key speech by Austin Albu, a Minister of State at the DEA, at the first of the periodic meetings of Council Chairmen with Ministers on 19 November 1965. He suggested they should concentrate their efforts on:

(*a*) Revision of the National Plan. The Government wanted to refine and expand what the Plan had to say about the regions. It was hoped that by 1967 each Council would be able to provide a fairly comprehensive analysis of the resources, trends, prospects, and needs of its region, which had been discussed thoroughly with the planning authorities and with representatives of labour and management;

(*b*) Long term growth of population. In view of the forecast increase in the UK population of 20 million by the end of the century, the Department of Economic Affairs, in conjunction with other government departments, had begun a review of population trends, and the pattern of settlement to the year 2,000, known as the Long Term Population Distribution Study. Councils' preliminary views on the review were wanted;

(*c*) Redeployment of manpower, Councils should consider what redeployment of uneconomic activities like coalmining meant for the economy of their region, and whether the Government's remedial measures were adequate;

(*d*) Public expenditure planning. Councils could be of greatest assistance to the Government by working out regional priorities. They would be asked to advise on priorities within concrete terms of expenditure and cost. Mr Albu said:

Look at priorities within your region, and be prepared, if necessary, to say sometimes what should get less as well as what should get more. We, the Government, will do our best to take your views into account in actual decisions.[22]

THE PASSING OF RESPONSIBILITY FOR THE PLANS FROM
THE BOARDS TO THE COUNCILS

At the outset it was envisaged that the plans would be produced by the Boards with the advice and assistance of the Councils. Thus in their terms of reference the Councils were asked to *assist* in the formulation of regional plans and *advise* on their implementation on the basis of information and assistance provided by the Boards.[23] On the other hand the Boards' functions were described as being:

To prepare the draft plan (or plans) for the region and to co-ordinate the work of the various government departments in implementing the final plan.[24]

The assigning of responsibility for preparing the plans to the Boards rather than the Councils created the impression that, following the precedent set by the 1963 White Papers on Central Scotland and the North East, the plans would commit the Government. It was also a more satisfactory arrangement from the point of view of certain departments in Whitehall, such as the MHLG, that were suspicious of the Councils.

In March 1966 the Government transferred responsibility for preparing the plans from the Boards to the Councils.[25] While the Councils were now free to publish their proposals the corollary was that the plans would not appear as official Government documents which could be expected to bind the Government.

This alteration constituted an important departure from the original blueprint, which placed a strong emphasis on the role of the regional representatives of central government as producers of the plans, and, as has been noted, bore a close resemblance to the system of regional planning in France. The passing of responsibility for preparing the plans from Boards to the Councils constituted a shift away from the French model.

One may speculate on the reasons for this change. The most likely explanation is that the Councils had been exerting pressures to be given a more prominent role, and that while the Government wished to experiment with regional plans, they were not yet ready to make a commitment to implement the results. By transferring responsibility for preparing the plans from the Boards to the Councils, the Government was able to provide the Councils with an opportunity to carve out a more definite role for themselves, and leave open the possibility of a more substantial commitment at a later stage.

A number of factors contributed to the Government's reluctance to invest formal powers in the Councils and Boards too quickly. Firstly it had just made a substantial commitment to a plan produced by the new machinery in Scotland.[26] This plan had 'represented a statement of Government policy and involved a number of major decisions on investment, on development programmes, and on objectives for employment.'[27] Moreover its impact had been strengthened by the simultaneous announcement of a strong new programme of regional aid which was of particular benefit to Scotland.[28] The Chairman of the Scottish Economic Planning Board subsequently implied that the need to provide resources to implement the Scottish plan had influenced the decisions on the expanded regional aid programme.[29] These events had highlighted the economic risks that might be entailed if the Scottish plan set a precedent for the English regions.

Secondly, there was anyway a risk that too strong a commitment would require a higher degree of interdepartmental coordination than it was practicable to expect the English Economic Planning Boards to achieve. The Scottish Economic Planning Board was better equipped to produce an interdepartmentally agreed regional programme than its English counterparts in several respects. First, its members had much longer experience of collaboration on regional plans as participants in the Scottish Development Group; secondly, it had the support of the Scottish Office and the Secretary of State for Scotland with a seat in the Cabinet; thirdly, it had the support of the Regional Development Division in the Scottish Office which advised the Secretary of State on economic planning in Scotland; and fourthly it included officials from the four Scottish departments and its task of getting relevant departments to think in terms of the region was correspondingly lessened.[30]

Thirdly, there was the further complication that the Councils had seized the initiative from the Boards in some regions. Thus, for example, rather than co-operate with the Board in extending the analysis in the North West study, the North West Council had taken an independent line and produced a short report in February 1966,[31] containing proposals which have been described as a 'personal credo from the then Chairman of the Planning Council reflecting his own aspirations for the future development of the region.'[32]

Whilst their acquisition of responsibility for preparing the plans could be expected to enhance the standing of the Councils *vis-à-vis* the Boards, they had to continue to rely on staff provided by the Boards whose primary loyalty lay with their masters in Whitehall. The Government gave an undertaking to publish their views on the Councils' plans, and this left the members of the Boards in the odd position of having, in the first place, to assist the Councils in the preparation of the plans, and then, as the senior regional representatives of their departments, advise the Government what to say in reply.

THE FAILURE OF THE NATIONAL PLAN AND THE EFFECT ON REGIONAL PLANNING

Faced with a worsening balance of payments crisis, in July 1966 the Government introduced deflationary measures involving large cuts in public expenditure, an increase in interest rates and a six months statutory freeze on incomes, which left the forecasts and targets of the National Plan in disarray. The Plan had to be abandoned and, in the words of one commentator:

Not only did the particular Plan of a particular Government come to an end on 20 July, the experiment begun by NEDC in 1962, with the object of raising the nation's growth rate, and endorsed by successive Governments from both main parties, suffered a resounding defeat. One particular approach to economic policy had lost its credibility in the country for the rest of this decade, and probably beyond.[33]

Shortly afterwards George Brown left the DEA to become Foreign Secretary, and was replaced by Michael Stewart. The influence and authority of the DEA in Whitehall had largely stemmed from the powerful position which George Brown had occupied as First Secretary of State and Deputy Prime Minister. After his departure a lot of the impetus went out of the department. Moreover, his replacement, Michael Stewart, had no great inclination to move the new regional machinery too quickly in the direction of regional government, and had, when Opposition spokesman on Housing and Local Government, reached the conclusion that an additional regional tier of government between central and local government was both unnecessary and undesirable.[34]

The abandonment of the National Plan produced uncertainty about the future role of the Councils and Boards since they could no longer be expected to work within the detailed national framework which the Plan had provided.

A review of the future work of the Councils and Boards was carried out in the DEA in the early part of 1967. Its main conclusion was that it was no longer practicable to expect the Councils and Boards to produce plans with timetables tied to investment programmes on the French model, and that in future they should concentrate on generating new ideas about the longer term planning of their regions.[35]

These conclusions were set out in a paper which Michael Stewart discussed with Council Chairmen in March 1967. The paper suggested that all Councils should aim to produce a strategy for the development of their region to 1981, with a general look beyond, against which the investment decisions of central and local government and public and private industry could be taken. It should cover:

(*a*) population growth and location;
(*b*) industrial location and employment growth;
(*c*) major communications;
(*d*) major countryside and amenity policies;
(*e*) social services, e.g. health and education;
(*f*) regional services e.g. water;
(*g*) broad policy objectives for the major urbanized areas.

Those subject headings were only offered as general guidance, and the intention was that the Councils should be driven sufficient discretion to evolve an approach best suited to the needs of their region.[36]

At the meeting Council Chairmen stressed that they would need additional staff to produce such strategies, since Board members and their staff were generally heavily engaged on departmental duties and had little time to spare for additional tasks. Michael Stewart subsequently persuaded the Cabinet to authorize the recruitment of additional research staff to work on regional strategies at headquarters and in the regions.

During the next three years every Council compiled and published a regional strategy.[37] While these documents differed in content, methodology, and impact, they all contained proposals for improving the physical, social, and economic fabric of their region, and guidance, in more or less detail, on the pattern of development. The South West strategy pointed out that regional planning had not yet reached a stage at which it was possible to provide detailed targets and forecasts. It said:

It has come to be recognized that it is too soon in the experience of regional planning to aim at providing a set of Government approved plans, which will neatly dovetail with each other, and which, in numbers of population, distribution of manpower, growth and location of industry, scale and disposition of public investment etc. will in aggregate coincide with the forecasts, intensions and capabilities envisaged by the Government for the economy as a whole.[38]

One might have expected that when a regional study already existed, the Council concerned would have adopted it as a starting point for its own strategy. However, in some regions, particularly in those where the ideas of the Council ran contrary to those of the Board, there was a tendency to discard the earlier reports. For example, the North West and Northern Councils' strategies did not extend the analysis in the earlier studies. Other Councils built on the earlier proposals. The West Midlands Council's strategy, for example, updated and carried forward the West Midlands Study. However it was followed by an invitation from the MHLG to the West Midlands Planning Authorities Conference (WMPAC) to carry out a planning study of the West Midlands conurbation and a wide surrounding area.[39] This move took the initiative away from the West Midlands Council. WMPAC subsequently set up a local authority based planning team, to which central government officials were seconded, which produced the West Midlands Regional Strategy in 1971.[40]

It was in regions where the Council both had something original to contribute and was able to work effectively with the Board, that the Councils produced more worthwhile strategies. Good examples were the South West and South East strategy reports.

The South West strategy went beyond simply assembling basic data as the basis for a shopping list of bids for extra resources, and attempted to frame its recommendations in the light of a framework of development which made optimum use of available resources.[41] This approach reflected the regional planning expertise of the Council Chairman, Professor R. C. Tress, Professor of Political Economy at Bristol University. Effective lobbying by the South West Council subsequently persuaded the Government to extend Portbury Dock in Bristol.

The South East strategy[42] also had a considerable impact. The Council was helped by its Chairman, Maurice Hackett, who was George Brown's brother-in-law. From the outset he viewed the preparation of a regional plan as one of the Council's prime tasks.[43] However it was not clear what the components of an economic planning strategy should be in the South East, whose problems were physical congestion and overcrowding. Moreover the Government had just completed a review of the South East Study,[43] and the Council was faced with the dilemma of justifying a strategy of its own when a Government approved strategy already existed. The solution it found was to formulate proposals for the period to 1991, thereby extending the South East Study by a further ten years.

The Council's strategy contained bold proposals for corridors of development on the main communications networks out of London, and filled a gap in the South East Study, which had recommended counter-magnets at the fringes of the region, without providing any specific guidance for development closer to the capital, where the pressures were greatest. It encountered strong opposition from the Standing Conference on London and South East Regional Planning, the body representing local planning authorities in the region, on the grounds that the Conference was preparing an alternative planning strategy,[44] and that a purely advisory body should not be permitted to undermine local authorities on planning matters.[45] However having encouraged the Council to plan boldly, the Secretary of State could hardly ignore such definite if generalized proposals.

The Government persuaded the South East Council and Standing Conference to join with it in commissioning a fresh planning strategy for the region. A planning team headed by the Chief Planner in the MHLG, and staffed by officers from central and local government, was set up to carry out the study. Their report,[46] which appeared in 1970, proved generally acceptable to the commissioning parties, and was approved by the Government in October 1971. This formula of tripartite commissioning of regional strategies by central government, local government, and the relevant Planning Council, thus emerged fortuitously in the South East as an *ad hoc* solution to a temporary administrative difficulty.

The variety in the scope, approach, and timing of the strategies produced during 1967-70 was a natural consequence of the Government's decision to leave the Councils a wide measure of freedom to evolve an approach best suited to the needs of their region. However, one result was that the Government found it difficult to integrate the various strategies at national level. The vacuum created by the collapse of the National Plan was not adequately filled, and as a result the Councils tended to become regarded as pressure groups and parochial regional advocates.[46] In these circumstances it is not surprising that the Council's proposals were frequently ignored or rejected. Their credibility, which in large measure depended upon how much notice the Government took of what they said, was badly damaged.

The DEA has been castigated for:

Failing to provide adequate guidelines for the Councils and Boards to ensure that what emerged proceeded from the same national premises about the distribution of population and employment, and that similar methods were used by all regions.[47]

The same authors argued that in the absence of such guidelines the strategies were unable to provide a meaningful basis for integrating national and regional priorities or reconciling the claims of competing regions. However it is open to question whether the DEA was in a position to produce a fully worked out national framework in the aftermath of the collapse of the National Plan; and, moreover, the Councils had been encouraged to evolve an approach suited to the needs of their region in the belief that in the absence of consensus about the nature and purpose of regional planning, experimentation with different approaches offered the best way forward.

In 1969 the DEA took steps to draw together the experience of Councils in strategy preparation. A discussion paper on regional strategies[49] led to the formation of a working party in July 1969, to prepare an agreed synopsis of the elements that should form the framework of a regional strategy. The working party met in Nottingham and was known as the Nottingham Group. Their report[50] was still in preparation when the DEA was abolished, and it was subsequently submitted to the Secretary of State for Local Government and Regional Planning alongside proposals by the tripartite approach pioneered in the South East to other regions.

THE ABOLITION OF THE DEPARTMENT OF ECONOMIC AFFAIRS AND THE REORGANIZATION WHICH FOLLOWED

After the demise of the National Plan, and the replacement of George Brown by Michael Stewart as Secretary of State for Economic Affairs, the prestige of the DEA in Whitehall progressively declined, and it was eventually abolished in October 1969. Major changes in the machinery of government with important consequences for regional planning followed.

In October 1969 a new Secretary of State for Local Government and Regional Planning was appointed and placed in overall charge of the MHLG and the Ministry of Transport. The bulk of the DEA's regional responsibilities, including the Councils and Boards, were transferred to an enlarged MHLG, although the section responsible for regional industrial policy passed to an enlarged Ministry of Technology, which incorporated the Ministry of Power and most of the Board of Trade. The decision to transfer the Councils to the MHLG had the unfortunate consequence that it meant that although the Councils were mainly concerned with economic matters, their recommendations had to be made to a department which did not have responsibility for economic policy.

This difficulty became increasingly acute as the climate in which the Councils operated changed from one in which the key planning issues concerned the physical pattern of economic and population growth, to one in which the primary concern of most if not every Council became industrial decline and unemployment. In such circumstances it was not surprising that the Councils' recommendations came increasingly to be aimed at the Departments of Industry and Employment.

With hindsight it would perhaps have made more sense if the Councils had been more closely tied with the economic departments. However, in 1969 it probably seemed sensible to emphasize the links between regional and local planning by passing responsibility for the Councils and Boards to the department responsible for the local planning system.

The need to integrate local development plans with the regional planning process had been emphasized in a report on the future of development plans in 1965.[51] The report formed the basis of the 1968 Town and Country Planning Act, which included a requirement that local authority structure plans should be drawn up having regard to 'current policies with respect to the economic planning and development of the region as a whole'.[52]

Local government has responded to the establishment of the Councils and Boards by setting up Standing Conferences of local planning authorities in each of the economic planning regions. The Standing Conferences had the tacit approval of the MHLG, which wanted to emphasize the distinction between regional physical planning, and regional economic planning, and their formation can be seen as an attempt on the part of local government to protect its responsibilities in the field of regional physical planning from encroachment by central government's Councils and Boards.

By 1969 the rivalry that had developed between the Councils and the Standing Conferences meant that there was a risk of conflicting strategies being produced in some if not all regions, and no means of ensuring that the differences could be resolved without central intervention and much delay and friction. The regions in which relations between the Councils and Standing Conferences were most difficult included the West Midlands (see above p. 180) and the East Midlands, where an initiative by Richard Crossman at the MHLG in 1965 had led to the commissioning of sub-regional studies of the major industrial areas in the region by the local authorities concerned.

Following the completion of these studies,[53] the Standing Conference had set up a full-time Technical Unit to monitor their implementation and produce a wider strategy for the region as a whole.

The benefits that were expected to flow from transferring the Councils and Boards to the MHLG were alluded to in a White Paper on local government reform published by the Secretary of State for Local Government and Regional Planning in February 1970. It said:

> The valuable work of the Regional Economic Planning Councils, to which the Government attach great importance, must continue—and indeed enter a new phase. We have completed the phase of outline regional strategies; we now need to develop firmer regional plans which can be linked with specific physical planning. To this end the Government intend to make arrangements to develop co-operation between the Councils and the Standing Conferences.[54]

Contrary to expectations the Conservatives were returned to power at the June 1970 Election. In October 1970 the new Conservative Government took the changes of October 1969 a stage further by setting up two giant departments—the Department of the Environment (DOE), and the Department of Trade and Industry. The DOE incorporated the MHLG and the Ministries of Public Building and Works and Transport; and the Department of Trade and Industry was based on the functions of the Board of Trade and Ministry of Technology. The Secretary of State for the Environment became responsible for the Councils and Boards, and was assigned the leading responsibility for regional policy.[55] Responsibility for regional industrial policy was transferred from the Minister of Technology to the Secretary of State for Trade and Industry.

During 1972 new integrated regional offices were formed in the DOE based on the functions of the former regional offices of the DEA, Ministry of Transport and MHLG. They were headed by Under-Secretary level Regional Directors who combined this role with that of Board Chairman. In the same year the regional organization of the Department of Trade and Industry in the assisted areas was strengthened by the devolution of decision-making on selective assistance under Section 7 of the 1972 Industry Act to Under-Secretary level Regional Directors assisted by Regional Industrial Directors, recruited on secondment from the private sector, and Regional Industrial Development Boards.

Although the DOE's statutory responsibility for physical planning, housing, and transport appeared to equip its Regional Directors to make a more effective contribution to the framing and implementation of regional strategies than their DEA predecessors, their independence in their role of Board Chairmen, and hence their credibility, particularly with the economic departments, was called into question when the Boards had to resolve conflicts on matters on which there was a departmental DOE interest.

The Conservative manifesto had included a commitment to reduce the overall level of government activity, and, in September 1970, a review of advisory bodies and their usefulness was put in hand. The poor public image of the Councils and their association with the previous Labour Government led to an expectation that they were unlikely to be retained.

A White Paper outlining revised Conservative proposals for a two-tier county/district system of local government, in place of the one tier system of unitary authorities proposed by the previous Labour Government, appeared in February 1971. Although the impetus to develop the regional tier was reduced by the decision to introduce a two-tier system of local government, the White Paper announced that long-term decisions on the future of the regional machinery had been deferred pending the report of the Royal Commission in the Constitution. The Government had probably concluded it would be a retrograde step to abolish the Councils in the face of the devolutionary pressures which the Commission had encountered. A further factor was the important admission in the White Paper that regional plans would continue to be needed because the proposed metropolitan counties would not be able to solve their planning problems within their own boundaries.[56] This consideration underlay the Government's decision to:

continue to pursue the preparation of regional strategies by the creation of teams comprising the Standing Conference of local planning authorities, and the Regional Economic Planning Councils and Central Government.[57]

This reference to the continued existence of the Councils put an end to any speculation that they might be abolished.

However their role was diminished since they contributed to tripartite strategies as just one of three commissioning parties. Moreover the Conservatives saw their main function as being to provide a source of independent advice, and a forum in which a wide range of interests could be consulted, and they did not see the Councils primarily as producers of regional plans. It was consistent with this approach that while Secretary of State for the Environment, Peter Walker pursued a policy of appointing younger members from industry and commerce to serve on the Councils. Having been encouraged to develop their consultative role the Councils concentrated their efforts on *ad hoc* advice on particular issues as they arose.

The Labour Governments which held office from February 1974 to May 1979 had no new ideas about how to develop the Councils, and they continued a gradual extension of the tripartite approach to regional planning. One innovation was the creation of a Standing Committee on Regional Affairs in 1975.[58] Regional strategy documents were debated by the Committee, and although the Government took account of the views expressed in formulating their replies to the strategies, the debates were too often marred by the making of constituency points. The report of the Royal Commission on the Constitution only recommended the creation of Regional Advisory and Consultative Councils in England,[59] and a consultative document on the English Dimension of Devolution, which appeared in November 1976,[60] held out little prospect of the creation of regional authorities in England in the short to medium term.

THE REGIONAL STRATEGIES OF THE SEVENTIES

In January 1972 a Junior Minister at the DOE announced that the Government hoped that tripartite strategies would eventually be produced for all the English regions, although the detailed arrangements and timing would vary from region to region.[61] By the end of the decade tripartite strategies had been produced in the North West, [62] East Anglia,[63] and the Northern region,[64] and tripartite strategic reviews had appeared in the South East,[65] and the West Midlands.[66] Tripartite strategies were not produced in the remaining regions, although the Yorkshire and Humberside Planning Council carried out a review of its strategy.[67]

Powell[68] has noted the evolutionary pattern which can be traced through the tripartite strategies as each of the planing teams made advances on the work of their predecessors, and Cherry[69] has also remarked on the considerable technical advances in regional planning achieved during this period. However both these and other writers[70] have suggested that weaknesses in the institutional framework acted as constraints on the effectiveness of the strategies, and that technical progress has been accompanied by an absence of any real development of governmental structures through which regional planning might be achieved.

An analysis of the content of tripartite regional strategy documents conducted by Skelcher[71] revealed a shift in their primary orientation from spatial, land-use matters to a concentration on the regional economy, social welfare, and allocation of public expenditure, together with issues relating to implementation. Although this change was most marked in the contrast between the original South East and West Midlands strategies and the up-dated strategies for those regions, the Strategic Plan for the North West (SPNW) was the first tripartite strategy to consider economic, industrial, and public expenditure issues in any depth, and the Strategic Plan for the Northern Region (SPNR) took this process further still. The SPNR Director was an economist from the World Bank—the local authorities had agreed to help finance the setting up of the team on condition that it should have an 'independent' leader who was not drawn from the ranks of either central or local government, and the approach in SPNR bore some resemblance to a World Bank programme for an underdeveloped country. Its centre piece was the detailed costing of the measures needed to promote a self-sustaining regional economy.

However this broadening in the issue agenda of regional strategies was seen by local authorities as offering an opportunity to make advocacy statements to central government.[72] This advocacy paid little regard to the implications for other regions or national priorities. Central government responded defensively and the Departments of Industry and Employment viewed the implicit or explicit assessment of the efficiency of their policies in the strategy team reports as expansionism on the part of DOE. The need to obtain interdepartmental agreement to the Government replies to the strategy reports resulted in long delays, and replies which were brief and bland, and which tended to assimilate the strategy to government thinking rather than to accept suggestions for changes in policy.[73]

Monitoring organizations were only established in the South East and the West Midlands, although a DOE commissioned report[74] based on the SPNW drew attention to the need to establish such organizations in all regions once the strategy teams were disbanded.

Implementation problems resulted from the non-involvement of major infrastructure and service agencies, such as the Regional Water Authorities, in the planning process. On the other hand available evidence suggests that approved regional strategies, which comprised the strategy team's final report taken together with the Government's response, tended to get reflected in structure plans.[75]

A change of direction in regional planning followed the election of a Conservative Government with a strong commitment to disengagement policies in May 1979. The Planning Councils were abolished in August 1979, and although the Planning Boards were retained, a shift in their role was indicated when they were subsequently renamed interdepartmental Regional Boards. The Departments of Employment and Industry withdrew from regional strategy work, and, in September 1979, over two years after the publication of the original report, it was made known that there would be no Government response to the Strategic Plan for the Northern Region. However DOE Ministers made it clear that they saw a continuing need for the provision of regional guidance as a framework for structure plans, although in future this guidance would be limited to specific issues which needed to be resolved.[76]

The Government response to the tripartite updating of the West Midlands strategy,[77] and further regional strategic guidance provided to the Standing Conference on London and South East Regional Planning,[78] suggest that for the next few years regional planning will be limited to strategic land-use planning issues. It is unlikely that further overall assessments of the problems and potentials of regions of the type pioneered first by the Planning Councils and Boards and subsequently by the tripartite strategy teams will be attempted during the lifetime of the present Government. On the other hand regional issues are unlikely to go away, and it would be premature to write an obituary for regional planning.[79]

CHAPTER 9

Public expenditure in the English regions[1]

JOHN SHORT

INTRODUCTION

PREVIOUS chapters have discussed the structure of regional organizations, their operations, and their relationships with each other, with central government, and with local authorities. The purpose of all this activity is not internal to government; it is ultimately concerned with the delivery of services to citizens. Despite the fact, brought out in previous chapters, that the regions do not enjoy a coherent government system, the total public sector, in the guise of the central government, local authorities, and public corporations does play an important role in the determination of the lives of the citizens in each region. The apparent lack of co-ordination between the various arms of government (in its widest sense) in the regional context does not preclude the governmental sector from having a large impact on the regions.

Although relatively few regional organizations or offices are directly involved in the final delivery of services, many perform roles, including budgetary allocation, which shape the delivery of services to citizens. Public expenditure provides the most useful indicator for comparison across regions, because it provides a common denominator for all policies, though it is not a direct measure of quantity or quality of service. There are a number of advantages in adopting a regional focus on public expenditure variations. Figures for local authority expenditure comprise only part of total public expenditure in the localities. Total figures for the United Kingdom conceal important variations between areas in the total and composition of public expenditure. Comparisons between Scotland, Wales, Northern Ireland, and England as a whole conceal differences within England and similarities in some programmes between some English regions and the other nations of the UK. In terms of possible reforms, the introduction of a regional dimension into the planning and control of public expenditure would provide a potential for a more efficient allocation of resources for each region and within each region, and therefore for the country as a whole.

Regional budgets for the government sector do not exist. Public expenditure is not planned so that a regional dimension is incorporated into the allocation system. True, certain functional programmes are organized on a regional basis, health and water being the prime examples, but they do not fit into a pattern of consistent regional boundaries where the level of spending in one programme may be related to the level of spending in other programmes, and where judgments can be made about the correct allocation of resources according to need. Despite this lack of regional budgets in the planning stage, estimates of public expenditure in the regions can be produced once the money has been spent since public expenditure across all programmes does, of course, take place in regions.

However, before examining the regional incidence of public expenditure, it is necessary first to determine the scope of such expenditure in the regional context.

Public expenditure in the regions can be viewed in two ways. One classification system comprises all expenditures made within the geographical boundary of the region irrespective of whether the benefits accrue partly to the region concerned and partly to other regions, or whether the expenditures are for the production of a final good or service, or for the production of the inputs into the final goods or services. Here, the important factor is the location of the production of the inputs into the final goods or services provided by the public sector through public expenditure. Spending on education, for example, would be broken down according to where the teachers are located (wages and salaries), and to where the other main inputs (equipment) are produced irrespective of where the education was consumed. With respect to the defence programme, spending would be broken down to the regions where the equipment is produced and the wages and salaries of personnel are earned irrespective of where the beneficiaries of the defence programme are located.

Regionally relevant expenditures, the second category, comprise only those expenditures made in a region, the purpose of which is for the benefit of that region, irrespective of where they are produced. These do not include expenditure on programmes of a national character. Such national expenditure may be defined as expenditure on national programmes, the benefits of which cannot be attributed to any particular region, but are fully attributed to all regions. Programmes such as defence, overseas services, other public services, common services, prisons, and debt interest are treated in this manner.[2]

The classification system which is of interest here is the regionally relevant one. This shows the spending in each region by central government, local authorities, and certain public corporations (such as new towns, water authorities, Housing Corporations, etc.) which is made for the benefit of that region. It provides figures on the consumption of public expenditure on various services in each region. Furthermore, it is a good measure of the role of the public sector in each region. The other classification system looks more at the ability of each region to produce goods and services for consumption by the public sector (both regionally and nationally).[3]

The remainder of this chapter is organized as follows. Figures on regionally relevant expenditures are presented for the 1969/70 to 1973/4 period for the pre-April 1974 standard regions. These are followed by the data for the 1974/5 to 1977/8 period for the post local government reorganization standard regions. Both of these sets of figures are examined as to their regional incidence, but only the latter figures are analysed in terms of the factors which determined the levels of expenditure in each region.

For both periods, the analysis is carried out using the average expenditure expressed in constant prices over the period. The price level used for the earlier period is the 1974 survey prices and for the later period 1978 survey prices both of the *Public Expenditure White Paper*. Each period has been averaged to ensure that a large capital programme in any one year does not give an atypical picture for a particular region. Each region's share of expenditure is examined in terms of its total expenditure, its distribution between capital and current expenditure; spending by central government, local authority, and public corporations; and finally by spending programme. Figures for Scotland and Wales in both periods and for Northern Ireland in 1974/5 to 1977/8 are also given to provide wider comparisons.

PUBLIC EXPENDITURE IN THE REGIONS, 1969/70–1973/4

Over the whole of Great Britain, regionally relevant public expenditures averaged £21.2 billion over the period. Central government was the largest of the three spending authorities, and more was spent on the current account in each region. Social security accounted for the greatest spending of the programmes in each region followed by education and health. These details are presented in Table 9.1.

However, regional comparisons of total spending are meaningless unless a suitable yardstick is introduced. Population seems to be the most relevant yardstick, since public expenditure as a whole is related to the needs of people. Consequently, certain anomalies are likely to result in so far as some programmes do not necessarily relate to population directly (parts of agriculture, fishery, and forestry, and trade, industry, and employment, for example). However, on the whole, population would appear to be the most suitable yardstick.

Table 9.2. shows the per capita distribution of regionally relevant expenditure. The salient feature of this table is the differences that exist in per capita expenditure levels between the programmes for each region and between each region. Scotland received £474 per head of population compared with £332 in the West Midlands, receiving £90 per head more of central government spending and £50 more of local authority spending; and nearly £100 more in current expenditure, and £46 more in capital expenditure.

In each programme there was a wide range of expenditure levels between the regions. The North region received £50 per head in trade, industry, and employment compared with £16 in the West Midlands; Scotland had £62 per head spent on housing while the South West had £23; the North received £31 per head on roads and the East Midlands £16 per head. As

Table 9.1. Regionally relevant public expenditure 1969/70–1973/4 average £m (1974 survey prices)

Programme	N	YH	EM	EA	SE	SW	WM	NW	W	S	GB
Agriculture, fisheries and forestry	35.6	42.8	31.7	41.9	86.2	55.6	32.9	22.3	42.4	96.0	487.4
Trade, industry, and employment	185.0	78.0	107.0	27.5	295.0	120.4	81.7	200.7	108.7	240.7	1,444.7
Roads and transport	103.6	95.8	54.8	35.5	401.9	113.9	108.4	172.4	81.9	144.8	1,313.0
Housing	152.7	137.6	94.7	54.3	903.8	88.2	158.7	246.7	89.2	325.7	2,251.6
Other environmental services	87.4	116.9	92.7	56.0	491.6	116.6	128.9	187.2	93.3	168.4	1,539.0
Law, order and protective services	46.8	54.4	45.0	20.1	307.0	52.2	62.7	95.3	35.1	76.1	794.7
Education and libraries, science and arts	231.5	332.5	239.8	127.9	1,388.5	254.4	347.2	480.6	206.8	459.5	4,068.7
Health and personal social services	186.4	282.0	196.6	95.9	1,195.3	235.4	275.3	401.5	176.0	375.5	3,419.9
Social security	405.4	547.6	345.8	169.8	1,752.5	427.7	510.1	790.1	345.5	602.1	5,896.6
Total	1,434.4	1,687.6	1,208.1	628.9	2,821.8	1,464.4	1,705.9	2,596.8	1,178.9	2,488.8	21,215.6
Central government	875.4	1,025.2	715.3	376.9	3,729.9	924.7	975.8	1,537.2	732.4	1,481.8	12,374.6
Local authorities	527.0	629.2	453.3	223.7	2,948.7	493.9	676.8	994.0	409.7	944.5	8,300.8
Public corporations	32.0	33.2	39.5	28.3	143.2	45.8	53.3	65.6	36.8	62.5	540.2
Current expenditure	1,019.9	1,359.2	944.9	467.0	5,106.1	1,133.5	1,314.1	1,953.7	889.3	1,845.0	16,032.7
Capital expenditure	414.5	328.4	263.2	161.9	1,715.7	330.9	391.8	643.1	289.6	643.8	5,182.9

Source: J. Short, 'The regional distribution of public expenditure in Great Britain, 1969/70–1973/4', Regional Studies, vol. 12, pp. 499–510.

Table 9.2. Regionally relevant public expenditure 1969/70–1973/4 average per capita £m (1974 survey prices)

Programme	N	YH	EM	EA	SE	SW	WM	NW	W	S	GB
Agriculture, fisheries, and forestry	10.8	8.9	9.3	25.0	5.0	14.7	6.4	3.3	15.7	18.3	9.0
Trade, industry, and employment	56.1	16.2	31.4	16.4	17.1	31.8	15.9	29.7	40.2	45.9	26.7
Roads and transport	31.4	19.9	16.1	21.2	23.3	30.1	21.1	25.5	30.3	27.6	24.3
Housing	46.3	28.6	27.8	32.4	52.4	23.3	30.9	36.5	33.0	62.1	41.6
Other environmental services	26.5	24.3	27.2	33.4	28.5	30.8	25.1	27.7	34.5	32.1	28.5
Law, order, and protective services	14.2	11.3	13.2	12.0	17.8	13.8	12.2	14.1	13.0	14.5	14.7
Education and libraries, science, and arts	70.2	69.1	70.4	76.3	80.5	67.2	67.6	71.1	76.5	87.6	75.2
Health and personal social services	56.5	58.6	57.7	57.2	69.3	62.2	53.6	59.4	65.1	71.6	63.2
Social security	122.9	113.8	101.5	101.3	101.6	113.0	99.3	116.9	127.8	114.8	109.0
Total	434.9	350.5	354.5	375.1	395.6	386.8	332.2	384.4	436.3	474.4	392.3
Central government	265.4	212.9	209.9	224.7	216.3	244.3	190.0	227.5	271.1	282.4	228.8
Local authorities	159.8	130.7	133.0	133.4	171.0	130.5	131.8	147.1	151.6	180.0	153.5
Public corporations	9.7	6.9	11.6	16.9	8.3	12.1	10.4	9.7	13.6	11.9	9.9
Current expenditure	309.2	282.4	277.3	278.5	296.1	299.4	255.9	288.9	329.2	351.7	296.4
Capital expenditure	125.7	68.2	77.2	96.6	99.5	87.4	76.3	95.5	107.2	122.7	95.8

Source: as for Table 9.1.

Table 9.3. Regionally relevant public expenditure 1969/70–1973/4 average
per capita index GB = 100

Programme	N	YH	EM	EA	SE	SW	WM	NW	W	S
Agriculture, fisheries, and forestry	120.0	98.9	103.3	277.8	55.6	163.3	71.1	36.7	174.7	203.3
Trade, industry, and employment	210.1	60.7	117.6	61.4	64.0	119.1	59.6	111.2	150.6	171.9
Roads and transport	129.2	81.9	66.3	87.2	95.9	123.9	86.8	104.9	124.7	113.6
Housing	111.3	68.8	66.8	77.9	126.0	56.0	74.3	87.7	79.3	149.3
Other environmental services	93.0	85.3	95.4	117.2	100.0	108.1	88.1	97.2	121.0	112.6
Law, order, and protective services	96.6	76.9	89.8	81.6	121.1	93.9	83.0	95.9	88.4	98.6
Education and libraries, science, and arts	93.4	91.9	93.6	101.5	107.0	89.4	89.9	94.5	101.7	116.5
Health and personal social services	89.4	92.7	91.3	90.5	109.7	98.4	84.8	94.0	103.0	113.3
Social security	112.8	104.4	93.1	92.9	93.2	103.7	91.1	107.2	117.2	105.3
Total	110.9	89.3	90.3	95.6	100.8	98.6	84.7	98.0	111.2	120.9
Central government	116.0	93.1	91.7	98.2	94.5	106.6	83.0	99.4	118.5	123.4
Local authorities	104.1	85.1	86.6	86.9	111.4	85.0	85.9	95.8	98.8	117.3
Public corporations	98.0	69.7	117.2	170.7	83.8	122.2	105.1	98.0	137.4	120.2
Current expenditure	104.3	95.3	93.6	93.9	99.9	101.0	86.3	97.5	111.1	118.7
Capital expenditure	131.2	71.2	80.6	100.8	103.9	91.2	79.7	99.7	111.9	128.1

Source: as for Table 9.1.

already mentioned social security, education, and health were the three highest spending programmes nationally. However, in the North region trade, industry, and employment was the next highest programme followed by housing. In Scotland, housing was ranked fourth, followed by trade, industry, and employment. By contrast in the South West, housing was ranked eighth.

The interregional difference on the level of spending between regions in the same programmes is shown in Table 9.3, which gives the per capita expenditure levels in terms of Great Britain. The variations in regionally relevant expenditure can be seen more clearly in the table. Scotland had almost 40 per cent more public expenditure than the lowest region—the West Midlands. Both the North region and Wales had over 10 per cent more expenditure than the average. The West Midlands has 15 per cent less than the national average. Central government contributed most to the three above-average regions while spending less in the regions with the lowest expenditure. Although current expenditure in the North, Scotland, and Wales was above the national average, capital spending was also above average to a significant degree. Within the programmes the width of the variations in spending are also highlighted in this table.

PUBLIC EXPENDITURE IN THE REGIONS, 1974/5-1977/8

The statistics on regionally relevant public expenditure for the 1974/5-1977/8 period are presented in Tables 9.4, 9.5, and 9.6 along the same lines as the previous section. Public expenditure averaged £49.5 billion over the period, and with inflation between 1974 and 1978 survey prices as just over 100 per cent, this represented a higher level of provision of about 15 per cent over the previous period. As before, social security, education, and health programmes accounted for the largest spending in each region with central government and the current account the longest agency and account. This is so for each region except Northern Ireland where trade, industry, and employment is the third highest replacing health and personal social services. However, direct comparison between the spending agencies in the English regions and Wales with Scotland

Table 9.4. Regionally relevant public expenditure 1974/5-1977/8 average £m (1978 survey prices)

Programme	N	YH	EM	EA	SE	SW	WM	NW	W	S	NI	UK
Agriculture, fisheries, and forestry	103.3	128.3	97.3	62.1	375.8	140.9	127.2	142.0	122.1	279.8	121.8	1,700.6
Trade, industry, and employment	419.4	238.4	208.0	62.1	668.9	213.7	269.7	440.1	255.0	549.1	268.4	3,592.8
Roads and transport	203.4	235.3	139.9	87.9	1,039.0	207.6	230.2	321.0	178.2	362.8	84.6	3,089.9
Housing	339.8	355.3	346.6	157.1	2,168.2	230.3	464.6	585.7	234.7	647.7	161.8	5,691.8
Other environmental services	193.1	227.3	164.4	98.5	930.7	178.6	255.6	323.8	162.3	379.8	83.2	2,997.3
Law, order, and protective services	96.2	150.7	102.9	47.7	670.3	119.9	143.3	203.8	79.3	166.4	184.6	1,965.1
Education and libraries, science, and arts	459.3	753.3	535.1	260.8	2,795.3	551.0	735.3	963.5	450.0	976.5	280.2	8,760.3
Health and personal social services	429.5	650.5	464.4	227.4	2,706.3	581.8	646.8	927.2	403.4	888.7	259.2	8,185.2
Social security	834.2	1,218.7	838.7	388.7	3,818.8	1,072.5	1,149.4	1,738.1	761.3	1,325.6	411.8	13,557.8
Total	3,078.2	3,957.8	2,897.3	1,392.3	15,173.3	3,296.3	4,022.1	5,645.2	2,646.3	5,576.4	1,855.6	49,540.8
Central government	1,886.7	2,398.1	1,707.3	838.1	8,480.2	2,162.2	2,344.8	3,478.4	1,658.8	3,343.2	1,536.1	29,833.9
Local authorities	1,101.1	1,494.8	1,112.1	479.0	6,408.0	1,076.4	1,557.8	2,017.4	928.8	2,118.7	221.6	18,515.7
Public corporations	90.4	64.8	77.8	75.0	284.9	57.8	119.4	149.4	58.7	114.5	98.1	1,190.8
Current expenditure	2,354.2	3,314.0	2,328.2	1,098.8	12,313.6	2,795.8	3,235.2	4,641.8	2,124.2	4,417.0	1,428.3	40,051.1
Capital expenditure	724.0	643.7	569.1	293.3	2,859.6	500.6	786.8	1,003.4	522.0	1,159.4	427.4	9,489.3

Source: J. Short, The Distribution of Public Expenditure and Taxation in the Regions 1974/75 to 1977/78 (Gower Press, Farnborough, 1980).

Table 9.5. Regionally relevant public expenditure 1974/5–1977/8 average per capita £m (1978 survey prices)

Programme	N	YH	EM	EA	SE	SW	WM	NW	W	S	NI	UK
Agriculture, fisheries and forestry	33.1	26.3	26.1	34.5	22.3	33.2	24.6	21.7	44.2	53.7	79.1	30.4
Trade, industry, and employment	134.2	48.8	55.7	34.5	39.6	50.4	52.2	67.2	92.2	105.5	174.3	64.3
Roads and transport	65.1	48.2	37.5	48.8	61.6	48.9	44.6	49.0	64.4	69.7	54.9	55.3
Housing	108.8	72.7	92.8	87.2	128.5	54.3	90.0	89.4	84.9	124.4	105.1	101.8
Other environmental services	61.8	46.5	44.0	54.7	55.1	42.1	49.5	49.4	58.7	73.0	54.0	53.6
Law, order, and protective services	30.8	30.9	27.6	26.5	39.7	28.3	27.8	31.1	28.7	32.0	119.9	35.2
Education and libraries, science, and arts	147.0	154.2	143.3	144.7	165.6	129.8	142.4	147.1	162.7	187.6	182.0	156.7
Health and personal social services	137.5	133.2	124.4	126.2	160.3	137.1	125.3	141.6	145.9	170.7	168.3	146.5
Social security	267.0	249.5	224.6	215.7	226.3	252.7	222.6	265.4	275.3	254.6	267.4	242.6
Total	985.2	810.3	775.8	772.7	899.0	776.8	779.1	861.9	956.9	1,071.2	1,205.0	886.4
Central government	603.8	491.1	457.2	465.1	502.4	509.5	454.2	531.1	599.8	642.2	997.5	533.8
Local authorities	352.4	306.1	297.8	265.8	379.7	253.7	301.7	308.0	335.9	420.4	143.9	331.3
Public corporations	28.9	13.3	20.8	41.6	16.9	13.6	23.1	22.8	21.2	22.0	63.7	21.3
Current expenditure	753.5	678.5	623.4	609.8	729.6	658.8	626.7	708.7	768.1	848.5	927.5	716.6
Capital expenditure	231.7	131.8	152.4	162.9	169.4	118.0	152.4	153.2	188.8	222.7	277.5	169.8

Source: as for Table 9.4.

Table 9.6. Regionally relevant public expenditure 1974/5–1977/8 average per capita index (regions in England, Wales, and Scotland GB = 100; Northern Ireland UK = 100)

Programme	N	YH	EM	EA	SE	SW	WM	NW	W	S	NI
Agriculture, fisheries, and forestry	114.1	90.6	90.0	118.9	76.8	114.4	84.7	74.8	152.3	185.0	260.2
Trade, industry, and employment	219.6	79.9	91.1	56.5	64.8	82.5	85.4	110.0	150.9	172.6	271.1
Roads and transport	117.8	87.2	67.9	88.3	111.5	88.5	80.7	88.7	116.6	126.2	117.4
Housing	107.0	71.5	91.3	85.8	126.4	53.4	88.5	87.9	83.5	122.4	103.2
Other environmental services	115.4	86.8	82.1	102.1	102.9	78.6	92.4	92.2	109.6	136.3	100.7
Law, order, and protective services	94.1	94.4	84.3	81.0	121.3	86.5	84.9	95.0	87.7	97.8	340.6
Education and libraries, science, and arts	94.3	98.9	91.9	92.8	106.2	83.3	91.4	94.4	104.4	120.3	116.1
Health and personal social services	94.4	91.4	85.4	86.6	110.0	94.1	86.0	97.2	100.1	117.2	114.9
Social security	110.5	103.2	92.9	89.3	93.6	104.6	92.1	109.8	113.9	105.4	110.2
Total	112.4	92.4	88.5	88.2	102.6	88.6	88.9	98.3	109.2	122.2	135.9
Central government	116.1	94.4	87.9	89.4	96.6	97.9	87.3	102.1	115.3	123.5	186.9
Local authorities	104.8	91.0	88.6	79.0	112.9	75.4	89.7	91.6	99.9	125.0	43.4
Public corporations	143.9	66.2	103.6	207.2	84.2	67.7	115.0	113.5	105.6	109.6	299.4
Current expenditure	106.1	95.6	87.8	85.9	102.8	135.0	88.3	99.8	108.2	119.5	129.4
Capital expenditure	139.1	79.1	91.5	97.8	101.7	70.8	91.5	92.0	113.3	133.7	163.4

Source: as for Table 9.4.

and Northern Ireland is not possible. This is because the responsibility for certain programmes in Northern Ireland differs from the rest of the country (particularly regarding local authorities), and in Scotland, water is a local authority responsibility where in England and Wales the agencies involved are public corporations.

Table 9.5 shows the per capita distribution of regionally relevant public expenditure. Northern Ireland is the recipient of the largest amount of expenditure over the period followed by Scotland, with East Anglia, East Midlands, South West, and West Midlands closely bunched together in ascending order at the other end of the scale, with a difference of £430 between Northern Ireland and East Anglia. As before there was a wide range of expenditure levels between the different regions in each programme. Northern Ireland received £174 in the trade, industry, and employment programme compared to East Anglia's £35. The South East had £129 spent on housing while the South West had £54. Roads and transport expenditure in Scotland was £70 while that in the East Midlands was £38.

Ignoring Northern Ireland, the difference between the highest spending region (Scotland) and East Anglia, the lowest, was 34 per cent, a narrowing of the differential from the earlier period. However, there was a bunching of four regions at the bottom end of the scale with East Anglia, East Midlands, South West, and West Midlands all receiving over 13 per cent less than the national average. At the other end, five regions had a greater than average share. Northern Ireland, the North and Wales all receiving considerably more, while the South East received 2.6 per cent more. In the four highest spending regions central government contributed most, while they were above average both on the current and capital accounts. Of the individual programmes, these four regions benefited most from the trade, industry, and employment programme ranging from over 50 per cent above average in Wales to 171 per cent above in Northern Ireland.

While it is not altogether correct to compare the two time periods directly because of the different price basis used in the tables, it is possible to look at the two periods together by using the coefficient of variation which shows the regional difference within each programme on a standardized basis.

This technique highlights those programmes where there is considerable spread among the regions, and those where the differences are not so great.

Table 9.7 shows that in both periods the variation in spending was lowest and stable between the periods in social security,

Table 9.7. Coefficients of variation for public expenditure between the regions

	1969/70-1973/4	1974/5-1977/8
Agriculture, fisheries, and forestry	0.54	0.31
Trade, industry, and employment	0.44	0.45
Roads and transport	0.20	0.19
Housing	0.37	0.23
Other environmental services	0.11	0.17
Law and order and protective services	0.13	0.12
Education and libraries, science and arts	0.08	0.10
Health and personal social services	0.09	0.10
Social security	0.09	0.08
Total	0.11	0.12

health, education, and law and order. The variation in other environmental services grew larger since the earlier period. Roads and transport, and trade, industry, and employment had greater but stable coefficients. The two remaining programmes, housing and agriculture, showed the largest differential between the regions.

The spread is least in those programmes where there is a statutory provision of a minimum level of service, and therefore the score for achieving regional differences is considerably less: social security, health, education, and law and order. Those programmes which show a large variation are those where regional differences in spending are built into the system (trade and industry), where the demand for the expenditure is dependent on regional factors (agriculture, and to a lesser extent transport), or where regional preferences favour one type of market arrangement as opposed to another (housing).

WHY ARE THERE REGIONAL DIFFERENCES IN LEVELS
OF PUBLIC EXPENDITURE?

That differences in the distribution of public expenditure on regionally relevant programmes exist as between regions has been highlighted over two separate periods in the previous sections. Population has been used as a yardstick for inter-regional comparison. Many explanations lie behind the diverse pattern of expenditure both in total and by programmes be-tween the regions. While the relative size of each region's total population was the single most important factor in determining the absolute total, per capita differences resulted from factors such as:

(*a*) the incidence in each region of particular groups in the population who were eligible for specific expenditures (e.g. pensioners, school children, etc.);

(*b*) government policies designed deliberately to influence the regional allocation of resources (e.g. expenditures to promote industrial growth in the development areas);

(*c*) the time phasing of certain national programmes in their application to the various regions (e.g. the importance of roads expenditure in regions such as the North region in the late 1960s and early 1970s, whereas such expenditure had pre-viously been relatively more important in the South East and Midlands);

(*d*) differences in the priorities attached to certain expendi-tures by the local authorities in each region (e.g. relatively high expenditures on public sector housing in the North region and Scotland);

(*e*) the geographic location of certain projects (e.g. new towns, subsidized industries);

(*f*) geographic variations in the cost of providing nominally the same service (e.g. high cost of housing in the South East com-pared with other regions);

(*g*) differences in the availability of finance to local authorities in each region arising from such factors as the resources gener-ated by rates and the workings of the particular formulae determining central government grants to local authorities;

(*h*) different standards of provision of nominally the same services by local and regional authorities in one region relative to those in another (e.g. doctors and dentists per head of population);

(*i*) different demands due to social attitudes (e.g. children staying on at school); and (*j*) the success of various pressure groups in lobbying for their areas.

By examining each region in terms of the major factors which influence the distribution of spending in each programme, it is possible to advance in very broad terms the reasons for the regional distributions which have existed in the years under consideration. For instance, the majority of educational spending is on schools; therefore it is likely that the school population in each regions will influence the regional spending in the wider education, libraries, science, and arts programme. Spending on higher education, museums, libraries, and arts are not likely to influence the overall distribution of spending as they are small in relation to schools education. Similarly, the spending in the housing programme is determined more by the spending on housing by local authorities and new towns rather than by option mortgages or housing association spending. A profile of each region showing the major factors which determine each region's expenditure in each programme is presented in an attempt to explain these differences. This profile relates to the post-April 1974 regional boundaries.

However, it is necessary to point out a general caveat that these regional profiles are presented in a very broad brush manner, and that exactitude is not intended. What is intended is to draw attention to the relevance of various factors as an explanation of why expenditure levels are of the order they are in relation to the overall national average. These factors can be seen as a rough measure of need, and a more detailed analysis has been undertaken by the Treasury in a *Needs Assessment Study* for the four countries of the UK.[4] Moreover, insofar as there is a degree of artificiality in the boundaries of the various English regions, characteristics may vary within regions while straddling boundaries.

The North Region

The region had 6.0 per cent of all agricultural land in the UK compared to 5.6 per cent of the nation's population, partly indicating why the region had a higher than average per capita expenditure in the agriculture, fisheries, and forestry programme. The very much higher than average spending in the trade, industry, and employment programme can be accounted for in terms of the development area status which covered the whole region, and the special development grants, regional employment premium (until this was ended in 1977) and selective assistance under Section 7 of the 1972 Industry Act. The region had 6.0 per cent of the surfaced roads length in the UK, but the high expenditure level in the region was boosted by the Tyneside Metro which was being constructed in the period under consideration. Housing expenditure in the region was higher than the national average due to lower owner-occupation and higher renting from local authorities and new towns. 41.0 per cent of the region's population rented from the authorities compared to 32.0 per cent nationally (in 1977). Higher than average spending in the other environmental services is due to the Keilder Reservoir Scheme and the improvements to combat environmental pollution, particularly on the rivers Tyne and Tees. Expenditure on law and order was higher than in most regions reflecting in part the higher rate of indictable offences recorded by the police. Although the region had a slightly higher percentage of under-fifteen-year-olds in the population compared to the UK (22.6 per cent compared to 22.5 per cent), the percentage of pupils aged sixteen remaining after the statutory leaving age was considerably lower (19.3 per cent compared to 25.6 per cent in England and Wales). This provides a partial explanation of why spending in the education programme was below the UK average using population as the index. The North region had 5.6 per cent above average list size for general medical practititioners and 36.4 per cent above average list size for general dental practitioners, and had just below the average number of available hospital beds per head. In addition, but offsetting this, it had the highest ratio of staff in local authorities social services departments per head in the regions of England and Wales. Public expenditure in the health and personal social services on average was 6.0 per cent below the UK level. There were fewer people of retirement age in the region compared to the country as a whole, but unemployment was considerably above the national average, as were days of certificated incapacity due to sickness or invalidity for the purpose of obtaining benefit. These ensured that the region had above average payments in the social security programme.

Yorkshire and Humberside

Yorkshire and Humberside has 8.7 per cent of the UK population. 6.3 per cent of all agricultural land in the UK is in the region, and even though the region had a large fishing industry spending in the agriculture, fisheries, and forestry programme was below average. Although the region had intermediate area status to obtain some regional assistance, the amount of aid it received compared to development and special development areas meant that spending on the trade, industry, and employment programme was below the national average. Surfaced road lengths amounted to 7.5 per cent of the UK total, and the per capita expenditure levels reflected this. However, in 1977/8 spending in the programme was high due to increased spending on trunk roads and local authority current spending (reflecting in part the higher public transport subsidies in South Yorkshire), and this higher spending boosted the overall average. There are no new towns in the Yorkshire and Humberside region; average house prices in the region were the lowest in the country and 33 per cent of the region's dwellings were rented from local authorities (compared to 32 per cent nationally). The combination of these factors provides an explanation of the region's low expenditure on housing. The region has slightly more under-fifteens in its population than the nation, but considerably fewer stay on at school beyond the statutory leaving age. The low per capita spending in health and personal social services is due to the above average list sizes for both general practitioners and dentists (6.5 per cent and 17.9 per cent above respectively), and the below average hospital beds available in the region's hospitals. These could not be offset by the high rate of personal social services provided in the region. The presence of more people of retirement age in the region (as a proportion of its population) ensured that spending in the social security programme was above average.

East Midlands

6.7 per cent of the UK population reside in the East Midlands. However, spending in the agriculture programme was below average despite the region having 7.1 per cent of all agricultural

land. Spending in the trade, industry, and employment programme was above average in 1974/5 because of payments to
the aircraft industry, but in other years (and on average) it
was below average due to the non-assisted area status of the
region and the falling off of payments for aircraft. Spending
on roads was low even though 7.3 per cent of total surfaced
roads were in the region. Capital spending by both central and
local authorities was depressed in the period due to higher
capital spending in earlier periods. Spending on education was
below average even though the region had an above average
population of under-fifteen-year-olds; however, offsetting this,
fewer stayed after their sixteenth birthday. The region had
the highest ratio of pupils to teachers of regions other than
Northern Ireland. The extremely low spending on health and
personal social services reflects the position of the region,
having the lowest rate of available hospital beds, 34 per cent
above average list size for dentists, and 6 per cent higher list
sizes for general medical practitioners. The region's below
average unemployment rate in addition to the percentage of
its population aged sixty-five and over being below the national
average made the region's spending in the social security programme low.

East Anglia

The population of East Anglia grew from 3.2 per cent of the
UK's total in 1974 to 3.3 per cent in 1977. The region had
5.8 per cent of all agricultural land and the percentage of the
region's total land area used for agricultural purposes was
higher than in other regions. Expenditure in the relevant programme was almost 14 per cent above average. The region was
not a major beneficiary of the trade, industry, and employment programme as it was not an assisted area, and did not
have any of the industries which were aided in this programme.
Roads and transport spending was below average although
the region had 5.3 per cent of surfaced road length. Owner
occupation was above the UK average, and the percentage of
houses rented from local authorities was much lower than the
national average. Accordingly, spending on housing was lower
than average even though the region had an expanding new
town (Peterborough). Spending on law and order was the

lowest of all regions reflecting the lowest rate of indictable offences recorded by the police per head in England and Wales. Capital spending by the regional water authorities in the region in 1974/5 and 1975/6 was high and ensured that spending in the other environmental services was above average. The region has a smaller percentage of its population under fifteen than nationally, and fewer stayed on at school after their sixteenth birthday. Consequently, education spending per head was below average. Although the region had a slightly greater number of general medical practitioners per head of population, the number of dentists per head was below average; allied to this, the region had fewer available hospital beds than the national average. Additionally, staff of local authority social services departments was below average. Consequently, spending on health and personal social services was well below the national average. The region had a lower rate of unemployment than nationally, and even though those over sixty-five form a slightly higher proportion of the population than nationally, the combination of all the factors brought spending on the social security programme to a below average level.

South East

The population of the South East fell from 30.3 per cent of the UK population in 1974 to 30.1 per cent in 1977. The region had only 9.9 per cent of the country's agricultural land so consequently per capita expenditure in the agricultural programme fell below the national average. As the region was not an assisted area for obtaining regional aid, spending per head in the trade, industry, and employment was well below average. Spending on roads, housing, other environmental services, law, education, and health was above average. Part of the reason for this lies in the overall higher costs in the South East, particularly for land. The region had the largest regional network for roads; highest incidence of indictable offences in England and Wales; a larger percentage of pupils at school after the statutory leaving age; and more doctors and dentists per head of the population than nationally. Spending in the social security programme was below average reflecting the lower unemployment rate in the region. This more than offset the higher percentage of those in the sixty-five and above age groups.

South West

The population of the South West expanded from 7.5 per cent of the UK total in 1974 to 7.7 per cent in 1977. The region was the largest agricultural area in England and has 10.5 per cent of the UK's agricultural land. Spending in the relevant programme was above average. Although part of the South West was a development area in the period, the related expenditure was not enough to give the region an above average share per head in the trade, industry, and employment programme. Moreover, with the removal of the regional employment premium, and the switching to more selective measures, the regions's position in this programme declined in the latter part of the period. Although the region had 12.5 per cent of the nation's surfaced roads, spending on roads and transport was below average reflecting low capital expenditure levels by local authorities. The region had the lowest percentage of houses rented from local authorities and this shows in the low spending per head on housing. Spending on education was also below the national average reflecting both the lower percentage of the population under fifteen, and the lower rate of those staying on at school after their sixteenth birthday. The region had more doctors and dentists per head than average, but this is offset by having fewer available hospital beds and fewer staff in social services per head of population. Spending on health and personal social services was below average. The age structure of the region's population shows that a greater proportion of the over-sixty-five age group live in the region, while unemployment since 1975 has been above the national average. Combined, these ensure that spending on the social security programme is above average.

West Midlands

9.3 per cent of the country's population live in the West Midlands. Spending in the agriculture, fisheries, and forestry programme was below average reflecting the size of the region's agricultural sector as measured by agricultural land mass which was 5.9 per cent of the UK total. The region did not benefit from regional aid but gained from the introduction of more selective assistance to industry under Section 8 of the 1972

Industry Act and the National Enterprise Board, particularly to the motor vehicles and machine tool industries, resulting in a greater share in the trade, industry, and employment programme than would otherwise be expected. 7.8 per cent of the country's surfaced roads were in the region; the major road construction programme for trunk roads in the region had taken place previously. Capital spending by the regional water authorities in the West Midlands was particularly high in 1974/5, but other than that expenditure was below average in the other environmental services. Although the region had more children under fifteen than nationally, fewer stayed on at school after the statutory leaving age, and spending on education was below the national average. The region had more patients per general medical practitioner and dentist, and fewer available hospital beds per head than nationally. In addition, it had fewer staff per head employed in local authorities social services. Combined these gave the region a much lower per capita spending level on health than the country as a whole. The unemployment rate and the percentage of population aged sixty-five and over were both below the national average ensuring that the region's share of social security expenditures was below the national average.

North West

The population of the North West was 11.7 per cent of the UK's. The region is not an agricultural area compared to the other regions. Only 2.6 per cent of the UK agricultural area is to be found there. Accordingly, spending in the relevant programme is well below average. Part of the North West, Merseyside, was a special development area and the rest was an intermediate area during the period under consideration. In addition, the region has benefited from selective assistance under Sections 7 and 8 of the Industry Act and from the activities of the National Enterprise Board. When all these different sources of finance have been combined in single years, the region has above average spending in the trade, industry, and employment programme. However, the amount the region received in regional assistance alone has not been sufficient to ensure that spending in the programme will be above average as in other development area regions. Spending on roads, housing, education, and health are all below average. The region has 6.7 per cent of the country's surfaced roads. Fewer houses are rented from local authorities or new towns as a percentage of total dwellings, and the cost of housing in the region is below average. More in the under-fifteen age group are to be found in the region than nationally, but considerably fewer stay on after their sixteenth birthday. There are fewer general medical practitioners and dentists, and available hospital beds per head of population than in the country as a whole. Spending on law and order was the highest of the English regions outside the South East reflecting in part the second highest rate in the English regions of indictable offences reported by the police. Spending on the social security programme was above average reflecting the higher unemployment rate and the problems of Merseyside. Indeed the proportion of household incomes derived from social security benefits was higher in the region compared to the other English regions.

Wales

The population of Wales was 4.9 per cent of the UK's. The country accounted for 8.5 per cent of the nation's agricultural land, and 10 per cent of its forest area. After Scotland, it grazes most sheep. Accordingly, spending in the relevant programme was considerably above average. All of the country is an assisted area in terms of regional aid; most of it is a development area and parts are special development areas. As a result, spending in the trade, industry, and employment programme was well above average. 8.6 per cent of the UK surfaced roads are in Wales and apart from 1974/5 capital expenditure on trunk roads has been particularly high. Fewer houses are rented from local authorities and new towns than nationally and house prices are below the national average. Spending on the housing programme was below average, while spending on roads and transport above average. Spending on other environmental services was above average in all but 1974/5, and this was due to increased spending by local authorities particularly on the current account. Spending on education was above average even though the under-fifteen age group was smaller as a percentage of total population compared to the nation. However, Wales had a far greater proportion remaining on at school after their sixteenth birthday. Health spending was slightly above average with the country having slightly more doctors than the national average, but fewer dentists, while having the national average for available hospitals beds. However, fewer were employed in local authorities personal social services departments. Unemployment in Wales was well above the national average, and Wales had a greater percentage of its population aged sixty-five and over than the UK average. Spending on the social security programme was, therefore, above average.

Scotland

9.3 per cent of the UK's population resided in Scotland. Apart from one regionally relevant programme, public expenditure in Scotland was above average. 31.6 per cent of the UK's agricultural land, and half its forests are in Scotland. The whole country was an assisted area with large parts special development areas, and the majority of the remainder development areas. In addition, Scotland received considerable Section 7 aid. 13.6 per cent of the nation's surfaced roads are in Scotland and it has the largest system of trunk and principal roads. In the period under review, expenditure on non-trunk roads has been particularly high. Over 50 per cent of the houses in Scotland are rented from local authorities or new towns, by far the greatest regional percentage. Current spending by local authorities in the other environmental services programme has increased considerably since 1975/6. More pupils stay on at school after they reach sixteen and Scotland has a greater percentage of under-fifteens than nationally. There are more general medical practitioners per head of population than any other region, and only two regions (the South East and South West) have more dentists per head. In addition, there are considerably more hospital beds available. The unemployment rate is much greater in Scotland than nationally, but there are fewer pensioners, bringing spending on the social security programme nearer the national average than it would otherwise have been.

Northern Ireland

2.8 per cent of the UK population live in Northern Ireland. Its pattern of government is different from the remainder of the country, and many of the functions which are carried out by local authorities elsewhere are organized by the central government. 6.2 per cent of the UK's agricultural land is in Northern Ireland and spending in the agriculture, fisheries, and forestry programme is the highest per head of all regions. Special incentives to industry apply in Northern Ireland, compared to the other regions of the UK. As a result spending per head on the trade, industry, and employment programme is higher in Northern Ireland than in other regions. 6.5 per cent of the UK's road surfaces are to be found in the region; however, it is only in 1976/7 that spending on roads becomes above average. This is due to increases in both current and capital expenditure, and this increase is greatest in 1977/8 giving an above average spending level overall. A similar growth in the housing capital programme took place in 1976/7 and was continued in 1977/8. The percentage of houses rented from the public sector increased over the period, and by 1977 was seven percentage points above the national average. Spending in the other environmental services grew sharply in 1975/6 and continued to be above average thereafter. Both the capital and current accounts shared in this increase. The high spending in the law and order programme reflects the problems which the region has faced and the authorities' attempts to combat them. The region had the highest percentage of the under-fifteen age group and, although a small percentage stayed on after sixteen, spending in the education programme was above average. The region had the second highest number of general medical practitioners, the fourth highest number of dentists, and the second highest number of hospital beds available per head of population of all regions. Accordingly, spending on the health programme was above the national average. The unemployment rate was the highest regional one and social security payments were consequently high. The overall spending on the social security programme was lowered by the smaller percentage of over-sixty-fives in the population than in the country as a whole.

Patterns of Regional Variations

From these regional profiles, it is possible to group together four regions. Scotland, Wales, Northern Ireland, and the North

region all get some special assistance to develop their economies with higher than average spending on the trade, industry,
and employment, and roads and transport programmes. In
the former, this assistance covers the whole of each region in
one form or another. As a result, all of these regions have
above average spendings in total regionally relevant programmes. While parts of other regions such as Yorkshire and
Humberside, the North West, and the South West have assisted
area status, the spending on assistance is not a large part of
the total. The East Midlands, West Midlands, and East Anglia
do not benefit from the regional development aid in the same
way. However, when these regions do benefit in any year from
spending in the overall trade, industry, and employment programme from selective aid under the National Enterprise Board
and Section 8, or aid to specific industries such as aircraft,
their overall per capita index improves. The final region, the
South East can be treated separately. This has a per capita
index above the national average, but this has arisen not because the region was a beneficiary of the trade, industry, and
employment programme as in the regions noted above, but
because there was particularly high spending on several major
programmes for which the principal responsibility lay with
local authorities. The region had the second highest per capita
spending by this agency, which has sufficient to compensate
for below average central government and public corporation
spending. Even though higher costs in the South East have
pulled the index up, the role of local authorities expenditure
is significant.

Indeed, this broad grouping of regions, particularly the
above average ones, applies to both time periods examined in
this chapter. The position of the South West and East Anglia
has deteriorated, but these two regions have experienced relative increases in their population. In addition, spending on
trade, industry, and employment, and roads and transport
in the South West has fallen off dramatically. The position of
the West Midlands has improved due in part to the introduction
of more selective national assistance to industry, while that
of the East Midlands has lessened partly due to the run down
of aid to the aircraft industry.

CONCLUSIONS

This chapter has presented estimates of public expenditure on the spending programmes which have an impact on the supply of public services to individual regions rather than the nation as a whole. Such spending patterns have been related to population in order to facilitate comparison. The chapter has not made any attempt to relate these levels to need as such, but has tried to show the major factors which may influence the regional distribution. The question of need and the correct allocation of spending according to it is well beyond the scope of this chapter. Neither does the chapter profess to present regional budgets for the government sector. Such budgets do not exist; a major feature of such budgets would be the ability to switch spending between individual programmes, an option which is not available to any region. Nevertheless the government sector in its allocation of resources between different programmes does spend in different regions at differing levels. The compilation of these levels of spending by programme provides the first step in any attempt to assess the 'correct' level of expenditure in relation to 'need', and is a necessary input into the formulation of regional budgets, should the political changes necessary to implement them ever take place.

CHAPTER 10

Members of Parliament: a regional perspective?

JOHN F. McDONALD

How far do MPs recognize and make use of the planning regions, or alternative conceptions of region, when expressing views about regional policy on the floor of the House? In order to answer this question, it is important to test whether the delineation of the English regions has succeeded in accommodating existing social and cultural factors to a degree which facilitates identification by Members of Parliament with their regions. If it can be shown that Members are able to identify with those regions in which their constituencies fall, then it would be safe to assume that the regions are something more than artificially contrived units, that they have a natural community base, and can therefore offer a channel for political activity on a regional basis. If, on the other hand, it can be shown that Members do not typically identify with a region or regional cause, and that the level of interest of English MPs, as indicated by the number of speeches in Parliament referring to the regions, is low compared with that from Scotland and Wales, then it can be suggested that the English regions are merely administrative (there is considerable doubt as to what actual administrative purpose they serve: see Chapter 2) and not political or community units.

Governments concerned with designating regions have encountered the problem that at some point the classification must become arbitrary, or else result in designating as regions areas which occupy no more than a few square miles. In Britain, the designation has been such as to follow the broad economic and geographical composition of the country. The reason for this lies with the motives behind their establishment, namely the need for administrative areas to facilitate the development of certain areas of geographic and economic space. For example, the purpose of the planning regions established in 1964 was to facilitate, through the Regional Economic Planning Councils and Boards, the use of unused resources in the regions in the most efficient way possible by producing coherent and comprehensive strategies for the regions and for the co-ordination of plans, national, regional, and departmental.[1]

Successive governments in the United Kingdom appear to have taken the view that the manner in which regions are delineated should depend upon the purpose for which they are created, and there are as a result many types of region within the United Kingdom, amongst which those dealing with water, gas, electricity, and health may be cited as examples. The boundaries of each region are drawn up chiefly from the point of view of administrative convenience in distributing the commodity or service in question. The planning regions are concerned with a variety of fields of economic acitivity, so that in delineating these regions, social, geographic, and economic factors of many kinds have been taken into account.

Many different criteria, then, are likely to have been used in drawing up regional boundaries, resulting in areas having regional planning structures based upon different, and sometimes conflicting, criteria. Because of the conflict, some criteria will have been ignored, and some taken into account in the form of a compromise. The final regional unit which is adopted in practice can therefore always be made the subject of some degree of criticism, and it is not to be expected that the official designation of large areas of geographic space as 'regions' will have the effect of displacing and replacing traditional community loyalties. This having been said, however, it might be reasonable to expect that a successful regional division should be one which attempts to accommodate, rather than displace, such loyalties. It is necessary, therefore, to test whether Members of Parliament identify with their own regions as officially designated, or with some other areas of their own delineation.

The analysis undertaken here takes the form of a survey of all speeches[2] on regional policy made on the floor of the House of Commons during a period of time long enough for significant patterns in the characteristics of speeches to emerge. All speeches which referred to regional economic policy[3] over a period of nine Parliamentary sessions (1968-76) were identified for this purpose. The period studied covered two changes of government, and a total of 2,016 speeches were examined.

Each of the speeches showed a predominant direction of interest[4] which was in the form either of a concern with regional policy as a general economic and political issue, or of a concern with the policy for its effects upon a particular area. Regional interest could, on this basis, be placed within one of four categories: overall regional interest; planning region interest; constituency area interest; or, sub-regional interest, according to the identifiable predominant concern displayed within each speech. A speech which falls within the category of 'overall regional interest' is one in which the main emphasis of the speech is not concerned with the policy as it affects a particular area, but rather with the policy as a total economic strategy. In order for a speech to fall in this category, it need not necessarily be concerned with any particular economic argument, but all speeches within the category have this in common: that for whatever reason (whether perhaps to make party political capital, or to refer to the regions as one aspect of the economic difficulties experienced by Britain), they are mainly concerned with regional policy in the light of much wider policy objectives than that of how the policy affects any given area.

The other three categories refer to speeches which show a primary concern with the implications of the policy for some particular area, and in this respect, the 'planning region' and 'constituency area interest' categories are reasonably straightforward. For example, those speeches whose main concern is with an official planning region[5] and with the policy as it affects that region are categorized as 'planning region interest'. This covers cases where the Member making the speech identifies with and shows a concern for a particular planning region. The 'constituency area' speech category is reserved for speeches in which Members identify with areas which correspond to constituencies. For example, Mr Michael McGuire (1976) was concerned with the effects of a factory closure upon his constituency and the problems of employment therein, and not

for its effects upon the region or upon the impoverished regions
in general:

> Tomorrow the Thorn Colour Tube factory in Skelmersdale in my constituency will cease production. Over 1,300 workers will lose their jobs
> . . . the present male unemployment rate is must over 15%, and the female unemployment rate is just over 11%.[6]

Concern for a constituency does not necessarily mean that
the regional boundaries have failed to capture interest. It
would be expected that identification with a Member's own
constituency would be high, and an MP could identify with
both. However, in this case it might be expected that if the
regions do act as a focus for interest, then constituency concern would be articulated in a wider regional context, with
the region providing the focal point in the speech. It is, however, the existence of the sub-regional category which is most
significant.

A sub-regional speech is one in which the interest of the
Member extends beyond a simple constituency bias to an area
which, though not as large as that covered by the official
region, is too large to be explained as a mere reflection of the
fact that it is easier to identify with a small area than with a
large one. It encompasses a number of constituencies, and so
cannot be explained as the reflection by the Member of the
interests of his constituency as these most directly affect him.
Such a sub-regional bias indicates that certain MPs have identified with an area which does not conform to the official planning region and which is not as small as a constituency (the
more obvious focus of an MP's interest), but which is nevertheless perceived as having sufficient homogeneity, whether
cultural, geographic, or economic, to be a focus of interest
and concern for a number of MPs. The existence of such an
identification serves to suggest that some MPs think in terms
of alternative regional units to those provided by the planning
regions, and therefore raises the question of the success of
the official delineation. For example, Mr Bernard Conlan
(1969) stated that:

> . . . in the last nine years over 100,000 jobs have been lost in the basic
> industries. That is the problem. It has existed in the North East for a
> long time . . . We must therefore consider the whole problem of how we
> are to attract more industries and more firms to the North East.[7]

Once the speeches have been categorized, it is possible to identify patterns of interest in regional policy as shown by MPs. It is, for example, possible to show the frequency with which MPs indicate a concern with a particular area. It is accepted that frequency is not the same as intensity of interest, but it may nonetheless be considered as an indicator of that interest which is a necessary precondition for the regions to be considered as political units. It has been decided that, when analysing patterns of interest, speeches by MPs who were ministers at the time should be excluded from the analysis.

Table 10.1 shows the frequency with which speeches in the four categories of interest occurred during the period studied.

Table 10.1

Speech origins (interest bias)	Absolute frequency	Relative frequency %*
Overall regional interest	377	23
Planning region interest	462	28
Constitutency area interest	601	36
Sub-regional interest	233	14
Total	1673	100

* The column percentages have been rounded to the nearest whole number.

The Table indicates that most speeches are concerned with the policy as it affects a particular area, and are not necessarily directed towards regional policy as a general issue. The fact that 28 per cent of the speeches showed an identification with the official planning regions also indicates that the regional units have not been a total failure from the viewpoint of channelling Members' interest. However, as more speeches are concerned with a constituency or sub-regional area, it would seem that the areas with which MPs identify are not necessarily, or even usually, those geographic areas which are officially defined as planning regions. It is evident, rather, that there is a strong tendency for the implications of regional policy to be viewed from the perspective of its effects upon areas of the MPs' own delineation. Although it is recognized that the constituency interest is not an alternative to a region, its existence indicates a failure of the region to capture and channel political interest and demands.

Relative party strengths as between regions constitute a factor which could account for MPs focusing their speeches in a particular direction. Table 10.2 shows that Labour MPs speak more frequently on regional policy and show a higher level of interest in the policy as it affects a particular area than do MPs from the Conservative or Liberal parties. This is hardly surprising, considering that more Labour MPs have their seats in disadvantaged areas, and that the Liberals have so few seats. The Conservative and Liberal identification with the official regions is a little higher than that of Labour, but not high enough to lead to the supposition that these MPs use the regions significantly more often so that the region is the focus and channel of interest for MPs from that party. This, of course, is particularly so when compared to the focus of interest for Nationalist Members.

Table 10.2. Speech origins (interest bias)—number and percentage

Party	Overall regional interest	Planning region interest	Constituency area interest interest	Sub-regional interest	Row total
Labour	208	219	378	141	946
	22%*	23%	40%	15%	100%
Conservative	140	148	197	81	566
	25%	26%	35%	14%	100%
Liberal	28	19	15	7	69
	41%	27%	22%	10%	100%
Nationalist	1	68	11	4	84
	1%	81%	13%	5%	100%
Total	377	462	601	260	1673
	23%	28%	36%	14%	100%

* The row percentages have been rounded to the nearest whole number.

Another factor to be considered is the frequency of regional issues articulated in Parliament, and by what regions. It would be expected that where regional delineation has followed existing and accepted political, geographic, social, and cultural boundaries then there are likely to be more speeches made by MPs from these regions than from the regions where the boundaries have not followed accepted delineation criteria.

Table 10.3 compares the percentage of seats in Parliament from England, Scotland, and Wales with the percentage of speeches made on regional policy by MPs from those areas. If the interest in the regions and in regional policy were found to be similar in the case of Members from all three areas, it would be expected that the percentage patterns of speeches would be similar to the percentage pattern of seats. This, clearly, is not the case. Indeed, the Table shows a disproportionate interest on the part of Scottish and Welsh Members in the regions and regional policy, and that these Members are over-represented in the debate upon this policy.

Table 10.3.

	Percentage and number distribution of constituencies in Great Britain	Percentage and number of regional speeches	Ratio of proportion of speeches to constituencies
England	83%* 516	63% 1279	.77
Scotland	11% 71	23% 459	2.0
Wales	6% 36	14% 278	2.4
Total	100% 623	100% 2,016	

* The column percentages have been rounded to the nearest whole number.

Part of the explanation for this may be found in the economic and geographic situation of Scotland and Wales, in that both lie on the periphery. That is, there should be greater regional interest shown by Members whose constituencies lie in the disadvantaged regions furthest away from the economic and political domination of London and the South East. If this were the only factor, however, it would be expected that there would be a higher degree of interest from Scotland, relative to the distribution of seats, than from Wales, for, although they are both on the periphery, Scotland is further from the centre and since 1970 has on the whole experienced higher levels of unemployment. This is not the case: there is little difference between them, and such differences as do exist indicates a higher degree of interest from Welsh Members than from Scottish Members. Therefore, the hypothesis that geographic, economic, and cultural remoteness is the only explanation is invalidated.

One major factor is that, whereas Scotland and Wales are in a situation where political activity on a regional basis has been institutionally accommodated, this has not been the case for the English regions. There has been access through Scottish and Welsh institutions to Westminster, and so to decision-making in actual government. Both regions have Secretaries of State, served by an administrative civil service organization, which means direct channels of communication with the Government, often bypassing Members of Parliament. Furthermore, through the work of their Members of Parliament, there is usually greater time for debate on Scottish and Welsh matters compared to English regional matters, not only before the whole House, but also by means of the Welsh and Scottish Grand Committees. These constitutional arrangements recognize a political unity within both nation-regions, and by their very existence have consolidated and reinforced a 'regional' identification and interest. Thus, the belief that political demands in relation to Scottish and Welsh problems should be heard is accentuated. This is not to suggest that these channels have been considered completely successful, or that such demands have been or will be met, but it does mean that such demands have been seen to emerge within the nation-region context. Such a political region is therefore likely to engender the interest of its own Members of Parliament, who are thus more likely to identify with the region, than is the case for Members from non-political regions.

For the English regions, there are no channels of the type which exist for Scotland and Wales. Although in 1964 Mr W. Rodgers, one of the two Parliamentary Secretaries from the North East, was given special responsibility for regional affairs, this arrangement was largely concerned with economic development, and was relatively short-lived. The Standing Committee on Regional Affairs was set up in 1975, to deliberate on the English regions. However, there is little evidence that this has done anything to encourage regional interest and identity. Borthwick, for example, argues that the English

Committee is at a disadvantage in relation to the Scottish and Welsh Grand Committees.[8]

Table 10.4. Speech origins (interest bias)—number and percentage

Planning region	Overall regional interest	Planning region interest	Constituency area interest	Sub- regional interest	Row total
Northern	49 23%	18 9%	74 35%	72 34%	213 100%
North West	43 17%	23 9%	140 55%	21 20%	256 100%
Yorkshire/ Humberside	29 18%	32 20%	76 48%	21 13%	158 100%
West Midlands	22 33%	1 2%	41 61%	3 5%	67 100%
East Midlands	25 54%	2 4%	19 41%	0 0%	46 100%
South West	47 45%	19 8%	31 30%	7 7%	104 100%
South East	83 58%	7 5%	50 35%	4 3%	144 100%
East Anglia	5 19%	5 19%	16 59%	1 4%	27 100%
Scotland	52 13%	235 59%	88 22%	27 7%	402 100%
Wales	22 9%	111 45%	66 27%	48 19%	247 100%
Total	377 23%	462 28%	601 36%	233 14%	1673 100%

* The row percentages have been rounded to the nearest whole number.

It can be seen from Table 10.4 that, with the exception of Scotland and Wales, MPs from the regions show more concern with constituency or sub-regional areas than with the official planning regions. This, therefore, indicates that political interest and activity is not channelled by the official English regions. As might be expected, it is the constituencey of the MP which provides the main focus of interest, but the presence of a number of speeches showing a sub-regional identification is most significant. Even a 14 per cent frequency suggests that some MPs think in terms of alternative regional units, and therefore raises the question of the success of the official delineation. The significance of the presence of a percentage of speeches which focus upon a sub-region lies in the inference that the higher the percentage of sub-regional speeches from an area, the stronger the indication that the official delineation has not succeeded in selecting politically meaningful criteria. This is particularly so where there are few speeches which show an identification with the official region, indicating that in practice, effective alternative delineations are made by the people of that area and by their MPs. A low percentage of sub-regional speeches, however, does not of itself imply that the official planning boundary is beyond criticism. It may be that the area of space which has been designated as a region contains no realistic focus of interest of any sort, official or unofficial, so that the speeches will be found to be constituency-orientated or concerned with the problems of regional policy as a whole. Only where there appears a high percentage of speeches which acknowledge the official planning region, coupled with a relatively low percentage of sub-regional speeches, can it be assumed that the official delineation for that area is in practice satisfactory. As this only occurs for Scotland and Wales, it supports the view that it is only for these two nation-regions that the regional boundaries have been successfully drawn.

The pattern of Scottish and Welsh speeches are so distinctive that they should be considered together. Table 10.5 indicates that, of the 656 speeches by Scottish and Welsh MPs, 346 (53 per cent) have a predominant interest in the policy as it affects their official planning region. This is particularly significant in the light of the fact that there are only 462 planning region speeches in total shown in Table 10.4. Such a high percentage of speeches showing interest in the official regions strongly suggests that the designation of these areas accommodates the most realistic delineation criteria, and in comparison to the English regions, increases the doubt as to the success of the delineation of the latter.

Table 10.4 shows that for the English regions the number of speeches concerned with the official regions is generally low, and that for five regions the major interest is with the policy

Table 10.5. Speech origins (interest bias)—number and per-centage

Planning region	Overall regional interest	Planning region interest	Constituency area interest	Sub-regional interest	Row total
Scotland	52	235	88	27	402
	13%*	59%	22%	7%	100%
Wales	29	111	66	48	247
	9%	46%	27%	19%	100%
Total	81	346	154	75	656
	12%	53%	24%	11%	100%

* The row percentages have been rounded to the nearest whole number.

as it affects an area of the Members' own delineation. This, then, indicates that the regional units have not been such as to channel interest or commitment. In the case of the three regions for which the constituency or sub-regional percentage is not the highest, there is moreover no indication of satisfaction with the official regional units.

In the case of MPs from the first three English regions, it is quite clear that there is identification with, and commitment to, areas of their own delineation. The majority of speeches from each of these regions are concerned with a constituency or sub-regional area, and the lowest percentage of speeches is provided by those concerned with the official planning region. In fact, for the Northern and North-West regions, there are more speeches with a sub-regional bias than there are speeches which show an interest in the official planning region (see Table 10.4). This strongly suggests that the official delineation has not been successful in producing areas with which MPs can identify. In the case of the Yorkshire/Humberside region, there are relatively more speeches concentrated upon the official planning region, and fewer with a sub-regional bias, but even here, the sub-regional identification is significant enough to suggest that in this region also, if not so markedly, there must be a doubt as to the success of the official delineation. This view is further supported by even a cursory glance at the characteristics of these regions.

The Northern planning region is arguably the least homogeneous planning region in the United Kingdom. This is reflected in the high sub-regional bias in speeches made by MPs from this region, who identify more closely with areas of their own delineation, in the absence of any focus for common interest provided by the official division. The North Eastern portion of the region provides a telling illustration. This area, which runs from Morpeth in the north to Cleveland in the south, has an internal homogeneity provided by the severe economic problems which characterize the area throughout, and which have resulted in most of the area acquiring Special Development Area status and receiving the same assistance package. The problems throughout this area stem from the decline of the older heavy industries, particularly ship-building. There is a common economic history from the Industrial Revolution to the decline and obsolescence of the twentieth century. These factors, coupled with a tradition of uniting in order to demand help, have produced an area which has a strong image of itself as a region, and this image is reflected in a strong cultural identification in the North East, which provides a striking example of a tendency which can be observed, perhaps to a lesser degree, in parts of other planning regions. The inhabitants of the North East and their MPs have no reason to identify themselves with other areas of the region: Penrith and the Border, for example, is entirely different in terms of its geography, history, economic situation, population density, and local culture. It is hardly surprising, therefore, that the Northern region has such a high proportion of speeches having a sub-regional bias, particularly concentrated within the North East,[9] since the criteria which were used in delineating the official regional boundaries were not those which appear as natural divisions to those who live in that area. Mr A. J. Beith made the point in 1975 that the North East possesses a sense of separateness:

The North East faces very similar problems to those of Scotland. It has the same kind of industrial legacy, the same problems of under-development in terms of industrial progress, the same problems of unemployment, the same problems of outworn and outdated housing stock and the same problems of remoteness as those applying to Scotland. What is more, of course, the North East is further from London than all of Wales.[10]

Here, Mr Beith was arguing for the same degree of separate

treatment as that received by Scotland and Wales, but only for the North East, and not for the whole Northern Region. This is perhaps not too surprising given the homogeneity of the North East and the fact that, in terms of population and constituencies, it forms by far the largest part of the Northern Region. Therefore, most MPs speaking from the Northern Region have their constituencies in the North East, and tend to make little distinction between the sub-region of the North East and the planning region. However the economic problems within the planning region are different, there is relatively little recognition of the rest of the region. This might seem to indicate that a more sensible division is to treat the North East as a region in itself. The alternative might be to reverse the 1974 regional boundaries and accept domination from the North East.

The relatively low level of interest in the North West planning region, indicated by the low percentage of speeches concerned with the region as a whole and a relatively high sub-regional interest, would seem to suggest that this region also is not a good 'fit', although not so poor as the Northern region. The North West region covers a smaller area than the Northern region, and has common internal links in terms of its geographic position, its traditions, and its economic situation. Nonetheless, the region contains within it recognizably different areas having certain common characteristics which provide a focus for interest, in competition with the official region. An example is provided by the two major sub-regions most frequently identified in the speeches, those of Merseyside and North-East Lancashire. The older established industries of Merseyside, now in decline, are those associated with a seaport, such as ship-building, cargo-handling and refining. The area has received aid, in the form of Special Development Area and Development Area status, which has brought new industry, trading estates, and New Towns, with the result that Merseyside has become heavily dependent upon regional aid. In contrast, North-East Lancashire's unemployment problems have not been as great, and its traditional industries, also in decline, are largely based upon textiles and coal. The area has only relatively recently achieved assisted-area status after much pressure, a factor which has widened the gap between the two areas. Lastly, Merseyside claims a distinct cultural entity, deriving from its character as a seaport and its diversity of ethnic groups. The divisions which the inhabitants of Merseyside and North-East Lancashire perceive were reflected in a speech made by Mr Arthur Davidson (1972):

> I want to stress the words 'North East Lancashire' so that the minister does not fall into the trap which so many people who are not familiar with the area fall, in thinking that the problems of the North-West and Lancashire mean the problems of Greater Liverpool and Greater Manchester.[11]

In the Yorkshire/Humberside region, although the official delineation appears to have been more successful than that of the Northern and North West regions, the sub-regional interest is nevertheless significant, and reflects mainly a difference in county identification, north and south of the River Humber. The post-1974 boundary changes did affect this region, and part of the old region south of the Humber was absorbed into the East Midlands. However, unless the division could be made along the Humber, then the differences in identification are still likely to arise. There is an awareness of social and economic differences between the two areas, which has been accentuated by the greater benefits received by the northern part through regional aid, to the detriment of the southern portion of the region. Concern at this discrimination was voiced by Mr Jeffrey Archer (1973):

> We are worried in North Lincolnshire and in the area of Humberside that too much is given to the North Bank—in particular to Hull—and too little to the South Bank . . . too many people in Yorkshire imagine that the capital of the world is Leeds and the next most important city in Britain is Hull. It seems that no-one has ever heard of Lincolnshire.[12]

In the case of these three regions, there is clearly reason to suggest that the officially designated planning region does not channel or act as a focus for MPs' interest, and that a significant degree of interest is channelled through areas which are seen as alternatives to the region.

The South East, the East Midlands, and the West Midlands, on the other hand, produce a relatively low percentage of sub-regional speeches (see Table 10.4). This might, at first sight, indicate that the inhabitants of these regions perceive the official delineation as satisfactory. However, the interest shown in the official planning regions is very little higher. Although within these three regions there are no strong rival claims for an alternative, sub-regional identification, it cannot be said that they provide a focus for the interests of their MPs. There are within these regions a number of geographical, cultural, and occupational variations, but none of them appears strong enough to provide any major focus for sub-regional interest; on the other hand, there is uniformity of economic situation, a general lower than average level of unemployment[13] and above average unemployment concentrated only in certain specific areas.[14] In consequence, the economic situation within these regions does not produce any inequalities on a scale large enough to promote any alternative basis for identification. There are so many small-scale variations that it seems plausible to suggest that not only is there no incentive towards sub-regional interest, but no incentive towards interest in the official planning region either. If this is the case—and Table 10.4 certainly reveals little interest in the planning regions—then it may be said that the regional delineation has not been notably successful for these regions, not because it runs counter to alternative identification, but because it has failed to promote and concentrate an identification with the regions themselves, which thus remain little more than artificial conceptions.

The figures for the South West and East Anglia would appear to indicate a more successful regional delineation, in that the percentage of regional speeches is higher than those for most of the English regions considered, while the sub-regional percentage is relatively low (see Table 10.4). However, when compared to Scotland and Wales, their success appears somewhat diminished. The South West region is one in which certain areas receive separate treatment, and in which the economic situation shows certain variations. The area of Cornwall is treated separately, since it has more severe economic problems, and this economic division accounts for most of the sub-regional bias in speeches from this area, which tend to be concentrated upon Cornwall and to a lesser degree upon Devon. This is illustrated in a speech by Mr Robert Hicks (1971):

I should like to congratulate my honourable friend, the Member for Falmouth and Camborne (Mr Mudd) on raising the subject of this important development which could have many desirable consequences, not least for the economy of the West Country, particularly Cornwall. Most of Cornwall is in the South West Development Area and the remainder within the Plymouth intermediate area . . .[15]

Unlike the three earlier regions, there are recognizable social, geographic, and economic variations producing commitment to a large area within the region. Although there is more concern with the region itself, the large number of speeches devoted to the wider policy issues would suggest that there is no widespread commitment by the MPs to the officially designated South West region. East Anglia, on the other hand, is relatively homogeneous, consisting mainly of the counties of Norfolk, Suffolk, and Cambridgeshire. It is an area of relatively low population density, with little manufacturing industry, and an economy based largely upon agriculture, fishing, and tourism. There are no major geographic, economic, or social divisions which could serve to channel sub-regional interest, and the whole region receives the same treatment insofar as East Anglia receives no assistance. Its economic problems, which are chiefly those of low wages and a large number of small areas suffering high percentage unemployment, are common throughout the region, and so promote greater interest in the region as a whole. However, as the economic problems are concentrated in many small areas in the region, interest at a constituency level is high.

From this discussion, and from the Tables, it seems evident that in the case of the English regions the official units have had little success in acting as focuses for MPs when articulating their demands. It is true that there are variations in the patterns of interest as between the regions, but this only leads to the conclusion that it is the lack of success which varies, for generally speaking, the drawing of the English regional boundaries has not produced areas with which MPs identify. This may reflect the lack of any substantial political or administrative machinery associated with he planning regions, as the comparative evidence from Scotland and Wales suggests, or it may be that regional boundaries have been drawn in such a way that they fail to acknowledge or accommodate the existence of large areas with competing claims for consideration, as the percentage of sub-regional speeches suggests. Finally, it might be that, for a number of English Regions such as the South East, there is no characteristic feature which is sufficiently strong or important to produce an identification with the region, or with any other area within the region, and no effective use has been made of the region which might have had the effect of promoting interest. Although the evidence gained from the study of Members' speeches does not of itself warrant firm conclusions as to the reasons for such lack of interest, it can be said that the evidence shows that Members adopt a variety of focuses when speaking on regional policy. Nor surprisingly, given their roles as elected representatives of their constituences, these issues are frequently discussed in constituency terms. When MPs employ a wider geographical focus, they appear to make little use of the government's Economic Planning Regions as a framework for channelling demands. expressions of support, or other views to the centre. Further, in a significant number of cases MPs adopt their own labelling of regions or sub-regions which do not correspond to the planning regions and use these as a framework for the articulation of their views.

CHAPTER 11

The debate on regional reform

MICHAEL KEATING

THE theme of regionalism is a recurring one in writings on British Government and regional solutions have been advocated for a wide variety of problems. Yet the subject continues to be surrounded with confusion and the terms and concepts used continue to suffer from lack of rigorous definition. As Nevil Johnson has commented, 'we have a feeble grasp of the potential relationship between territory and power'.[1] There is a recognized rationale for local government in terms of local choice over divisible services and a tradition of municipal self-government to sustain it. What is lacking, however, is a well-developed theory of the state and the division of power within it, and a theory of intermediate administration, between the centre and the locality, such as are found both in federal states and in unitary states such as France. Thus there has been no common starting point for arguments about regionalism.

This chapter reviews the major arguments about regional reform this century, attempts to disentangle the values underlying the arguments and finally considers the arguments and possible future developments in terms of five models of regional administration.

THE SOURCES OF THE DEBATE

Four general values seem to underlie the academic and political arguments about regional reform. These are efficiency and effectiveness in government; accountability; local autonomy; and territorial justice. Of course, these values are difficult to specify and operationalize and their use has reflected the interests of the protagonists to the debate but they provide a useful starting point because most of the arguments advanced can be seen to be concerned with maximizing one or more of these. The sources of the debate can usefully be considered under five headings. The first of these concerns demands from the regions themselves, either for autonomy or for a larger share of resources in the name of some form of territorial justice. While both of these are 'regionalist', they differ in their constitutional implications, demands for resource allocation being implicitly or explicitly centralist as only the centre is in a position to redistribute. Secondly, there is the argument, heard especially in periods of reform and expansion in government, that both democracy and efficiency can be improved by devolving power from the centre—democracy through greater local autonomy and participation, and efficiency through reducing congestion at the centre and increasing the accountability of government. Thirdly, there is the concern about the proliferation of *ad hoc* bodies at the regional level and of regional arms of central government. Their existence has often been accepted as demonstrating the appropriateness, on grounds of efficiency and effectiveness, of the regional level for the allocation of certain functions of government but, because they do not fit into the traditional models of central or local government, these regional institutions are attacked as undemocratic, i.e. not reflecting local preferences or unaccountable. Fourthly, there has been, from time to time, interest in regional planning. This has arisen from geographers' conceptions of the region as an appropriate unit for planning and from the status of the region as a meeting place for types and levels of governmental institutions which need to plan and co-ordinate their activities for the sake of effectiveness and efficiency. Fifthly, regionalism has risen in the context of local government reform. Reformers have often sought more 'rational' units, based on economic and social geography, in order to plan, and larger units, to provide a greater resource base and exploit economies of scale in service provision. Efficiency and effectiveness would, it is claimed be enhanced and, as a result of this the local authorities would enjoy greater control over their environment and thus increased autonomy.

Prescriptions for regional reform have often confused these arguments or sought to serve contradictory purposes. At the same time, much of the writing on the subject has been incomplete, written from limited disciplinary perspectives. Thus planners and economists have often emphasized planning and industrial needs based upon notions of efficiency but have failed to recognize the existence of conflicts of value and interest and the need for political means for their resolution. Political scientists and politicians, on the other hand, have often emphasized local autonomy and accountability, skimming over difficult questions about the allocation of responsibilities for industrial and economic questions and their relation to efficiency and territorial justice.

THE DEBATE ON REGIONALISM

The first modern stirrings of interest in regionalism came before the First World War. In 1905, the Fabian Society launched their *New Heptarchy* series with W. Saunders' *Municipalisation by Provinces*.[2] Although often hailed as a prescription for devolution, Saunders' scheme in fact involved a greater centralization of transit, electricity, and water services under regional *ad hoc* boards. In many ways, the pamphlet foreshadows modern developments, not least in its advocacy of indirect election to secure the most 'efficient persons' for the boards. The impetus for the Fabian scheme came from dissatisfaction with the inability of local government as then organized to discharge these and other modern functions efficiently—a theme which was to recur with increasing frequency.

Around the First World War, there was a flurry of interest in regionalism stemming from concern about local government and the current theme of Home Rule All Round. As a contribution to the Home Rule debate, the geographer C. B. Fawcett produced *Provinces of England*,[3] which appeared in 1919. This drew up, on the basis of geographical factors, provinces into which England should be divided but said little about the powers of provincial councils. The interest in Home Rule and concern about the overload on government at the centre in view of the added responsibilities of the state led to the establishment of a Speaker's Conference on devolution in 1919-20.

This reached a surprising degree of agreement on the powers which could be given to devolved governments but not on their membership. As the two schemes which emerged both treated England as a unit for devolved government, they cannot strictly be considered as exercises in regionalism, and, in any case, the political impetus for devolution died down after the Irish Treaty.

Shortly afterwards, the distinction between regionalism for the purpose of central government administration and regionalism for local government purposes was asserted by G. D. H. Cole. In *The Future of Local Government*[4] he complained that the two had been confused and, while dismissing 'any proposal to set up a dozen or so "Parliaments" (as) manifestly absurd",[5] called for regional authorities at a level which we could recognize as the city-region or remodelled county.

While interest in devolution largely died out between the wars, concern with the problems of local government led many writers back to the case for city-regions. In the late 1930s, too, concern about the plight of the depressed regions brought the question of regional balance and regional development to the fore. The Commissioners for Special Areas, appointed in 1935, may have achieved little in practical terms, but they helped to bring regional problems to the attention of government and commentators on government. Two offshoots of their work, in particular, contributed to the debate. In 1937, a Royal Commission on Local Government in Tyneside[6] recommended the creation of a new county for the whole conurbation. In 1940, the Royal Commission on the Distribution of the Industrial Population[7] linked the issue of the economically depressed regions with that of the reform of local government advocating regional councils but without going into detail about their size or functions.

During the Second World War, interest in regionalism increased greatly as a result of the continuing interest in regional development, now seen in the context of post-war reconstruction; a revived concern about the inadeqacies of the existing local government structure, especially in the conurbations; the fashion for planning; and the experience of the wartime Commissioners for Civil Defence. There were ten of these

Commissioners in England, responsible for areas of 'provincial' size, with the task of co-ordinating defence work in the regions. They were assisted by regional offices of the main departments of government and, in the event of a complete breakdown of communications, were to assume full responsibility for the government of their respective regions.[8] Although their full potential powers were, in the event, never exercised, the commissioner system was unpopular, especially with local government, and there was a general determination that, after the war, both the Commissioners themselves and the large regions for which they were responsible should be swept away.[9] As Blackburn put it,

I know of nothing which would excite more unanimous opposition from all existing local authorities than a suggestion of regional administration on the scale of the Civil Defence regions, which would entirely remove the 'local' from all local government's major functions. It would be quite out of touch with the people . . . its administrative machinery would be unwieldy and bureaucratic, rather than democratic, control would be inevitable.[10]

Thus the debate during and after the War concentrated on the reform of local government and city-regionalism, though there were some efforts, such as those of the geographer Gilbert[11] to promote interest in a wider conception of regionalism. Among a spate of advocates of city-regions for planning purposes were Self, Blackburn, Robson, Taylor, Dickinson, the Labour Party, and NALGO,[12] with the latter also seeing a need for indirectly elected provincial councils. G. D. H. Cole returned to the subject, again stressing the distinction between regional organization for the purposes of central government administration, which would require regions of the scale for those of civil defence and regions for local planning, which should be based on the conurbations and counties.[13] Little came of all this. A Local Government Boundary Commission was appointed in 1945 but was dissolved in 1949 with none of its recommendations adopted.[14] In 1946, the Treasury attempted to introduce some uniformity into central government's arrangements by establishing nine 'standard regions', a measure which met with only limited success. Meanwhile, the regional arrangements made by the new nationalized industries further complicated the picture.

After the failure of the post-war local government reform movement, interest in regionalism died down. Government, too, became less regionally conscious in the 1950s, running down its own regional offices[15] and its regional economic policy.

The 1960s saw another revival of interest in regionalism, stemming from the renewed vogue for planning, the continuing shortcomings of the local government structure, concern about the depressed regions and, from the late 1960s, the revival of Scottish and Welsh nationalism. Those elements of the debate were to become increasingly confused.

The concern about regional development arose in the early 1960s. In 1962, Lord Hailsham was given special responsibility for the North of England and in 1963 regional development plans were produced by the Government for Central Scotland and North East England but these were essentially *ad hoc* 'one off' measures. Although indicative economic planning machinery had been re-established in the form of the NEDC in 1962, the lack of a regional dimension to its work was widely criticized. However, while there was a wide consensus on the need for regional development machinery, there was little agreement on what form it should take or what should be its relationship to central and local government. The Steering Group for the *Buchanan Report on Traffic in Towns*[16] adopted a highly technocratic approach, proceeding from the need to deal with traffic, to the need to redevelop urban areas, to advocating Regional Development Agencies which, operating at the level of the city-region, would largely displace the local authorities in this area. Peter Self[17] also argued for regional development corporations but, with a greater awareness of the political implications of the proposal, said that, ideally, they should be responsible to elected (city) regional governments. This would help to end the divorce between economic and physical planning and the confusion of planning responsibilities among different departments of central government. The policy of the Conservative Government was to support the idea of regional development but not regional government. As Sir Keith Joseph put it in 1964,

Regional plans yes; regional development yes; but these do not necessarily involve regional government in the sense of regional representative councils. What they do involve is strong regional arms of central government and a reorganised, more effective local government system.[18]

The Labour Party, too, saw regional planning as largely a function of central government. In the debate on the *Buchanan Report*, their spokesman, Michael Stewart, made this clear,

What we are driven to is that somewhere in our structure of government there has to be something which is not there already—really effective operation of regional representatives of central government.

We can leave open the question of whether they should be politicians or regional ministers . . . or whether they ought to be highly placed regional officials . . . My other reason for rejecting building up from local authorities is that, in the region, we are executing national policy.[19]

It is thus not surprising that local government should have regarded the proposed regional machinery with suspicion, as a means of tightening central control. Accordingly, when Labour came into power and established its regional machinery, it made several concessions. Development Corporations at the city-region level were not set up. Instead, at the 'provincial' level, the regional apparatus of Whitehall departments was strengthened and regional officials brought together in non-executive Regional Economic Planning Boards. These were to work with Regional Economic Planning Councils which would consist of persons chosen for their expertise and representatives of regional interests. There were two crucial ambiguities in the machinery from the outset. To calm the fears of local planning authorities and the Ministry of Housing and Local Government, the word 'economic' had been inserted in the titles of the councils and boards. This brought into question the role of the regional machinery in breaking down the barriers between physical and economic planning. Secondly, it was unclear from the constitution of the councils and the boards whether they were meant to achieve planning from the top down or from the bottom up, or to provide a meeting place for centre and locality. Some members of the Government appear to have seen the machinery as the basis for a future system of regional government but, in the event, the tension between the 'top-downwards' and the 'bottom-upwards' elements was resolved in favour of the former.[20] With the demise of the National Plan in 1966, regional economic planning, too, dwindled into insignificance.

The 1960s and 1970s also saw the re-emergence of the idea of the city-region as a solution to the problems of local government structure and demands for the devolution of power from the centre, the latter stimulated by the successes of Scottish and Welsh nationalism. However, disputes arose as to whether these two questions and the problems of regional economic planning were amenable to a common solution or should be treated separately. John Mackintosh, in a powerful pleas for reform,[21] argued for regional authorities at a 'provincial' level which could draw powers from both central and local government and plan the economic and physical development of their regions. The Liberal Party argued in a similar vein, as did the *Economist*.[22] Derek Senior,[23] on the other hand, distinguished between provinces, which he saw as appropriate to central government administration, and smaller city-regions, on which local government and planning should be based—an echo of Cole's earlier arguments.

In his Memorandum of Dissent to the report of the Royal Commission on Local Government,[24] Senior expanded these views. He proposed that the local government system should be based on thirty-five city-regions, with second-tier districts below them. The city-region, he considered, was the correct unit for planning purposes but tended to be too large for the provision of personal services, making a unitary system, as desired by the majority of the Commission, impossible. Senior also recognized the importance of the 'provincial' level for strategic planning and the need for a 'bridge' between central government, which had tended to be concerned with inter-regional economic planning, and local government, with its concern with intra-regional land use planning. There was a need to bring these two together, both territorially, at the provincial level and functionally, by breaking down the distinction between economic and land-use planning. The bridge could be provided by Ministers of State in each of five provinces, advised by an appointed council, drawn partly from local government. The provincial council would draw up a provincial plan, which it would submit to the Ministry to be 'reconciled with other regional plans. The resulting national strategy would be used as a basis for the approval of local authorities' structure plans.'[25] What is of interest here is the simultaneous awareness of the needs of national economic management and of local planning and the concept of the 'bridge' between the two levels of government, as an alternative to the idea of building a third tier of government as the 'intermediate' level. However, his description of the planning process might be criticized as being rather circular and the underlying assumption of political consensus begs important questions about the political control of planning.

The majority of the Redcliffe-Maud Commission also saw a need for organization between their proposed unitary authorities and national government. For this, they proposed 'provincial' councils at the level of the Economic Planning Regions, to co-ordinate the plans of local authorities at the strategic level. Their powers would be few and their status, based upon indirect election, uncertain, but this section of the report was taken up by regionalists as showing the need for organization at this level.

While the Redcliffe-Maud Commission was still sitting, the Government, worried about nationalist pressure in Scotland and Wales, established the Royal Commission on the Constitution, under Lord Crowther, who was later succeeded by Lord Kilbrandon. The terms of reference of the commissions on local government in England and Scotland and of the Commission on the Constitution and their interpretation illustrate well the lack of serious thinking about the relationship of power and territory in British political debate. For, while the terms of reference of the local government commissions restricted them to the existing functions of local government and thus ruled out devolution from the centre, the Commission on the Constitution contained in its terms no reference to local government, so precluding a recommendation of regional authorities drawing powers upwards from local government. The justification for this was that neither commission could trespass on the area of the other but this could equally be seen as a reason for creating a single commission or for dealing with the regional level and the allocation of powers first.

Despite its inability to look at local government structure, the Kilbrandon Commission[26] did produce proposals for English regional government. The signatories of the majority report divided three ways, with two members favouring 'executive devolution' to regional councils, eight favouring regional co-ordinating and advisory councils, partly indirectly elected by the local authorities and partly nominated, and one favouring a scheme of co-ordinating committees of local authorities. Perhaps of more interest was the minority report, by Lord Crowther-Hunt and Professor Peacock.[27] They discerned a regional level of government already in existence, consisting of the regional outposts of central government and the various *ad hoc* authorities, and proposed a system of elected regional councils to bring this level of government under control. Their reasoning has been criticized[28] for not distinguishing, as writers such as Cole and Senior had, between central government's regionally based functions in pursuit of national or inter-regional objectives and functions which can be organized on a purely intra-regional basis. However, their criticism of 'unaccountable' regional bodies added weight to arguments for regional government.

Despite this, however, regional government attracted little interest in England. The Government issued a discussion paper[29] which merely summarized possible schemes derived from Kilbrandon, without commitment. From the mid 1970s, however, the issue of territorial justice became more important, particularly among MPs and councillors in the north of England, where concern grew at the twin dangers of favouritism to Scotland in the form of devolution and the Scottish Development Agency and the run-down of regional policy as the recession began to affect formerly prosperous areas in the Midlands and the South. However, this regionalism suffered from a lack of focus, the campaigners undecided on whether the aim was to block Scottish devolution or to gain devolution for the North of England, to stop Scotland getting extra resources or to secure extra resources and a development agency for themselves.[30]

One group which did seem to have clear objectives was the Campaign for the North, a group whose aim was to create in the North of England the same sort of pressure which had secured so much for Scotland. However, this involved creating a somewhat artificial 'northern nationalism' and a great deal of dubiously relevant historical delving to try and demonstrate that the North could be equated with Scotland and that

England had never comprised a political unit. The Campaign also failed to develop a coherent economic strategy, merely asserting that UK regional policy had failed and implying that a self-governing Northern Region would actually be better off without it, in an attempt to link two separate elements of regionalism—the desire for more self-government and the desire for more resources.[31] Despite the adhesion of some Liberal and Labour MPs, the Campaign failed to gain widespread support.

In 1975, the Labour Party started a review of its policy on regional government. Partly, this was a reaction to the devolution proposals for Scotland and Wales but the main impetus came from opposition to the Conservative reforms of 1974 which had created the 'undemocratic' *ad hoc* regional health and water authorities and the two-tier system of local government. In particular, Labour controlled former county boroughs were resentful of the loss of powers to Conservative counties and were pushing for 'organic change' as a step to single-tier local government. The replacement of the counties by provincial-scale regions was seen as one way of achieving this. Following a discussion document.[32] the 1976 Party Programme included a commitment to

A dozen directly elected regional authorities, responsible for planning and for infrastructure development . . . they should take over from the *ad hoc* authorities for water and sewerage, health and economic planning, plus certain powers devolved from central government, certain of them already decentralised in the various departments' regional offices.[33]

In 1977, the National Executive Committee issued a more detailed document,[34] presenting two possible models for regional assemblies. The 'Local Government Model' would set up elected regional authorities for strategic planning, allocation of capital resources, and the provision of public facilities of a 'regional' nature, e.g. arts and sports centres, regional health administration (possibly), fire, police, and (possibly) universities. Local Government would retain its direct links with Whitehall, except that capital allocations would become a regional responsibility. The 'Welsh Model' provided for regional authorities with the powers of the proposed Welsh Assembly. This would involve taking over both central government responsibilities for the supervision of local government and central government executive responsibilities for health, personal

social services, housing, physical planning and the environment, roads and road transport, natural resources, and tourism.
Regional authorities would also take over the executive functions of the nominated *ad hoc* authorities, which would then
be abolished. They would also take over executive responsibility for the intra-regional allocation of capital resources
among services, as well as among local authorities and, with
the abolition of the counties, would take over those county
functions not allocated to districts.

The consultation document was discussed at regional conferences of the Party and produced widespread sentiment in
favour of Elected Regional Authorities (ERAs), especially in
the North, North West, and West Midlands. A 'fair degree of
regional self-consciousness' was found except in the South
East. There was, however, little agreement on the powers of
ERAs, except as a solution to the problem of *ad hoc* authorities and, in the North, as agencies for economic development, as a counterweight to the Scottish Assembly. In many
cases, the response was inconsistent, with delegates accepting
the case for ERAs but not wanting to take powers away from
a Labour Government or Labour-controlled counties. The
strongest strand in the responses was the opposition to the two-
tier system of local government and support for 'organic change'.

In the Party as a whole, there were strong interests working
against a radical change to elected regional government. The
Health Service unions resisted the proposal to bring the NHS
under ERAs, preferring to push for industrial democracy in
the service and local councillors resisted any suggestion of
subjecting local government to the regional tier, thus preju-
dicing its direct links with central government. Further, the
hydrologically determined boundaries of the water authorities
were not considered appropriate for any other function. Without control over health, water, or local government, ERAs
would lose much of their *raison d'être*. Against this, there was
no powerful force pushing *for* regional government.

In view of the mixed reaction to the proposals, the Party's
officers concluded that the only possible solution was to adopt
an 'organic' approach to the regional problem as well as the
local government one. Plans were floated for just two regional
authorities, for the North and for Yorkshire and Humberside,

on the ground that opinion in these regions was favourable and that no major boundary problems arose with the *ad hoc* authorities. The experience of these authorities in action might crystallize opinion elsewhere. This did not meet with the approval of the NEC and the only firm commitment made was to 'organic change' at the local level.

WHITHER REGIONAL REFORM?

All the years of debate about regionalism in England have produced very little in practical terms. The 1974 reform of local government took little cognizance of the regional principle, except in the metropolitan counties, where a truncated version of the city-region has been accepted for planning purposes. The failure of the Scottish and Welsh devolution plans has undermined the case for regional devolution which never, in any case, gathered much political support. Regional planning at the provincial scale has faltered and the abolition of the Regional Economic Planning Councils in 1979 has meant a reduction in the potential regional input to planning. Inter-regional industrial location policy, too, has been run down. It is possible, therefore, to take stock of the debate at this point and note the major outstanding questions and confusions, some of which are highlighted by the Labour Party debate.

The most obvious confusion remaining concerns the meaning of the term 'region'. While geographers and economists have been able to develop fairly precise operational definitions in terms of physical features and patterns of activity, students of politics and administration have had difficulty relating their concerns to these definitions and to the existing structure of government. Often, the terms 'regional' has been used in the study of government to refer to all institutions which cover areas larger than those of local authorities but smaller than the whole country. We have traced two principal meanings, the 'city-region' and the 'province'. The former is reasonably well understood and has formed the basis for recommendations for local government reform in England and Scotland. The latter, which has formed the basis for recommendations for devolution from the centre, requires much more rigorous definition if the potential relationship between territory and power is further to be explored.

Another area requiring further theoretical development is the relationship between territory and function. British local government has long been based on the formal principle that each tier of government must be statutorily independent and have responsibility for a defined range of functions. The complementary principle is that for each function of government there is an optimum size of territory and population. The reforms of the 1970s, which established two-tier systems of local government in England, Scotland, and Wales, maintained this principle, though the difficulties of putting it into effect gave rise to scepticism about its validity. There was, for instance, a difference of opinion within the Department of Education and Science about the optimum size for an education authority[35] while the water function was thought to require areas unsuitable for any other function. Other objections to the principle of division by function are that it runs contrary to modern aspirations for a more corporate approach in both central and local government and that the traditional functional divisions often fail to correspond to the problems arising in the community. The difficulties of maintaining a functional division of power have led students of federalism on to the more fruitful approach of 'intergovernmental relations' which concentrates on policy problems and power relations in government. Yet, very often, the question of regional reform has been approached as a problem of redistribution of functions. Such approaches, as the Labour Party's experience shows, soon run into the ground as it is discovered that there are no regional units optimal for all functions and that existing organizations often represent not only functionally appropriate units but also the power base of actors in the intergovernmental relations game. This is not to deny totally the functional principle. Operational efficiency can be improved by establishing service delivery agencies of the right size and the planning function does require an appropriate territory. The autonomy of units of government can be enhanced where they possess functions which are to a large extent self-contained. What is being denied is that such functions are usual, that the functional principle can be paramount in regional reform and that it can yield definitive solutions. As well as seeing regional reform in terms of the allocation of government functions, we need to see it in terms of maximizing the autonomy and power of groups of people, in communities or regions. This in turn, depends on political value judgements and on the nature of regional demands and aspirations.

The confusion here concerns the relationship between local autonomy and territorial justice as elements in regionalism. Some writers have suggested that there is a desire among people in the English regions for greater self-government. This belief underlay the recommendations of some members of the Kilbrandon Commission, although Kilbrandon's survey evidence on the desire for English devolution can be questioned on the ground that respondents were presented with the option of increased local power without any of the costs attached. Senior, on the other hand, has said that "Regionalism" in England, indeed, reflects dissatisfaction with our failure to achieve nationwide uniformity in standards of living, rather than any hankering for the social and economic diversity of provincial home rule.'[36] So, while some writers maintain that there is a drive to regional equality parallel with the drive to social and economic equality, others see a drive for regional diversity. For the latter, the problem arises as to how to reconcile this with the commitment of the welfare state to equity and equal provision. One answer is to separate the principle of territorial equity from that of social and economic equity, so that inter-regional equity would prevail though intra-regional allocations might differ. This would, of course, create inequity as between similar social groups in different regions. Whether this would be acceptable would depend on whether there is indeed within the regions widespread frustration at the present pattern of resource allocation and political support for those wishing to change it. Only when the issues of regional autonomy and central control are presented in such a way as to reveal both costs and benefits will it be possible to answer this question.

To clarify these issues and appraise the many proposals for reform which have been made, we will now look at five ideal-type models of regional administration which emerge from the debate. It will then be possible to see how they serve the values mentioned earlier and how far the differing approaches are compatible.

Firstly, we can see regional administration as an integral part of central government, an extension of central government departments into the regions. There have been advocates of this approach to regionalism among politicians at the centre who have seen regional machinery as a way in which an increasingly interventionist state can secure the implementation of its policies. Michael Stewart and Keith Joseph in the 1960s illustrate this approach and it has been argued[37] that many of the existing regional institutions should be seen in this light. The question of distribution of functions in this model does not arise as tasks are allocated purely according to operational convenience. There is not necessarily conflict between territorial and social equity as all resource allocation decisions are taken at the centre. Problems can arise, however, over co-ordination and over relations with local government. In so far as it is impractical for all co-ordination of government activity to take place in Whitehall, some discretion must be given to field offices to reallocate resources and mediate conflicts. If that is the case, local authorities are likely to resent the power of regional officials and raise questions about their accountability. The logic of this model is that it should develop into a full prefectoral system, but this has never seriously been advocated in peace time because of the strength of the traditions of autonomous local government and because of the unwillingness of politicians and officials at the centre to build a unified and unitary state machine which would involve them accepting responsibility for the minutiae of politics. This unwillingness has persisted despite some grand ambitions of the centre exemplified by Labour's proposals for economic planning in the 1960s and the Conservative plans to control local expenditure in the 1980s. In any case, the functional fragmentation of government responsibilities at the centre and ministers' individual responsibilities would render the creation of a prefectoral system very difficult.

Secondly, we can see the region as an arena for local government. Regional machinery has sometimes been advocated as a means of dealing with problems which transcend local authority boundaries, such as housing overspill or land-use planning, or as a method for the joint discharge of functions where economies of scale are available. Several of our writers, including the Redcliffe-Maud Commission, have advocated regional administration of this type, involving weak institutions with little independent power or effect on central-local relations. Others have wished to reconstitute local government itself on a regional basis. Usually this has involved the city-region, as a unit with geographical, social, and economic coherence within which many problems arise and can be resolved. This regional reform of local government can increase functional effectiveness and local autonomy. Generally, the 'province' type of region has been seen as too large for this purpose and lacking in the community base of local government and authorities based upon it as representing a diminution of local autonomy.

Thirdly, we can see the regional administration as 'intermediate', a 'bridge' between central and local government. It has been argued[38] that some of the existing regional institutions can be seen as intermediate but, with the notable exception of Derek Senior, few advocates of regional reform have attempted to develop the concept. As intermediate administration, the region could provide a meeting place for bodies representing diverse constituencies, defined both functionally and geographically and provide for co-ordination and mediation of differences. For this purpose, regional institutions should not be independent or possess legitimacy in themselves, but should be dependent on central and local institutions. The contributions and procedures of some existing institutions which appear 'intermediate' such as the RWAs, do not provide for this as their members, instead of operating in a representative capacity, are expected to develop a 'corporate' responsibility. Matters which could be dealt with through such machinery include the reconciliation of local and central objectives at the level of regional planning, the co-ordination of central, industrial, and local land-use planning, and the reconciliation of central and local priorities in higher education and health planning. Proposals for intermediate government have often been flawed by the assumption of consensus between centre and locality which allows their advocates to avoid the question of power relations. It would be more realistic in this model to recognize conflicts and differing objectives between centre and locality and to see regional institutions as an element in a complex process of intergovernmental relations involving two-way channels of influence and a bargaining process. Regional institutions would then be a channel of influence, a neutral meeting ground and perhaps a means of carrying out agreed tasks falling clearly neither to the centre nor to the locality.

The fourth and fifth models are of the region as a third level of government, inserted between the centre and the locality and independent of both. This approach depends on a number of assumptions about the regions. Usually, but not necessarily, its advocates have maintained that there are identifiable functions of government best performed at the regional level. These may include functions already vested in regional institutions as well as functions currently vested in local or central government. A more important assumption is that there is a demand within the regions for distinctive policies or combinations of policies and that inter-regional diversity, possibly combined with broad inter-regional equity in the global allocation of resources, is to be preferred to equity within given social groups across the whole nation. Further, it is usually believed that it is desirable to limit the power of the central government by devolving it to lower levels.

There are at least two approaches to the creation of a third tier of government. Our fourth model, associated with Peacock and Crowther-Hunt, takes existing regional institutions, which they see as already constituting a level of government, as its base. This level of government is seen as violating democratic norms of responsibility and accountability as found in British central and local government. The answer is to bring it within the pale of the constitution by placing it under the control of elected regional assemblies. The difficulty with this is that, as has been argued,[39] the existing institutions are mainly part of the centre or intermediate and that an elected third tier of government could neither perform the centre's inter-regional functions nor, because it would possess its own electoral constituency, act as a bridge between centre and locality or the public and private sectors. Indeed, it might itself require further sets of bridges, mechanisms linking it to central and local government and 'quangos' linking it to independent arenas such as that of the arts.

The fifth, more radical model, associated with J. P. Mackintosh, involved the redistribution of functions throughout government. Elected regional authorities would take over many of the responsibilities of central government and would make their own arrangements for systems of local government beneath them and subordinate to them. The traditional centre-local relationships would be replaced by centre-region relationships. The underlying rationale for such a reform is the devolution of power from the centre by the creation of politically powerful authorities representing distinctive regional constituencies. The regional authorities would not only administer the affairs of their own regions but would be a constraint on the autonomy and power of the centre. This model is thus effectively federalist and is the only one which really challenges the unitary state.

These are of course, ideal-type models of regional administration and in any system, complex patterns of inter-relations will develop. However, it is important to be clear, in relation to any proposed reforms, which model is appropriate and what values are to be maximized. So the first model might be seen an appropriate vehicle for maximizing efficiency and effectiveness, territorial justice, and possibly, through strict line management, accountability, but not local autonomy. The second model might promote greater local autonomy and effectiveness but not accountability and is of little relevance to territorial justice. The third model could serve to promote efficiency and, by providing non-hierarchical means of resolving centre-local differences, local autonomy. The fourth model is designed to overcome problems of accountability and to increase local autonomy. It may also serve to increase efficiency and effectiveness but raises serious questions about territorial justice. The same can be said of the fifth model, which would further raise questions about the functional effectiveness of central government in its remaining responsibilities.

We have not attempted here to build a new prescriptive theory of regional government but we have at least established that some of the approaches to regional reform in the past have been incompatible and that a much sounder base is needed for future proposals. This must include a well-developed approach not only to the question of regions but also to the nature of the centre and the state itself.

Notes

CHAPTER 1

[1] See also Ian McAllister, Richard Parry, and Richard Rose, 'United Kingdom Rankings: The Territorial Dimension in Social Indicators', *Studies in Public Policy*, No. 44 (Glasgow: University of Strathclyde, 1979). *Regional Statistics* (HMSO, annually) provides a wealth of social and economic data for the English standard regions and for Scotland, Wales, and Northern Ireland.

[2] See the discussion of various definitions and concepts of 'region' in John Glasson, *An Introduction to Regional Planning*, 2nd edition (London: Hutchinson, 1978) Chapter 2.

[3] See e.g. Harry W. Richardson (ed.), *Regional Economics: A Reader* (London: Macmillan, 1970); L. Needleman (ed.), *Regional Analysis* (Harmondsworth: Penguin, 1968).

[4] Glasson, *An Introduction to Regional Planning*, pp. 35–6.

[5] See C. Brett, 'The Lessons of Devolution in Northern Ireland', *Political Quarterly*, vol. 41, 1970, pp. 261–80.

[6] D. Birrell and A. Murie, *Policy and Government in Northern Ireland* (Dublin: Gill and Macmillan, 1980).

[7] Brian W. Hogwood, 'The Tartan Fringe: Quangos and other assorted animals in Scotland', *Studies in Public Policy*, No. 34 (Glasgow: University of Strathclyde, 1979).

[8] First Report from the Committee on Welsh Affairs, Session 1979–80, *The Role of the Welsh Office and Associated Bodies in Developing Employment Opportunities in Wales, Volume 2: Minutes of Evidence and Appendices*, HC 731-II/485, Q. 1448.

[9] Richard Parry, 'Territory and Public Employment: A General Model and British Evidence', *Journal of Public Policy*, vol. 1, No. 2 (1981).

[10] I attempt to unravel similar issues in the context of Scottish devolution in Brian W. Hogwood, 'Models of Industrial Policy: The Implications for Devolution', *Studies in Public Policy*, No. 5, (Glasgow: University of Strathclyde, 1977), pp. 19–23.

[11] See Nevil Johnson, *In Search of the Constitution* (London: Methuen, 1977), pp. 89–90.

[12] See Johnson, *In Search of the Constitution*, p. 89; L. J. Sharpe, 'Modernising the Localities: Local Government in Britain and Some Comparisons with France,' in J. Lagroye and V. Wright (eds.), *Local Government in Britain and France* (London: Allen & Unwin, 1979), p. 43.

[13] See R. A. W. Rhodes, 'Research into Central-Local Relations in Britain: A Framework for Analysis', in Social Science Research Council, *Central-Local Government Relationships* (London: SSRC, 1979); R. A. W. Rhodes, 'Analysing intergovernmental relations', *European Journal of Political Research*, vol. 8 (1980)

pp. 289–322; A. Maass, *Area and Power: A Theory of Local Government* (Glencoe, Illinois: Free Press, 1959); Deil S. Wright, *Understanding Intergovernmental Relations* (North Scituate, Massachusetts: Duxbury Press, 1978). Similarly the operation in practice of the French system reflects the interdependence of the prefects and the local notables; see M. Crozier and Jean-Claude Thoenig, 'The regulation of complex organised systems', *Administrative Science Quarterly*, vol. 2 (1976) pp. 547–70.

[14] See A. Barker, D. C. Hague and W. J. M. Mackenzie (eds.), *Public Policy and Private Interests: The Institutions of Compromise* (London: Macmillan, 1975); A. Barker (ed.), *Quangos in Britain* (London: Macmillan, 1982).

[15] Maass, *Area and Power*, p. 16.

[16] According to Wright, *Understanding Intergovernmental Relations*, pp. 46–7, the term 'marble cake' was created in the early 1940s by Professor Joseph McLean, but was popularized by Morton Grodzins, 'The Federal System', in *Goals for Americans: Report of the President's Commission on National Goals and Chapters Submitted for the Consideration of the Commission* (Prentice-Hall, Spectrum, 1960) pp. 265–82.

[17] Grodzins, 'The Federal System', p. 265, quoted in Wright, *Understanding Intergovernmental Relations*, p. 47.

[18] Grodzins, 'The Federal System', p. 266, quoted in Wright, *Understanding Intergovernmental Relations*, p. 47–8.

[19] Rhodes, 'Research into Centre-Local Relations'.

[20] cf. J. D. Thompson, *Organisations in Action* (New York: McGraw Hill, 1967).

[21] Edward Page, 'Grant Consolidation and the Development of Intergovernmental Relations in the United States and the United Kingdom' (paper prepared for the Fifth Conference of the PSA Workgroup on United Kingdom Politics, Cardiff, September 1980) makes similar points in relation to the analysis of centre-local government relations in Britain, especially pp. 22–5.

[22] J. J. Richardson and A. G. Jordan, *Governing under Pressure* (Oxford: Martin Robertson, 1979) pp. 109–13.

[23] Richardson and Jordan, *Governing under Pressure*, p. 113.

[24] My thanks to Bleddyn Davies for his comment which led me to develop this point. See also F. Wirt, 'Professionalism and Political Conflict', *Journal of Public Policy*, vol. 1 (1981) pp. 61–93.

[25] For an overview of explanations of the growth of public expenditure see P. D. Larkey, C. Stolp, and M. Winer, 'Theorizing About the Growth of Government: A Research Assessment', *Journal of Public Policy*, vol. 1, No. 2 (1981).

[26] Jim Bulpitt, 'Territory and Power: Some Existing Approaches Assessed', paper presented to the Fourth Annual Conference of PSA Work Group on United Kingdom Politics, Warwick, 1979, especially pp. 16–17.

CHAPTER 2

[1] We would like to thank those in a large number of government departments and other public organizations who have provided us with information about their regional organizations.

[2] For a much earlier attempt to measure the use of regional boundaries, see W. Thornhill (ed.), *The Case for Regional Reform* (London: Nelson, 1972) pp. 96–9.

[3] Memorandum by the Treasury to the Select Committee on Estimates in *Sixth Report of the Select Committee on Estimates: Regional Organisation of Government Departments*, HC 233, Session 1953/54 (HMSO, 1954).

[4] See B. C. Smith, *Regionalism in England: Regional Institutions: A Guide* (London: Acton Society Trust, 1964).

[5] For a discussion of the failure of regional economic planning see the chapter on the framework of regional planning by Peter Lindley in this volume and also M. Watson, 'The regional dimension of planning', and M. Wright and S. Young, 'Regional planning in Britain', both in J. Hayward and M. Watson (eds.), *Planning Politics and Public Policy* (Cambridge: Cambridge University Press, 1975), pp. 237–48. For evidence of the continued proliferation of boundaries see Commission on the Constitution, *Written Evidence* vol. 4 (HMSO, 1970).

[6] See especially A. Dunsire, C. Hood, and K. S. Thompson, *Measuring Administrative Structure in British Government*, Occasional Paper No. 3, Machinery of Government Project (York: Institute of Social and Economic Research, University of York, 1978); and C. Hood, A. Dunsire, and K. S. Thompson, 'So you think you know what government departments are . . .', *Public Administration Bulletin*, No. 27 (1978) pp. 20–32.

[7] Hood *et al.*, 'So you think you know what government departments are . . .'.

[8] See Chapter 3 by Keating and Rhodes on the West Midlands; on the South West, the West Midlands, and Wales, see J. A. Cross, 'The regional decentralisation of British government departments', *Public Administration*, vol. 48 (1970), pp. 423–41. For general discussion see Watson, 'The regional dimension of planning', and Wright and Young, 'Regional planning in Britain'.

[9] See P. Hennessy, *The Times*, 4 November 1979.

[10] See Watson, 'The regional dimension of planning'.

CHAPTER 3

[1] N. Johnson, *In Search of the Constitution: Reflections on State and Society in Britain* (Oxford: Pergamon, 1977), p. 89.

[2] Ibid.

[3] Royal Commission on the Constitution 1969–73, Vol. II, *Memorandum of Dissent* by Lord Crowther-Hunt and Professor A. T. Peacock, Cmnd. 5460-1, (HMSO, 1973), p. 79.

[4] J. P. Mackintosh, *The Government and Politics of Britain* (London: Macmillan), p. 182.

[5] Interview with regional civil servant.

[6] L. A. Gunn and P. Lindley, 'Devolution: Origins, Events and Issues', *Public Administration Bulletin* (1977).

[7] A. Maass, *Area and Power: A Theory of Local Government* (Glencoe, Illinois: Free Press, 1959).

[8] R. A. Dahl, *After the Revolution: Authority in a Good Society* (New Haven and London: Yale University Press, 1970).

[9] Interview with Lord Winstanley, *Guardian*, 29 January 1979.

[10] Royal Commission on the Constitution, *Memorandum of Dissent*, para. 160.

[11] See Chapter 4.

[12] Countryside Commission, *10th Annual Report* (London, 1978).

[13] M. Keating and M. Rhodes, 'Is There a Regional Level of Government in England?', *Studies in Public Policy No. 49*, Centre for the Study of Public Policy, University of Strathclyde, 1979. See also M. Keating and M. Rhodes, 'Looking for "Regional" Government', *Municipal Journal*, 8 August 1980.

[14] R. A. W. Rhodes, *Research into Central-Local Relations in Britain: A Framework for Analysis* (London: Social Science Research Council, 1979).

[15] See Chapter 4.

[16] D. Gillingwater and D. A. Hart (eds), *The Regional Planning Process* (Farnborough: Saxon House, 1978).

[17] J. Friend, J. Power, and K. Yewlett, 'Processes of Public Planning: the regional dimension', in Gillingwater and Hart, op. cit.

[18] A. W. Paterson, 'The Machinery of Economic Planning, 3, Regional Economic Planning Councils and Boards', *Public Administration*, 44 (1966).

[19] A. G. Powell, 'Strategies for the English Regions: Ten Years of Evolution', *Town Planning Review*, vol. 49, no. I (January 1978).

[20] *H. C. Deb.*, Vol. 689, col. 141, 10 February 1964.

[21] J. P. Mackintosh, *The Devolution of Power* (Harmondsworth: Penguin, 1968).

[22] See M. Wright and S. Young, 'Regional Planning in Britain' in J. Hayward and M. Watson (eds.), *Planning, Politics and Public Policy: The British, French and Italian Experience* (Cambridge: Cambridge University Press, 1975).

[23] P. Lindley, 'Regional Planning Studies and Strategies, 1964–76: The National Background', unpublished paper, Civil Service College.

[24] Ibid.

[25] Friend, Power, and Yewlett, 'Processes of Public Planning', p. 113.

[26] Ibid.

CHAPTER 4

[1] This paper has debts quite out of proportion of its length. I am most grateful to the civil servants in London and the regions, and to the local authority politicians and officers who have given their time to answer my questions. In the interests of open government they must, of course, remain anonymous. My thanks also go to those academic colleagues who have discussed earlier drafts of this piece with me. I am of course solely responsible for the remaining inperfections. I hope others will look further both at the issues that are discussed here, and at those which have had to be omitted.

[2] Reports from the Estimates Committee, HC 241, Session 1960–1 (HMSO) p. ix, and Appendix II.

[3] See *Policy for the Inner Cities*, Cmnd 6854 (London: HMSO, 1977); and P. Lawless, *Urban Deprivation and Government Initiative* (London: Faber, 1979) pp. 69ff.

[4] See the Annual Reports under the 1972 Industry Act.

[5] One of the main recommendations of the Central Policy Review Staff's report *Relations Between Central Government and Local Authorities* (HMSO, 1977), was a call for a more corporate interdepartmental approach from central government departments.

[6] See D. Rigby, *The Problems of Operating the Community Land Act*, unpublished dissertation, Manchester University Department of Town and Country Planning.

[7] See *The Effectiveness of Local Plans in Inner Urban Areas*, a paper prepared by B. Adcock, Principal Planner, Wirral MBC, 1979.

[8] J. M. Lee & B. Wood, *The Scope of Local Government Initiative* (Oxford: Martin Robertson, 1974), Chapter 2.

[9] P. Hall *et al*, *The Containment of Urban England* (London: Allen and Unwin, 1973).

[10] Schemes were drawn up later to use Derelict Land Grants to return the site to agricultural use. This was in itself unusual as such grants are normally only available if there is a more tangible after-use.

[11] J. A. G. Griffith, *Central Departments and Local Authorities* (London: Allen and Unwin, 1966) p. 330.

[12] These arrangements were altered by the Local Government, Planning and

Land Act of 1980, which was introduced by the Conservative Secretary of State, Michael Heseltine.

[13] Griffith, *Central Departments*, p. 310.

[14] Ibid., p. 313.

[15] Ibid., p. 310.

[16] W. A. Roberts discusses the West Midlands in the early 1970s in Chapter 9 of *The Reform of Planning Law* (London: Macmillan 1976).

[17] *Municipal Engineering*, 3 June 1980.

[18] See for more detailed discussion, a paper prepared by S. C. Young for the ECPR Conference in March 1980 in Florence, 'British Urban Authorities as Interest Groups'.

[19] The start of this campaign is noted in C. Painter, 'The Repercussion of Administrative Innovation: The West Midlands Economic Planning Council', *Public Administration*, vol. 50 (1972) pp. 467–84.

[20] D. Rigby, *The Problems of Operating the Community Land Act*, pp. 9, 12; and S. Barrett *et al.*, *Implementation of the Community Land Scheme*, SAUS, 1978.

[21] See some of the memoranda presented to the Trade and Industry Sub-Committee of the Expenditure Committee while it produced *The Motor Vehicle Industry* HC 617, Session 1974-5 (London: HMSO) Good examples are T45, T51, T55, and T67, which graphically explain the nature of the decline of the vehicles and associated industries in the West Midlands.

[22] See *HC Debates*, 17 December 1980, cols. 306/7 (WA); *Guardian* Diary, 12 December 1980.

CHAPTER 5

[1] For an overview of all four systems see my chapter in P. Madgwick and R. Rose (eds.) *The Territorial Dimension in United Kingdom Government* (London: Macmillan, forthcoming). I would like to thank the officials who provided me with information and those who have commented on drafts of this and related papers.

[2] See D. Lee, *Regional Planning and the Location of Industry*, revised edition (London: Heinemann, 1970) pp. 7-11.

[3] B. C. Smith, *Regionalism in England: Vol. I: Regional Institutions: A Guide* (Acton Society Trust, 1964).

[4] G. M. Field and P. V. Hills, 'The Administration of Industrial Subsidies', in A. Whiting (ed.), *The Economics of Industrial Subsidies* (HMSO, 1976) p. 5.

[5] Ibid., pp. 7-11.

[6] J. A. Cross, 'The Regional Decentralisation of British Governments', *Public Administration*, vol. 48 (1970) pp. 423-41.

[7] Expenditure Committee (Trade and Industry Sub-Committee), *Regional Development Incentives: Minutes of Evidence (from October 1972 to June 1973) and Appendices* (HMSO, 1973) p. 96.

[8] Field and Hills, 'The Administration of Industrial Subsidies', p. 12; *Eighth Report from the Expenditure Committee, Session 1977–78: Selected Public Expenditure Programmes: Chapter II: Regional and Selective Assistance to Industry*, HC 600-II/281 i and ii, Session 1977/8 (HMSO, 1978), Q. 192-3.

[9] *Eighth Report* 1977/8, Q. 194. It will be noted that the role of the DOI in processing applications for EEC Regional Fund money for industrial projects is not discussed here; this is because it is not regarded as a substantive activity, since funds obtained by the British government in this way from the EEC are simply used to offset expenditure already allocated in the usual way.

[10] *Industry Act 1972 Annual Reports* (HMSO).

[11] Mr Lippitt, Deputy Secretary at DOI, in *Eighth Report* 1977/8.

[12] *Eighth Report* 1977/8, Q. 141-2.

[13] Ibid., Q. 111.

[14] For a discussion of monitoring of industrial assistance, see B. Hogwood, 'Monitoring of Government Involvement in Industry: The Case of Shipbuilding', *Public Administration*, vol. 54 (1976) pp. 409-24.

[15] *Eighth Report from the Expenditure Committee, Session 1975-76: Public Expenditure on Chrysler UK Ltd.: Volume II*, HC 596-II, Session 1975-6 (HMSO, 1976), Q. 3258.

[16] *Third Report from the Committee of Public Accounts*, HC 303, Session 1974 (HMSO, 1974), p. 278.

[17] *Eighth Report*, 1977/8. Q. 131-2.

[18] I am grateful to Stephen Young for pointing this out to me.

[19] *Development Fund Accounts 1973/4*, HC 97, Session 1974-5 and *Development Fund Accounts 1978/9*, HC 395, Session 1979-80 (HMSO). COSIRA ceased to operate in Wales from 1 April 1977.

[20] See Smith, *Regionalism in England*, pp. 78-85.

[21] M. Wright and S. Young, 'Regional Planning in Britain', in J. Hayward and M. Watson (eds.), *Planning Politics and Public Policy* (Cambridge: Cambridge University Press, 1975) p. 238.

CHAPTER 6

(Note: Department of Health and Social Security is indicated by DHSS)

[1] DHSS, *The Administrative Structure of the Medical and Related Services in England and Wales* (HMSO, 1968).

[2] DHSS, *The Future Structure of the National Health Service* (HMSO, 1970).

[3] DHSS, *National Health Service Reorganisation: England* (White paper) (HMSO, 1972) Cmnd. 5055.

[4] DHSS, *Patients First*, Consultative Paper on the Structure and Management of the National Health Service in England and Wales, (HMSO, 1979).

[5] DHSS, *Management Arrangements for the Reorganised National Health Service* (HMSO, 1972), para. 2.27.

[6] R. Levitt, *The Reorganised National Health Service* (Croom Helm, 1976), p. 40.

[7] DHSS, *Circular HC(80)8* Health Service Development Structure and Management (July 1980).

[8] DHSS, *Regional Chairmen's Enquiry into the working of the DHSS in relation to Regional Health Authorities* (1976).

[9] DHSS, *National Health Service Reorganisation*, op. cit. paras. 33 and 34.

[10] D. L. R. Smith and D. C. Hague (eds), *The Dilemma of Accountability in Modern Government* (Macmillan, 1971). See particularly the paper by D. Z. Robinson, 'Government Contracting for Academic Research: Accountability in the American Experience'.

[11] Royal Commission on the National Health Service, *Report*, Cmnd. 7615 (HMSO, 1979), para. 19.10.

[12] DHSS, *National Health Service Reorganisation*, op. cit., para. 84.

[13] DHSS, *National Health Service Reorganisation*, Consultative Document (1971), para. 14. DHSS, *National Health Service Reorganisation*, op. cit., para. 96.

[14] To one-third of the total membership. The decisions were announced in 1975 in the wake of a consultative paper: DHSS, *Democracy in the National Health Service* (HMSO, 1974).

[15] H. J. Elcock and S. C. Haywood, *The Buck Stops Where? Accountability and Control in the National Health Service* (Institute for Health Studies, University of Hull, 1980).

[16] DHSS, *Management Arrangements for the Reorganised National Health Service*, op. cit., para. 2.8.

[17] DHSS, *National Health Service Reorganisation*, op. cit., para. 134.

[18] DHSS, Circular (73)22, *Membership and Procedure of Regional and Area Health Authorities* (1973).

[19] DHSS, Circular HC(79)1, LAC(79)1, *Health Services Management Appointments to Area Health Authorities* (April 1979).

[20] DHSS, *National Health Service Reorganisation*, op. cit., para. 128.

[21] H. J. Elcock, 'Regional Government in Action', *Public Administration* vol. 56, no 4 (1978). Subsequent references to RHA members are taken from this article and the associated research.

[22] Royal Commission on the National Health Service, *Research Paper no 1* (HMSO, 1978).

[23] S. C. Haywood *et al.*, *The Curate's Egg . . . Good in Parts: Senior Officer Reflections on the NHS* (Institute for Health Studies, University of Hull, 1979).

[24] W. E. Hall and P. A. Hunt, *The Authority Member* (National Association of Health Authorities, 1979) p. 6.

[25] Committee on the Management of Local Government (The Maud Committee), *Vol. 2: The Local Government Councillor* (HMSO, 1967) chap. IV.

[26] DHSS, *The Future Structure of the National Health Service*, op. cit., para. 1.

[27] S. C. Haywood and A. Alaszewski, *Crisis in the NHS: the Politics of Management* (Croom Helm, 1980). The planning system was under review at the time of writing, with a view to its simplification.

[28] This account is taken from H. J. Elcock and S. C. Haywood, op. cit.

[29] Outer Circle Policy Unit, *Health First: a comment on Patients First* (London, 1980) para. 2.6.

[30] Royal Commission on the National Health Service, op. cit., Ch. 19.

[31] DHSS and Welsh Office, *Patients First*, op. cit., para. 6.

[32] Ibid. para. 5 (foreword), para. 5.

CHAPTER 7

[1] D. A. Okun, *The Regionalisation of Water Management* (Barking: Applied Science Publishers, 1977) pp. 4–7, 310–21; E. Porter, *Water Management in England and Wales* (Cambridge: Cambridge University Press, 1978) pp. 3–19.

[2] Figures from Department of the Environment, *The New Water Industry: Management and Structure* (HMSO, 1973) pp. 6–7.

[3] A. G. Jordan, J. J. Richardson, and R. H. Kimber, 'The Origins of the Water Act of 1973', *Public Administration*, vol. 55 (1977) pp. 317–34.

[4] P. Cordle and C. Willetts, 'Links Between Regional Water Authorities and Local Authorities', *Corporate Planning*, vol. 3 (1976) pp. 39–50; P. Cloke, *Key Settlements in Rural Areas* (Cambridge: Methuen, 1979); C. Skelcher, 'The Changing Shape of Regional Planning', *Town Planning Review*, vol. 51 (1980) pp. 324–9.

[5] D. A. Okun, op. cit., pp. 41–6; A. G. Jordan *et al.*, 'The Origins of the Water Act of 1973', op. cit., pp. 321–4.

[6] D. J. Parker and E. C. Penning-Rowsell, *Water Planning in Britain* (London: George Allen and Unwin, 1980) pp. 47–51 and 243–4.

[7] Central Advisory Water Committee, *The Future Management of Water in England and Wales* (London: HMSO, 1971); A. G. Jordan and J. J. Richardson, 'Outside Committees and Policy-Making: The Central Advisory Water Committee', *Public Administration Bulletin*, number 24 (1977) pp. 41–58.

[8] Department of the Environment, *New Water Industry*.

[9] Throughout this chapter 'managerial' and 'technical' criteria are differentiated from 'political' criteria in that the first two are concerned with choices between means towards accepted ends while the last is concerned with choices between both means and ends. In terms of the water industry these can be seen as differences between professional and social values.

[10] 'Functions' in this context are the individual services that the WAs provide— water supply, sewerage, etc.—'functional' refers to the structure and organization of the WAs as they affect these functions. Reorganization led to a unification of water functions within the WAs but led to a functional fragmentation of services between the WAs and local authorities.

[11] C. Kirby, *Water in Great Britain* (Harmondsworth, Middlesex: Pelican, 1979) p. 16-42.

[12] Central Advisory Water Committee, *Future Management*.

[13] C. J. Gray, *Organisational Contingencies and Water Authority Structure* (Hendon: Middlesex Polytechnic, Geography and Planning Paper No. 3, 1980).

[14] J. Pullin, 'Multifunctionalism', *The Surveyor* (2 April 1976) pp. 15-16.

[15] Department of the Environment, *New Water Industry*, (Ogden), and *The Water Services: Economic and Financial Policies, Second Report*, (Jukes) (HMSO, 1974).

[16] Sewerage agencies are discussed below. Water Companies are statutorily controlled organizations providing water supplies to some areas of the country. These twenty-eight Companies supply water to about 25 per cent of the population of England and Wales. They act as agents for the WAs and their forward plans must be submitted to, and agreed by, the WAs. While officially autonomous they tend to act as operational divisions for the WAs, with their plans being tied into the regional strategies of the WAs. See: Water Companies Association, 'The Water Company—After Reorganisation', *Water* (October 1975) pp. 32-3; B. Redknap and W. Scott, 'The Local Authority Agency for Sewerage', *Water Pollution Control*, vol. 75 (1976) pp. 257-65; D. J. Parker and E. C. Penning-Rowsell, op. cit., pp. 35-6.

[17] A. G. Jordan and J. J. Richardson, 'Outside Committees and Policy-Making: The Central Advisory Water Committee', op. cit., pp. 48-53.

[18] J. Naughton, 'Looking Back and Forward', *The Surveyor* (7 March 1975) pp. 45-60; H. Van Oosterom, 'The Structure and Functions of the Regional Water Authorities', in P. J. Drudy (Ed.), *Water Planning and the Regions* (London: Regional Studies Association, 1977) Discussion Paper 9, pp. 11-18.

[19] C. D. Andrews, *We Didn't Wait For The Rain* (London: National Water Council, 1976).

[20] National Water Council, *Water Industry Review, 1978* (London: National Water Council, 1978) pp. 5-12.

[21] Department of the Environment and The Welsh Office, *A Background to Water Reorganisation in England and Wales* (HMSO, 1973) p. 30.

[22] Ministry of Agriculture, Fisheries and Food, *Guidance Notes for Water Authorities: Water Act 1973, Section 24 Surveys* (Internal Memorandum, 1974); Department of the Environment, *Guidance on Water Authorities' Annual Plans and Programmes* (Internal Memorandum, updated to 1977).

[23] J. J. Richardson, A. G. Jordan and R. H. Kimber, 'Lobbying, Administrative Reform and Policy Styles: The Case of Land Drainage', *Political Studies*, vol. 25 (1978) pp. 47-64; E. Porter, op. cit., pp. 95-101.

[24] The other major statutory body is the Water Space Amenity Commission, (WSAC), which is concerned with water-based recreation.

[25] M. Greenfield, 'National Water Council—Watchdog or Lapdog?', *Municipal Journal* (4 April 1975) pp. 21-2.

[26] T. King, 'Learning Financial Discipline', *Water*, (May, 1980), pp. 2-4.

[27] D. A. Okun, op. cit., p. 241; National Water Council, *Annual Report and Accounts, 1978–79* (London: National Water Council, 1979) p. 5.

[28] See *The Times*, 24, 25 February, and 5 March 1981, and *The Guardian*, 3 March 1981.

[29] D. A. Okun, op. cit., pp. 57–9; A. G. Jordan *et al.*, op. cit., p. 330; B. Rednap and W. Scott, op. cit.

[30] See Chapter 2.

[31] Department of the Environment, *Circular 100/73, Water Authorities and Local Authorities*; B. Payne, *Water Authorities and Planning Authorities: A Study of Developing Relationships* (Manchester: Manchester University, Occasional Paper No. 1, 1977); B. Stanley, 'The Thames Water Authority, *The Planner* (January, 1979) pp. 20–2.

[32] P. Cloke, op. cit., pp. 160–2; B. Stafford, 'Water Services', *Town Planning Review*, vol. 51, (1980), pp. 315–18.

[33] J. Thackray, pp. 20–38 in R. J. S. Baker (Ed.), *Planning, Forecasting and Frustration in the Public Services* (Sheffield, Yorkshire and Humberside Regional Management Centre Occasional Paper, 1979).

[34] D. A. Okun, op. cit., pp. 214–17; Editorial, 'Looking Beyond The Inheritance', *Municipal Journal, Engineering Supplement* (4 April 1975).

[35] D. A. Okun, op. cit., pp. 324–6.

[36] J. J. Richardson and A. G. Jordan, *Governing Under Pressure* (Oxford: Martin Robertson, 1979) pp. 109–13.

[37] P. Cloke, op. cit., pp. 92–4, 160–2.

[38] B. Stanley, op. cit., and G. Carpner, untitled reply, *The Planner* (January, 1979) p. 22, for one example.

[39] See N. Johnson, 'Defining Accountability', *Public Administration Bulletin*, No. 17 (1974) pp. 3–13.

[40] See Chapter 11; and P. Self, *Econocrats and the Policy Process* (London: Macmillan, 1975).

[41] This is, of necessity, a highly generalized statement concerning the whole area of public accountability. See Johnson, *Accountability*, and J. Stanyer, 'Divided Responsibilities: Accountability in Decentralised Government', *Public Administration Bulletin*, No. 17 (1974) pp. 14–30.

[42] See Chapter 3.

[43] A. G. Jordan and J. J. Richardson, 'Outside Committees and Policy-Making: The Central Advisory Water Committee', op. cit., pp. 50–3.

[44] Department of the Environment, *Constitution of Regional Water Authorities, Water Reorganisation Consultation Document 8* (London: Department of the Environment, 1972); *Circular 82/71, Reorganisation of Water and Sewage Services.*

[45] A. G. Jordan *et al.*, 'The Origins of the Water Act of 1973', op. cit., p. 330.

[46] Department of the Environment, Welsh Office and Ministry of Agriculture, Fisheries and Food, *Review of the Water Industry in England and Wales; A Consultative Document* (HMSO, 1976) p. 15.

[47] Department of the Environment, Welsh Office and Ministry of Agriculture, Fisheries and Food, *The Water Industry in England and Wales, The Next Steps*, (HMSO, 1977) p. 16; D. Howell in *Hansard*, HC Vol. 965, No. 86, Cols. 1322–45 (4 April 1979).

[48] D. A. Okun, op. cit., p. 61; Department of the Environment *et al.*, *Review*, pp. 15–16; E. Griffiths, 'A Conservative View of the Review',*Water* (1976) pp. 2–4.

[49] Department of the Environment,*New Water Industry*, pp. 13–14; N. Johnson, op. cit., pp. 3–4.

[50] Jordan *et al.*, 'The Origins of the Water Act of 1973', op. cit., pp. 318–20; J. J. Richardson and A. G. Jordan, *Governing Under Pressure*, pp. 46–8.

[51] For example, 66 District Councils in the Anglian WA area appoint 10 members between them, and 71 Districts in the Severn-Trent area appoint 16 members.

[52] National Water Council, *Review*, p. 88. This includes Water Company revenue expenditure; if this is excluded the relevant figure is 91 per cent.

[53] E. J. Gilliand, 'Financial Problems', pp. 21–32 in Institution of Water Engineers and Scientists, *Symposium on Water Services: Financial, Engineering and Scientific Planning* (London: IWES, 1977); M. Broady, '"Welsh Water": The Politics of Water Supply', pp. 19–30 in P. J. Drudy (ed.), *Water Planning and the Regions*.

[54] Ibid, p. 28; D. A. Okun, op. cit., pp. 233–9.

[55] Ibid, pp. 240–1.

[56] Welsh Office, *Committee of Inquiry into Water Charges in the Area of the Welsh National Water Development Authority* (Cardiff: HMSO, 1975); Department of the Environment *et al.*, *Review*, op. cit., pp. 21–8; Department of the Environment *et al.*, *The Water Industry in England and Wales*, op. cit., p. 11; A. Porter, 'Equalisation Explained', *Water* (March, 1978) p. 23.

[57] J. Lingard and W. Dugdale, 'Universal Metering', *Water* (No. 4, 1975) pp. 6–10; J. A. Rees, 'Rethinking Our Approach to Water Supply Provision', *Geography*, vol. 61 (1976) pp. 232–45, and *The Management of Urban Domestic Water Services* Unpublished Ph.D. Thesis, London: University of London, 1978).

[58] D. J. Parker and E. C. Penning-Rowsell, op. cit., pp. 84–92.

[59] National Water Council, *Annual Report, 1978–79*, pp. 60–1.

[60] R. C. Jenking, 'Financing the Water Cycle', *Water Pollution Control*, vol. 75 (1976) pp. 244–56; National Water Council, *Paying For Water* (London: National Water Council, 1976); Department of the Environment *et al.*, *Review*, p. 17.

[61] Department of the Environment, *The Water Services: Economic and Financial Policies, Third Report* (HMSO, 1974).

[62] National Water Council, *Review*, p. 91; E. J. Gilliand, op. cit., p. 27.

[63] The effect of sewage disposal to rivers on the extraction of water for drinking purposes downstream, for example: the relationship of water quality and quantity was an important rationale for reorganization. See D. A. Okun, op. cit., pp. 6, 23–6; A. G. Jordan *et al.*, 'The Origins of the Water Act of 1973', op. cit., pp. 320–1.

CHAPTER 8

[1] P. J. O. Self, 'Regional Planning Britain', *Urban Studies*, vol. I, no. I (1964).

[2] G. E. Cherry, 'Prospects for Regional Planning—A Review of Metropolitan Strategies for the West Midlands', *Local Government Studies* (May/June 1980), p. 42.

[3] Barlow Report, *Royal Commission on the Distribution of the Industrial Population*, Cmd. 6153 (HMSO, 1940).

[4] Scottish Council (Development and Industry), *Inquiry into the Scottish Economy* (Edinburgh, 1961).

[5] T. D. Haddow, 'The Administration of Redevelopment', *Public Administration*, vol. 42 (Autumn 1969).

[6] Scottish Development Department, *Central Scotland: Programme for Development and Growth*, Cmnd. 2188 (HMSO, 1963).

[7] Secretary of State for Trade, Industry, and Regional Development, *The North East: A Programme for Regional Development and Growth*, Cmnd. 2206 (HMSO, 1963).

[8] Ministry of Housing and Local Government, *The South East Study* (HMSO, 1964).

[9] *South East England*, Cmnd. 2308 (HMSO, 1969).

[10] Ibid. Paras 1, 5, 14, 30. The White Paper was presented to Parliament jointly by the Secretary of State for Industry, Trade, and Regional Development, and the Minister of Housing and Local Government and Minister of Welsh Affairs.

[11] P. J. O. Self, 'Regional Planning and the Machinery of Government', *Public Administration*, vol. 42 (Autumn 1964); and G. McCrone, 'The Next Steps in Regional Planning', in T. Wilson (ed.), *Papers on Regional Development* (Oxford: Blackwell, 1965).

[12] National Economic Development Council, *Conditions Favourable to Faster Growth* (HMSO, 1963) pp. 14-29.

[13] C. Buchanan, *Traffic in Towns*, (HMSO: 1963). The recommendation to set up regional development agencies was contained in Sir Geoffrey Crowther's preface to the report.

[14] *H. C. Debates*, vol. 703, no. 639, col. 1829 (10 December 1964).

[15] G. Brown, *In My Way: The Political Memoirs of Lord George-Brown* (London: Gollancz, 1971) pp. 108-9.

[16] Richard Crossman, *The Diaries of a Cabinet Minister: Volume One: Ministry of Housing 1964-66*, (London: Hamish Hamilton and Jonathan Cape, 1975) p. 93.

[17] G. Brown, op. cit., pp. 108-9.

[18] Author's interview with Right Hon. William Rodgers MP, 17 April 1980.

[19] DEA, *The North West: A Regional Study* (HMSO, 1965). DEA, *The West Midlands: A Regional Study* (HMSO, 1965).

[20] DEA, *The National Plan*, Cmnd. 2764 (HMSO, 1965) p. 85.

[21] Ibid., p. 95.

[22] I. R. Gough and T. E. Chester, 'Regionalism in the Balance: Whitehall and Town Hall at the Cross Roads', *District Bank Review*, (March 1966).

[23] DEA, *Progress Report: Industrial and Regional*, Number 3, (March 1965).

[24] Ibid.

[25] DEA, *Minutes of Meeting Between Secretary of State for Economic Affairs and Council Chairmen*, Internal Paper (March 1966).

[26] Scottish Office, *The Scottish Economy 1965 to 1970: A Plan for Expansion*, Cmnd. 2864. (HMSO, 1966).

[27] J. M. McGuinness, 'Regional Economic Development—Progress in Scotland', *Journal of the Town Planning Institute* (March 1968).

[28] DEA, *Investment Incentives*, Cmnd. 2874 (HMSO, 1966).

[29] J. M. McGuinness, 'Regional Economic Development', op. cit.

[30] M. Wright and S. Young, 'Regional Planning in Britain', in J. Hayward and M. Watson (ed.), *Planning, Politics and Public Policy. The British, French and Italian Experience* (Cambridge University Press, 1975), p. 241.

[31] North West Economic Planning Council, *Preliminary Thoughts on a Planning Strategy for the North West* (HMSO, 1966).

[32] DEA North West Region Research Section, *The Formation of Regional Planning Strategies*, Internal Paper (1968).

[33] S. Brittan, *Inquest on Planning in Britain*, (PEP, 1967).

[34] Author's Interview with Right Hon. Michael Stewart MP, 4 December 1978.

[35] DEA, *The Future Work of the Regional Economic Planning Councils and Boards*, Internal Paper (March 1967).

[36] Ibid.

[37] West Midlands Economic Planning Council, *The West Midlands Patterns of Growth* (HMSO, 1967).

South West Economic Planning Council, *A Region With a Future: A Draft Strategy for the South West* (HMSO, 1967).

South East Economic Planning Council, *A Strategy for the South East* (HMSO, 1967).

North West Economic Planning Council, *Strategy II: The North West of the 1970s* (HMSO, 1968).

East Anglia Economic Planning Council, *East Anglia: A Study* (HMSO, 1968).

Northern Economic Planning Council, *Northern Region: An Outline Strategy of Development to 1981* (HMSO, 1969).

East Midlands Economic Planning Council, *Opportunity in the East Midlands* (HMSO, 1969).

Yorkshire and Humberside Economic Planning Council, *Yorkshire and Humberside: Regional Strategy* (HMSO, 1970).

[38] South West Economic Planning Council, *A Region With a Future*, op. cit.

[39] West Midlands Planning Authorities Conference, *A Developing Strategy for the West Midlands: Report of the West Midlands Planning Authorities Conference With Statement by the Secretary of State* (Birmingham, 1974) p. 1.

[40] West Midlands Planning Authorities Conference, *A Developing Strategy for the West Midlands* (Birmingham, 1971).

[41] M. B. Gahagan, *Regional Economic Planning in Great Britain 1959–72* (M. A. Thesis, University of Manchester, 1973) pp. 149–53.

[42] South East Economic Planning Council, op. cit.

[43] Author's interview with Professor P. J. O. Self, former member of South East Economic Planning Council, October 1975.

[44] Ministry of Housing and Local Government, *Circular 90/66, Review of the South East Study* (HMSO, 1966).

[45] P. Hall, *Urban and Regional Planning* (Penguin Books, 1974).

[46] South East Joint Planning Team, *Strategic Plan for the South East* (HMSO, 1970).

[47] Author's interview with William Oslow, former Chairman Yorkshire and Humberside Economic Planning Board, January 1976.

[48] M. Wright and S. Young. 'Regional Planning in Britain', op. cit., pp. 252–3.

[49] DEA, *The Preparation of Regional Strategies*, Internal Paper (1969).

[50] DEA, *Report of the Working Group on Regional Strategies* (The Nottingham Report), Internal Paper (1969).

[51] Ministry of Housing and Local Government, Ministry of Transport, and Scottish Development Department, *The Future of Development Plans: A Report by the Planning Advisory Group* (HMSO, 1965), pp. 10–11.

[52] *Town and Country Planning Act 1968*, S.2(4) (9), (HMSO, 1968). This requirement was repeated in the main DOE circular on structure plans—*Structure Plans 55/77*.

[53] Leicester City Council and Leicestershire County Council, *Leicester and Leicestershire Sub-Regional Planning Study* (1969).

Nottinghamshire County Council, Derbyshire County Council, Nottingham City Council, Derby County Borough Council, *Nottinghamshire and Derbyshire Sub-Regional Study* (1969).

[54] Secretary of State for Local Government and Regional Planning, *Reform of Local Government in England*, Cmnd. 4276 (HMSO, 1970), para. 12.

[55] Prime Minister and Minister for the Civil Service, *The Reorganization of Central Government*, Cmnd. 4506, (HMSO, 1970), para. 31.

[56] Secretary of State for the Environment, *Local Government in England: Government Proposals for Reorganization*, Cmnd. 4584, (HMSO, 1971), para. 32.

[57] *Local Government in England*, op. cit., para. 37.

[58] *H. C. Debates*, vol. 903, cols. 165–203 (9 June 1975).

[59] *Royal Commission on the Constitution 1969-1973: Volume I: Report.* Cmnd. 5460 (HMSO, 1973) Ch. 25.

[60] Lord President of the Council, *Devolution: The English Dimension: A Consulation Document* (HMSO, 1976).

[61] *H. C. Debates*, vol. 829, no. 882, Written Answers, col. 181 (19 January 1972).

[62] SPNW Joint Planning Team, *Strategic Plan for the North West* (HMSO, 1974).

[63] East Anglia Joint Planning Team, *Strategic Choice for East Anglia* (HMSO, 1974).

[64] Northern Region Strategy Team, *Strategic Plan for the Northern Region* (HMSO, 1977).

[65] South East Joint Planning Team, *Strategy for the South East: 1976 Review Development of the Strategic Plan for the South East* (HMSO, 1976).

[66] Joint Monitoring Steering Group, *A Developing Strategy for the West Midlands Updating and Rolling Forward of the Regional Strategy to 1981* (West Midlands Regional Study, Birmingham, July 1979).

[67] Yorkshire and Humberside Economic Planning Council, *Yorkshire and Humberside Regional Strategy Review: The Next Ten Years* (HMSO, 1976).

[68] A. G. Powell, 'Strategies for the English Regions: Ten Years of Evolution', *Town Planning Review*, vol. 49, no. I (January 1978).

[69] G. E. Cherry, 'Prospects for Regional Planning', op. cit.

[70] J. Mawson and C. Skelcher, 'Updating the West Midlands Regional Strategy, A Review of Inter-Authority Relationships', *Town Planning Review*, vol. 51, no. 2 (April 1980).

[71] C. Skelcher, 'The Changing Shape of Regional Planning', *Town Planning Review*, vol. 51, no. 3 (July 1980).

[72] C. Skelcher, 'The Changing Shape of Regional Planning', op. cit.

[73] A. G. Powell, 'Strategies for the English Regions', op. cit., p. 10.

[74] F. Wedgwood-Oppenheim, D. A. Hart, and B. W. Cobley, *An Exploratory Study in Strategic Monitoring, Establishing a Regional Performance Evaluation and Policy Review Unit for the North West* (Inlogov, University of Birmingham, 1974).

[75] A. G. Powell, 'Strategies for the English Regions', op. cit., p. 11.

[76] Speech by Marcus Fox, MBE, MP, Parliamentary Under Secretary of State, DOE, to Royal Town Planning Institute Annual Conference in Norwich, 30 April 1980.

[77] Letter from Secretary of State for the Environment to the Chairman of the West Midlands Planning Authorities Conference, 18 July 1980. Attached to DOE Press Notice 288 1980.

[78] Letter from Secretary of State for the Environment to the Chairman of the Standing Conference on London and South East Regional Planning, 7 August 1980. Attached to DOE Press Notice 322 1980.

[79] P. J. O. Self 'Whatever Happened to Regional Planning', *Town and Country Planning* (July/August 1980).

CHAPTER 9

[1] The data presented in this chapter for the period 1974/5 to 1977/8 were produced as part of a research project into regional money flows undertaken at the University of Durham, and sponsored initially by the Department of the Environment and subsequently by the Social Science Research Council. The data for the period 1969/70 to 1973/4 were obtained while the author was working at the Northern Region Strategy Team.

[2] See J. Short, *The Distribution of Public Expenditure and Taxation in the Regions 1974/75 to 1977/78* (Farnborough: Gower Press, 1980).

[3] Estimates of this for the period 1974/5 to 1977/8 can be found in J. Short, *A Study of Regional Money Flows in the UK Regions* (Farnborough: Gower Press, 1980).

[4] HM Treasury, *Needs Assessment Study—Report* (HMSO, 1979).

CHAPTER 10

[1] George Brown, First Secretary of State and Secretary of State for Economic Affairs, *H.C. Deb.*, vol. 703, cols. 1829–31 (10 December 1964).

[2] The speeches were found in seventeen categories of debate, namely: Adjournment, supply, consolidated fund, Finance Bills, Budget, Queen's Speech, Debate on Report, Debate on resolutions, Debate on orders, Debate on statement, Debate on motion, Debate on White Paper, Scotland, Wales, E.E.C. and Committee of the Whole of the House.

It is not possible to ascribe a single motive for the making of each speech. What can be done, however, is to give the number of speeches which were concerned with making demands, and the number expressing other views, bearing in mind that in some cases demands will be made as well as other views expressed. For example, a speech for aid might also make political points by criticizing or supporting the policy of a particular party in addition to putting forward a particular conceptual viewpoint as to the solution to the problem; that is, the answer could be found in the use of the market mechanism or direct government control.

Speech	Number
Demands for help	903
Critical of Labour policies	399
Critical of Conservative policies	443
Support for Conservative policies	342
Support for Labour policies	476
Conceptual	142
Nationalist	47
Maiden	22
Total	2,774

[3] The term 'regional economic policy' should be taken to mean any policy designed to deal with economic problems within the planning regions, whether these are, for example, problems of congestion and overheating in the South East or above average unemployment and underused resources in the North West. Speeches on general economic policy focused on how it affects, for example, unemployment in the regions or a particular region or area have also been included.

[4] Where a speech refers directly and consistently to regional policy as it affects a particular area then it may be said that the predominant direction of interest (even if it is the only direction of interest) in the speech is towards that area, whether it be constituency, planning region, or sub-region. Where the speech refers directly and consistently to regional policy as it affects other economic policy or a party standpoint or ideological bias then it may be said that the predominant direction of interest (even if it is the only direction of interest) is towards overall policy. In a number of speeches reference has been made to all four categories: in this case a decision was taken as to the focus of the MP's interest. In most cases the decision was relatively simple as the main area of interest was quite clear, but in some cases the focus was less clear and required the making of a value judgement.

⁵ The set of boundaries used in this survey are those in existence before 1974. The changes in 1974 could not be accommodated in the method of analysis and it was considered that although changes in some cases tended to move towards MPs' identification, e.g., the post-1974 Northern Region, the pattern of speeches for the smaller part of the survey (1974-6) followed the trends identified and did not alter the main conclusions.

⁶ Michael McGuire, *H.C. Deb.*, vol. 903, cols. 1661-2 (2 January 1976).

⁷ Bernard Conlan, *H.C. Deb.*, vol. 792, cols. 955-6 (1 December 1969).

⁸ R. L. Borthwick, 'When the Short Cut May Be a Blind Alley: The Standing Committee on Regional Affairs', *Parliamentary Affairs*, vol. XXXI, no. 2 (Spring 1978) p. 207.

⁹ An example to illustrate this point was the debate on the Northern Economic Planning Region in December 1969. There were sixteen speeches, thirteen of which were by MPs from the North East speaking about the North East. *H.C. Deb.*, vol. 892, cols. 915-79 (1 December 1969).

¹⁰ A. J. Beith, *H.C. Deb.*, vol. 893, cols. 183-4 (9 June 1975).

¹¹ Arthur Davidson, *H.C. Deb.*, vol. 841, col. 449 (18 July 1972).

¹² Jeffrey Archer, *H. C. Deb.*, vol. 866, cols. 376-7 (11 December 1973).

¹³

Unemployment Rates (percentages)								
Region	1968	1969	1970	1971	1972	1973	1974	1975
U.K.	2.5	2.5	2.6	3.5	3.9	2.7	2.7	4.1
S.E.	1.6	1.5	1.6	2.1	2.2	1.5	1.6	2.8
E. Mid.	1.8	1.9	2.2	2.9	3.1	2.1	2.2	3.6
W. Mid.	2.0	1.8	2.0	3.0	3.6	2.2	N.A.	4.1

Source: Central Statistical Office *Regional Statistics* No. 11 (HMSO, 1975) p. 123 and No. 12 (HMSO, 1976) p. 118.

¹⁴ This problem of 'pockets' of above average unemployment has given rise to locally biased speeches like that of Mr Christopher Mayhew. 'The prospect, therefore, looks a lot less cheerful, especially against the unemployment problems of the area. Unemployment has been a severe problem in my constituency in recent years. We used to be a traditional full employment area but we are no longer. Unemployment has risen from about 500 in the early 1960s to 2,000 quite recently ... Such discouragement has been given to employers to come to Greenwich that applicants for I.D.C.s are put off.' (Christopher Mayhew, *H.C. Deb.*, vol. 840, cols. 1809-10 (12 July 1972)).

¹⁵ Robert Hicks, *H.C. Deb.*, vol. 822, col. 1542 (3 August 1971).

CHAPTER 11

¹ N. Johnson, *In Search of the Constitution: Reflections on State and Society in Britain* (Oxford: Pergamon, 1977) p. 89.

² W. Saunders, *Municipalisation by Provinces* (New Heptarchy series, No. 1) (London: Fabian Society, 1905).

³ C. B. Fawcett, *Provinces of England* revised edition, edited by W. G. East and S. W. Wooldridge (London: Hutchison, 1961).

⁴ G. D. H. Cole, *The Future of Local Government* (London: Cassell, 1921).

⁵ Quoted in W. Thornhill (ed.), *The Case for Regional Reform* (London: Nelson, 1972).

⁶ Royal Commission on Local Government in the Tyneside Area, *Report*, Cmd. 5402 (HMSO, 1937).

[7] Royal Commission on the Distribution of the Industrial Population (Barlow Commission) *Report*, Cmd. 6153 (HMSO, 1940).

[8] B. C. Smith, *Regionalism in England. 2. Its Nature and Purpose, 1905–1965* (London: Acton Society Trust, 1965). See also B. C. Smith, *Regionalism in England. Regional Institutions: A Guide* (London: Acton Society Trust, 1964).

[9] See 'Regionaliter', 'The Regional Commissioners', *Political Quarterly*, vol. 12, No. 2 (1941). Partly reproduced in Thornhill, *Regional Reform*.

[10] F. Blackburn, *Local Government Reform* (Altrincham: John Sherrat, 1947) p. 43.

[11] E. W. Gilbert, 'Practical Regionalism in England and Wales', *Geographical Journal* (July 1939); E. W. Gilbert, 'Areas of Regional Organisation', *Public Administration*, 27 (1949).

[12] P. Self, *Regionalism* (London: Fabian Publications and George Allen & Unwin, 1949); Blackburn, *Local Government Reform*; W. A. Robson, *The Development of Local Government* (London: Allen & Unwin, 2nd edn., 1948); E. G. R. Taylor, 'Land and Plan', *Architect and Building News*, (17 October 1941) reproduced in Thornhill, *Regional Reform*; R. E. Dickinson, *City Region and Regionalism* (London: Kegan Paul, 1947); Labour Party, *The Future of Regional Government* (London: The Labour Party, 1943); National Association of Local Government Officers, *Reform of Local Government* (London: NALGO, 1943), quoted in Thornhill, *Regional Reform* and Blackburn, *Local Government Reform*.

[13] G. D. H. Cole, *Local and Regional Government* (London: Cassell, 1947).

[14] V. Wiseman, 'Regional Government in the United Kingdom', *Parliamentary Affairs*, vol. XIX (1965–6).

[15] Thornhill, *Regional Reform*.

[16] *Traffic in Towns*, Report of Steering Group and Working Group Appointed by the Minister of Transport (London: HMSO, 1963).

[17] P. Self, 'Regional Planning and the Machinery of Government', *Public Administration*, 42 (1964).

[18] K. Joseph, 'Local Authorities and Regions', *Public Administration*, 42 (1964).

[19] *H.C. Deb.*, vol. 689, col. 141 (10 February 1964).

[20] See Chapter 3.

[21] J. P. Mackintosh, *The Devolution of Power* (Harmondsworth: Penguin, 1968).

[22] Liberal Party, *Parliaments for the Future* (London: Liberal Party Research Department, 1970); *Economist*, 18 May 1963.

[23] D. Senior, 'The City Region as an Administrative Unit', *Political Quarterly*, 36 (1965).

[24] Royal Commission on Local Government in England, 1966–9, *Memorandum of Dissent* by Mr D. Senior, Cmnd. 4040–1 (London: HMSO, 1969).

[25] Ibid. p. 140.

[26] Royal Commission on the Constitution, *Report*.

[27] Royal Commission on the Constitution, Vol. 11, *Memorandum of Dissent*, Cmnd. 5460–1.

[28] M. Keating and M. Rhodes 'Is there a Regional Level of Government in England?', *Studies in Public Policy*, (University of Strathclyde, 1979).

[29] *Devolution: The English Dimension—Consultative Document* (HMSO, 1976).

[30] For an account of the diverse aims of the devolution opponents in the North East, see R. Guthrie and I. McLean, 'Another Part of the Periphery: Reactions to Devolution in an English Development Area', *Parliamentary Affairs* (1978).

[31] P. Temperton (ed.), *Up North* (Hebden Bridge: Campaign for the North, 1978).

[32] Labour Party, *Devolution and Regional Government in England. A Discussion Document for the Labour Movement* (London: Labour Party, 1975).

[33] Labour Party, *Labour's Programme, 1976* (London: Labour Party, 1976).

[34] Labour Party, *Regional Authorities and Local Government Reform. A Consultation Document for the Labour Movement* (London: Labour Party, 1977).

[35] P. G. Richards, *The Reformed Local Government System* (2nd edn.) (London: George Allen & Unwin, 1975).

[36] Senior, *Memorandum of Dissent*, p. 136.

[37] See chapter 3.

[38] Ibid.

[39] Ibid.

Index